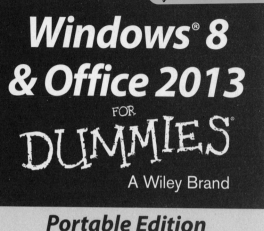

Windows® 8 & Office 2013

FOR DUMMIES®

A Wiley Brand

Portable Edition

by Andy Rathbone and Wallace Wang

FOR
DUMMIES®
A Wiley Brand

Windows® 8 & Office 2013 For Dummies® Portable Edition

Published by
John Wiley & Sons, Inc.
111 River Street
Hoboken, NJ 07030-5774

www.wiley.com

For general information on our other products and services, please contact our Customer Care Department within the U.S. at 877-762-2974, outside the U.S. at 317-572-3993, or fax 317-572-4002.

For technical support, please visit www.wiley.com/techsupport.

Wiley also publishes its books in a variety of electronic formats. Some content that appears in print may not be available in electronic books.

Library of Congress Control Number: 2013935668

ISBN: 978-1-118-66953-2 (pbk), 978-1-118-73925-9 (ebk), 978-1-118-73926-6 (ebk), 978-1-118-73928-0 (ebk)

Manufactured in the United States of America

10 9 8 7 6 5 4 3 2 1

About the Authors

Andy Rathbone started geeking around with computers in 1985 when he bought a 26-pound portable CP/M Kaypro 2X. Like other nerds of the day, he soon began playing with null-modem adapters, dialing computer bulletin boards, and working part-time at Radio Shack.

He wrote articles for various techie publications before moving to computer books in 1992. He's written the *Windows For Dummies* series, *Upgrading and Fixing PCs For Dummies*, *TiVo For Dummies*, *PCs: The Missing Manual*, and many other computer books.

Today, he has more than 15 million copies of his books in print, and they've been translated into more than 30 languages. You can reach Andy at his website, www.andyrathbone.com.

The author, **Wallace Wang,** currently exists as a carbon-based life form, consuming precious natural resources for his own survival at the expense of the rest of the planet. Despite his dislike of unnecessary complexity, the author actually enjoys what computers can do, even if they tend to fail spectacularly in everyday use at the worst possible time (details, details . . .). Besides writing computer books, the author also enjoys studying movies and performing stand-up comedy just to do something creative that involves human beings as opposed to machines. In addition, the author also refers to himself in the third person in imitation of professional athletes and other personages who like pretending that they're more important than they really are.

Authors' Acknowledgments

Special thanks to Dan Gookin, Matt Wagner, Tina Rathbone, Steve Hayes, Nicole Sholly, Virginia Sanders, and Russ Mullen. Thanks also to all the folks I never meet in editorial, sales, marketing, proofreading, layout, graphics, and manufacturing who work hard to bring you this book.

—*Andy Rathbone*

I'd like to thank all the friendly people who helped put this book together. Additional thanks go to my radio co-hosts (Wes Sample, Dane Henderson, Sherri Diaz, and Joe Shattuck) at My107.9FM in beautifully isolated Alpine, California, where we host a weekly radio show called *Notes From the Underground*. Thanks also go to Johannes Gutenberg for inventing the printing press, which is currently being defeated by armies of people dismissing the invention of mass printing by refusing to read any books at all.

—*Wallace Wang*

Publisher's Acknowledgments

We're proud of this book; please send us your comments at http://dummies.custhelp.com. For other comments, please contact our Customer Care Department within the U.S. at 877-762-2974, outside the U.S. at 317-572-3993, or fax 317-572-4002.

Some of the people who helped bring this book to market include the following:

Acquisitions and Editorial

Project Editor: Charlotte Kughen

Executive Editor: Steve Hayes

Editorial Manager: Jodi Jensen

Editorial Assistant: Anne Sullivan

Sr. Editorial Assistant: Cherie Case

Composition Services

Sr Project Coordinator: Kristie Rees

Layout and Graphics: Jennifer Creasey

Proofreader: Christine Sabooni

Indexer: BIM Indexing & Proofreading Services

Publishing and Editorial for Technology Dummies

    Richard Swadley, Vice President and Executive Group Publisher

    Andy Cummings, Vice President and Publisher

    Mary Bednarek, Executive Acquisitions Director

    Mary C. Corder, Editorial Director

Publishing for Consumer Dummies

    Kathleen Nebenhaus, Vice President and Publisher

Composition Services

    Debbie Stailey, Director of Composition Services

Contents at a Glance

Table of Contents

● ●

Introduction

● ●

*W*elcome to *Windows 8 & Office 2013 For Dummies,* your resource for Microsoft's new operating system and office productivity software. You're no dummy, that's for sure. But when it comes to Windows 8 and Office 2013, the fascination just isn't there. You want to get your work done, stop, and move on to something more important.

That's where this book comes in handy. Instead of becoming a Windows 8 and Office 2013 expert, you'll know just enough to get by quickly, cleanly, and with a minimum of pain so that you can move on to the more pleasant things in life.

About This Book

Don't try to read this book in one sitting; there's no need. Instead, treat this book like a dictionary or an encyclopedia. Turn to the page with the information you need and say, "Ah, so that's what they're talking about." Then put down the book and move on.

How This Book Is Organized

The information in this book has been well sifted. This book contains three parts. The first two parts are divided into chapters relating to the part's theme. Here are the categories (the envelope, please).

Part I: Windows 8

This part introduces you to Windows 8, including subjects like the following:

- ✔ Keeping your computer safe and secure
- ✔ Making sense of the new Start screen
- ✔ Finding, starting, and closing programs and apps
- ✔ Setting up a computer for the whole family to use
- ✔ Taking and viewing digital photos
- ✔ Interacting with others through social apps
- ✔ Fixing Windows 8 when it's misbehaving

Part II: Office 2013

To use Microsoft Office 2013, you need to know how to find the commands you need. This part of the book focuses on showing you how to use the Ribbon user interface that appears in all Office 2013 programs. By the time you finish this part of the book, you'll feel comfortable using any program in Office 2013.

This part of the book explains the basics of using Word, Excel, Outlook, PowerPoint, and Access. You become familiar with using Office and read about different techniques you can use to work with Office even faster than before. By the time you finish this part of the book, you'll be much more comfortable using Office 2013.

Part III: The Part of Tens

Everybody loves lists (except during tax time). This part contains lists of ten aggravating things about Windows 8 (and how to fix them) and ten tips you can use in Office 2013 to increase your productivity.

Icons Used in This Book

Icons highlight important or useful information.

This icon alerts you about juicy information that makes computing easier.

Don't forget to remember these important points. (Or at least dog-ear the pages so that you can look them up again a few days later.)

The computer won't explode while you're performing the delicate operations associated with this icon. Still, wearing gloves and proceeding with caution is a good idea.

Are you moving to Windows 8 from Windows Vista or Windows 7? This icon alerts you to areas where 8 works significantly differently from its predecessors.

Watch out! This signpost warns you that pointless technical information is coming around the bend. Swerve away from this icon to stay safe from awful technical drivel.

Controlled by fingertips rather than mice and keyboards, touchscreens are standard fare on tablets, as well as some laptops and desktop computer monitors. This icon appears next to information aimed directly at the touchy feely crowd.

Where to Go from Here

Now, you're ready for action. Give the pages a quick
flip and scan a section or two that you know you'll need
later. Please remember, this is *your* book — your weapon
against the computer nerds who've inflicted this whole
complicated computer concept on you. Please circle any
paragraphs you find useful, highlight key concepts, add
your own sticky notes, and doodle in the margins next to
the complicated stuff.

Part I
Windows 8

Visit www.dummies.com/go/Windows8 for great Dummies content related to this book.

In this part . . .

- ✔ Get a refresher on Windows basics.

- ✔ Find out what's new in Windows 8.

- ✔ Get the scoop on the new Start screen.

- ✔ Discover how to store files on your computer, on an external device, and in the cloud.

- ✔ Figure out how to work with apps.

- ✔ Customize Windows 8 to suit your needs and protect your data.

Chapter 1

Revealing Windows 8

*C*hances are good that you've heard about *Windows:* the boxes and windows that greet you whenever you turn on your computer. In fact, millions of people worldwide are puzzling over Windows as you read this book. Almost every new computer and laptop sold today comes with Windows preinstalled, ready to toss colorful boxes onto the screen.

This chapter helps you understand why Windows lives inside your computer, and I introduce Microsoft's latest Windows version, called *Windows 8.* I explain how Windows 8 differs from previous Windows versions, whether you should upgrade to Windows 8, and how well your faithful old PC and programs will weather the upgrade.

What Is Windows 8, and Why Are You Using It?

Created and sold by a company called Microsoft, Windows isn't like your usual software that lets you calculate income taxes or send angry e-mails to mail-order companies. No, Windows is an *operating system,* meaning it controls the way you work with your computer. It's been around for nearly 30 years, and the latest incarnation is called *Windows 8,* shown in Figure 1-1.

Figure 1-1: The newest version of Windows, Windows 8, comes preinstalled on most new PCs today.

The name *Windows* comes from all the little windows it places on your computer screen. Each window shows information, such as a picture, a program, or a baffling technical reprimand. You can place several windows onscreen simultaneously and jump from window to window, visiting different programs. Or, you can enlarge one window to fill the entire screen.

When you turn on your computer, Windows jumps onto the screen and begins supervising any running programs. When everything goes well, you don't really notice Windows; you simply see your programs or your work. When things don't go well, though, Windows often leaves you scratching your head over a perplexing error message.

In addition to controlling your computer and bossing around your programs, Windows 8 comes with a bunch of free programs and *apps* — miniprograms. These programs and apps let you do different things, such as write and print letters, browse the Internet, play music, and send your friends dimly lit photos of your latest meal.

And why are you using Windows 8? Well, you probably didn't have much choice. Nearly every computer sold since late October 2012 comes with Windows 8 preinstalled. A few people escaped Windows by buying Apple computers (those nicer-looking computers that cost a lot more). But chances are good that you, your neighbors, your boss, and millions of other people around the world are using Windows.

✔ Windows 8 introduces a radical new full-screen–sized Start menu that's designed for *touchscreens* — displays controlled with your fingertips. Now called a *Start screen,* it also appears on desktop PCs, oddly enough. Be prepared for some initial mouse awkwardness as you try to mimic a fingertip with your mouse pointer.

✔ The new automatic backup program in Windows 8, *File History,* greatly simplifies what you should have been doing all along: creating copies of your important files for safekeeping.

What's New in Windows 8?

You may have worked with earlier versions of Microsoft Windows. If so, toss away that hard-earned knowledge because Windows 8 starts from scratch. Why? Because Windows 8 tries to please two camps of computer owners.

See, some people are mostly *consumers*. They read e-mail, watch videos, listen to music, and browse the web, often while away from their desktop PC. Whether on the go or on the couch, they're consuming media (and popcorn).

Other people are mostly *creators*. They write papers, prepare tax returns, update blogs, edit videos, or, quite often, tap whichever keys their boss requires that day.

To please both markets, Microsoft broke Windows 8 into two very different sections:

✔ **Start screen:** For the on-the-go information grabbers, the Windows 8 Start screen fills the entire screen with large, colorful tiles that constantly update to show the latest stock prices, weather, e-mail, Facebook updates, and other tidbits. Shown earlier in Figure 1-1, that information appears before you touch a button. And *touch* is a keyword: The Start screen works best with a touchscreen monitor or tablet.

✔ **Desktop tile:** When it's time for work, head for the Start screen's *desktop* tile. The traditional Windows desktop appears, shown in Figure 1-2, bringing all its power — as well as its detailed, cumbersome menus.

Figure 1-2: The Windows 8 desktop works much as it did in Windows 7, but without a Start button.

Some people like the convenience of having both types of computers built into one. Others find the two experiences to be oddly disjointed.

✔ In a way, Windows 8 offers the best of both worlds: You can stay on the Start screen for quick, on-the-go browsing. And when work beckons, you can head for the desktop, where your traditional Windows programs await.

✔ The catch is that the Windows desktop no longer contains the traditional Start button and the Start menu that sprouted from the corner. Instead, you must retreat to the new, Start *screen*. To open a program, click or tap a program's tile from the Start screen, and Windows shuffles you back to the desktop, where the newly opened program awaits.

✔ Welcome to the split personality awaiting you in Windows 8! I explain the Start screen in Chapter 2; the Windows desktop awaits your attention in Chapter 3.

Should I Bother Switching to Windows 8?

In a word, no. Most people stick with the Windows version that came installed on their computers. That way they avoid the chore of figuring out a new version of Windows. Also, Windows 8 comes with a particularly steep learning curve because it's quite different from earlier Windows versions.

Also, many of the biggest changes in Windows 8 work best with *touchscreens* — those fingertip-controlled screens found on expensive cellphones, tablets, and some of the latest laptops. No matter what device it runs on, Windows 8 looks and behaves the same, whether it's controlled by fingers on a touchscreen tablet or by a mouse and keyboard on a desktop PC.

On the positive side, if you manage to figure out Windows 8 once, you'll know how to run it on *all* your Windows devices: a tablet, Windows phone, a laptop, a desktop PC, and perhaps even a touchscreen television. On the negative side, being designed for so many different things makes Windows 8 behave a little awkwardly on *all* of them.

Instead of upgrading, stick with the masses and stay with your current computer. When you're ready to buy a new computer, the latest version of Windows will be installed and waiting for you.

Windows 8 doesn't support *Windows XP mode,* a popular way to run a Windows XP desktop inside its own window within Windows 7. If you needed Windows XP mode in Windows 7, don't upgrade to Windows 8.

Can My Current PC Still Run Windows 8?

If you want to upgrade to Windows 8, your computer probably won't complain. Windows 8 should run without problem on any PC currently running Windows 7 or Windows Vista. In fact, Windows 8 may run faster on your old PC than Windows Vista did, especially on laptops.

If your PC runs Windows XP, it may still run Windows 8, but probably not at its best.

If you have a technogeek in your family, have him or her translate the following information, which describes the Windows 8 hardware requirements:

- ✔ **Requirements for x86 (32-bit) architecture:** 1 GHz processor, 1GB of RAM, DirectX 9 graphics device with WDDM 1.0 or higher driver, 16GB HDD free space

- ✔ **Requirements for x86 (64-bit) architecture:** 1 GHz processor, 2GB of RAM, DirectX 9 graphics device with WDDM 1.0 or higher driver, 20GB HDD free space

In common language, this information simply says that nearly any computer sold in the past five years can be upgraded to Windows 8 with little problem.

Windows 8 runs nearly any program that runs on Windows 7 and Windows Vista. It even runs some Windows XP programs, as well. Some older programs, however, won't work, including most security-based programs, such as antivirus, firewall, and security suites. You'll need to contact the program's manufacturer for an upgraded version.

Shopping for a new PC to run Windows 8? To see how well a particular showroom PC can handle Windows 8, point your mouse at any screen's bottom-left corner and click the right mouse button. When the menu appears, choose System. The Windows Experience Index appears. It has already tested the PC and given it a grade ranging from 1 (terrible) to 9.9 (extraordinary).

Don't know what version of Windows runs on your current PC? Go to the Start menu, right-click Computer, and choose Properties. The screen that appears lists your Windows version. (If your Start menu fills the screen with a bunch of colorful tiles, you're already running Windows 8. If so, right-click in the bottom-left corner, choose System from the pop-up menu, and the System window's Windows Edition section says which version of Windows 8 is running.)

The Four Flavors of Windows 8

Microsoft offers four main versions of Windows 8, but you'll probably want only one: the aptly titled "Windows 8" version.

Small businesses will choose Windows 8 Pro, and larger businesses will want Windows 8 Enterprise. Still, to clear up the confusion, here are descriptions of the versions:

✔ **Windows RT:** Designed for long battery life, this version only comes preinstalled, mostly on tablets. It runs the Start screen and apps, but its limited desktop won't run your own Windows programs. To compensate, Windows RT includes versions of Microsoft Word, Excel, PowerPoint, and OneNote.

✔ **Windows 8:** Aimed at consumers, this version includes the Start screen, apps, and a full-featured

Windows desktop that can run most Windows programs.

✔ **Windows 8 Pro:** Aimed at the business market, this version features everything from the Windows 8 version as well as tools used by small businesses: encryption, extra networking features, and similar business tools. If you buy a Media Center Pack upgrade, Windows 8 Pro can record TV shows through a TV tuner with Windows Media Center, as well as play DVDs. (To upgrade Windows 8 to Media Center, buy a Windows 8 Pro Pack.)

✔ **Windows 8 Enterprise:** Microsoft sells this large business version in bulk to large businesses.

Each version contains all the features of the versions preceding it. Windows 8 Pro contains everything found in Windows 8, for example.

Here are some guidelines for choosing the version you need:

✔ If you're considering a tablet with **Windows RT**, make sure you realize that it *can't run regular Windows programs.* You're limited to its bundled Office programs and any apps you download from the Windows Store.

✔ If you'll be using your PC at home, pick up **Windows 8.**

✔ If you need to connect to a domain through a work network — and you'll know if you're doing it — you want **Windows 8 Pro.**

Want to play DVDs or record TV shows with Windows Media Center in Windows 8 Pro? Then pull out your credit card and upgrade online for the Media Center Pack. (To upgrade the consumer-oriented Windows 8 with Windows Media Center, buy the Windows 8 Pro Pack.)

✔ If you're a computer tech who works for businesses, go ahead and argue with your boss over whether you need **Windows 8 Pro** or **Windows 8 Enterprise.** The boss will make the decision based on whether it's a small company (Windows 8 Pro) or a large company (Windows Enterprise).

Most computers let you upgrade to a more powerful version of Windows 8 from the desktop Control Panel's System area. (Reach for your credit card before clicking the I Want to Buy a Product Key Online button.)

Chapter 2

The Mysterious New Start Screen

● ●

In This Chapter

▶ Starting Windows 8

▶ Signing in to Windows 8

▶ Understanding the Start screen

▶ Switching among apps

▶ Finding shortcuts on the Charms bar

▶ Seeing all your apps and programs

▶ Customizing the Start screen

▶ Turning off your computer

● ●

*W*indows 8 comes with the traditional Windows desktop, but the new Start screen creates all the excitement. The Start screen's large, colorful tiles offer quick stepping stones for checking e-mail, watching videos, and sampling Internet fare.

On a touchscreen tablet, you could spend all day working within the Start screen's world of full-screen apps, deftly maneuvering through them with your fingertips.

On a desktop computer, however, armed with only a mouse and keyboard, you could spend all day trying to *avoid* the Start screen and find the traditional Windows desktop.

But love it or hate it, the new Start screen plays an integral role in Windows 8. This chapter explains how to make the most of it, whether you want to enjoy it or avoid it as much as possible.

When you stare glumly at the confusing new Start screen, try these tricks: Right-click a blank spot, or point at any screen corner with your mouse. Those actions fetch hidden menus, bringing you a glimmer of navigational hope.

If you're using a touchscreen computer, substitute the word *tap* when you read the word *click.* Tapping twice works like *double-clicking.* And when you see the term *right-click,* touch and hold your finger on the glass; lift your finger when the right-click menu appears.

Being Welcomed to the World of Windows 8

Starting Windows 8 is as easy as turning on your computer — Windows 8 leaps onto the screen automatically with a flourish. But before you can begin working, Windows 8 stops you cold: It displays a locked screen, shown in Figure 2-1, with no entrance key dangling nearby.

Figure 2-1: To move past this lock screen, drag up on the screen with your mouse or finger, or press a key on the keyboard.

Previous versions of Windows let you sign in as soon as you turned on your computer. Windows 8, by contrast, makes you unlock a screen before moving to the sign in page, where you type in your name and password.

How do you unlock the lock screen? The answer depends on whether you're using a mouse, keyboard, or touchscreen:

- **Mouse:** On a desktop PC or laptop, click any mouse button.

- **Keyboard:** Press any key, and the lock screen slides away. Easy!

- **Touch:** Touch the screen with your finger and then slide your finger *up* the glass. A quick flick of the finger will do.

When you're in the door, Windows wants you to *sign in* by clicking your name and typing in a password.

If you don't see an account listed for you on the Sign In screen, you have several options:

- ✔ **If you see your name and e-mail address listed, type your password.** Windows 8 lets you in and displays your Start screen, just as you last left it.

- ✔ **If you don't see your name, but you have an account on the computer, click the left-pointing arrow.** Windows 8 displays a list of *all* the account holders. You may see the computer owner's name, as well as an account for Administrator and one for Guest.

- ✔ **If you just bought the computer, use the account named Administrator.** Designed to give the owner full power over the computer, the Administrator account user can set up new accounts for other people, install programs, start an Internet connection, and access *all* the files on the computer — even those belonging to other people. Windows 8 needs at least one person to act as administrator.

- ✔ **Use the Guest account.** Designed for household visitors, this account lets guests use the computer temporarily.

- ✔ **No Guest account?** Then find out who owns the computer and beg that person to set up a username for you or to turn on the Guest account.

Don't *want* to sign in at the Sign In screen? The screen's two bottom-corner buttons offer these other options:

✔ **The little wheelchair-shaped button in the screen's bottom-left corner** customizes Windows 8 for people with physical challenges in hearing, sight, or manual dexterity. If you choose this button by mistake, click or touch on a different part of the screen to avoid changing any settings.

✔ **The little button in the screen's bottom-right corner** lets you shut down or restart your PC. (If you've accidentally clicked it and shut down your PC, don't panic. Press your PC's power button, and your PC will return to this screen.)

Even while locked, as shown in Figure 2-1, your computer's screen displays current information in its bottom-left corner. Depending on how it's configured, you can see the time and date; your wireless Internet signal strength (the more bars, the better); battery strength (the more colorful the icon, the better); your next scheduled appointment; a count of unread e-mail; and other items.

Understanding user accounts

Windows 8 allows several people to work on the same computer, yet it keeps everybody's work separate. To do that, it needs to know who's currently sitting in front of the keyboard. When you *sign in* by clicking your *username* Windows 8 presents your personalized Start screen, ready for you to make your own personalized mess.

When you're through working or just feel like taking a break, sign out (explained at this chapter's end) so that somebody else can use the computer. Later, when you sign back in, your messy desktop will be waiting for you.

Although you may turn your desktop into a mess, it's your *own* mess. When you return to the computer, your letters will be just as you saved them.

Until you customize your username picture, you'll be represented by a silhouette. To add a photo to your user account, click your username in the screen's corner and choose Change Account Picture. Click the Webcam button to take a quick shot with your computer's built-in webcam. No webcam? Then choose Browse to peek through existing photos. *Hint:* Click the word Files and choose Pictures to see all the photos on your PC.

Keeping your account private with a password

Because Windows 8 lets many people use the same computer, how do you stop Rob from reading Diane's love letters to Jason Bieber? Using a *password* solves some of those problems.

In fact, a password is more important than ever in Windows 8 because some accounts can be tied to a credit card. By typing a secret password when signing in you enable your computer to recognize *you* and nobody else. If you protect your username with a password, nobody can access your files. And nobody can rack up charges for computer games while you're away from home.

To set up or change your password, follow these steps:

1. **Summon the Charms bar and click the Settings icon.**

I cover the *Charms bar,* a shortcut-filled strip of icons — sometimes called *charms* — that hug every screen's right edge, later in this chapter. You fetch the Charms bar differently depending on whether you're using a mouse, keyboard, or touchscreen:

- *Mouse:* Move the mouse pointer to the top-right or bottom-right corners of your screen.

- *Keyboard:* Hold down the ▦ key and press the letter C.

- *Touchscreens:* Slide your finger from the screen's right edge inward.

When the Charms bar appears, click the Settings icon. The Settings screen appears.

2. **Click the words Change PC Settings at the very bottom of the Settings screen.**

   The PC Settings screen appears.

3. **Click the Users category on the left and then click the Change Your Password button. Or, to create a password, click the Create a Password button.**

   You may need to type your existing password to gain entrance.

4. **Type a password that will be easy to remember.**

   Choose something like the name of your favorite vegetable, for example, or your dental floss brand. To beef up its security level, capitalize some letters and embed a number in the password, like **Glide2** or **Ask4More**. (Don't use these exact two examples, though, because they've probably been added to every password cracker's arsenal by now.)

5. **If asked, type that same password into the Retype Password box, so Windows knows you're spelling it correctly.**

6. **In the Password Hint box, type a hint that reminds you — and only you — of your password.**

   Windows won't let you type in your exact password as a hint. You have to be a bit more creative.

7. **Click the Next button, and click Finish.**

   Suspect you've botched something during this process? Click Cancel to return to Step 3 and either start over or exit.

After you've created the password, Windows 8 begins asking for your password whenever you sign in.

- ✔ Passwords are *case-sensitive.* The words *Caviar* and *caviar* are considered two different passwords.

- ✔ Afraid that you'll forget your password someday? Protect yourself now: Make a *Password Reset Disk,* which is a special way of resetting forgotten passwords.

- ✔ Windows also offers to Create a Picture Password in Step 3, where you drag a finger or mouse over a photo in a certain sequence. Then, instead of entering a password, you redraw that sequence on the sign-in picture. (Picture passwords work much better on touchscreen tablets than desktop monitors.)

- ✔ Another new option in Step 3 is Create a PIN. A *PIN* is a four-digit code like the ones punched into Automated Teller Machines (ATMs). The disadvantage of a PIN? There's no password hint to a four-digit password.

✔ Forgotten your password *already?* When you type a password that doesn't work, Windows 8 automatically displays your hint — if you created one — which should help to remind you of your password. Careful, though — anybody can read your hint, so make sure that it's something that makes sense only to you. As a last resort, insert the Password Reset Disk you made.

Make Windows stop asking me for a password!

Windows asks for your name and password only when it needs to know who's tapping on its keys. And it needs that information for any of these four reasons:

✔ Your computer is part of a network, and your identity determines what goodies you can access.

✔ The computer's owner wants to limit what you can do on the computer.

✔ You share your computer with other people and want to keep others from signing in with your name and changing your files and settings.

✔ You want a Microsoft account so you can access apps that run on the Start screen.

If these concerns don't apply to you, purge the password by selecting Change My Password in Step 3 in the section "Keeping your account private with a password." In the next step, leave the New Password box blank and click Next.

Without that password, though, anybody can sign in, use your user account, and view (or destroy) your files. If you're working in an office setting, this setup can be serious trouble. If you've been assigned a password, it's better to simply get used to it.

Signing up for a Microsoft account

Whether you're signing in to Windows 8 for the first time, trying to access some Start screen apps, or just trying to change a setting, you'll eventually see a screen similar to the one in Figure 2-2.

Figure 2-2: You need a Microsoft account to access many of the Windows 8 features.

That screen appears because Windows 8 introduces a new type of user account. You can sign in with either a *Microsoft* account or a *Local* account. Each serves different needs:

- ✔ **Local account:** This account works fine for people working with traditional Windows programs on the Windows desktop. Local account holders can't run many of the Start screen apps bundled with Windows 8, including the Mail app. Nor can they download new apps from the Windows Store.

- ✔ **Microsoft account:** Consisting of an e-mail address and a password, this lets you download apps from the Windows Store and run all the bundled apps in Windows 8. You can link a Microsoft account with your social media accounts, automatically stocking your address book with your friends from Facebook, Twitter, and other sites. (Plus, you can access both your own and your friends' Facebook photos.)

You have two ways to sign in with a Microsoft account; they're ranked here according to simplicity:

- ✔ **Use an existing Microsoft account.** If you already use Hotmail, Outlook, Live, Xbox LIVE, or Windows Messenger, you already have a Microsoft account and password. Type in that e-mail address and password at the screen shown in Figure 2-2 and then click the Sign In button.

- ✔ **Sign up for a new Microsoft account.** Click the Sign Up for a Microsoft Account link, shown in Figure 2-2, and Microsoft takes you to a website where you can turn your existing e-mail address into a Microsoft account. (Signing up for a new Microsoft e-mail address is a better option, however, because it lets you use Windows 8's built-in Mail app.)

If you're signing into Windows 8 for the first time, and you don't want a Microsoft account, you see a Cancel button. Click Cancel, and the next screen shows a button that lets you sign in with a Local account instead.

But until you create a Microsoft account, the nag screen in Figure 2-2 will haunt you whenever you try to access a Windows 8 feature that requires a Microsoft account.

Figuring Out the New Start Screen in Windows 8

The new Start screen in Windows 8 whisks you away from traditional Windows desktop and drops you into a foreign land with no helpful translator at your side. That's right: Windows 8 no longer has a Start button *or* a Start menu.

Instead, the new Windows 8 Start *screen* (refer to Figure 2-1) appears whenever you turn on your computer. Whereas older Windows versions had a small Start menu on a desktop, the Windows 8 Start screen fills the entire screen with large tiles stretching beyond the right edge. Each tile represents a program installed on your computer.

As you work, you'll constantly switch between the screen-filling Start screen and the traditional screen-filling desktop, covered in the next chapter.

Despite the drastic remodel, the Start screen still offers a way to start programs; adjust Windows settings; find help for sticky situations; or, thankfully, shut down Windows and get away from the computer for a while. Some Start screen tiles needn't be opened to see their contents. For example, the Calendar tile constantly updates to show the current date and day, as well as your next few appointments.

Your Start screen changes as you add more programs and apps to your computer. That's why the Start screen on your friend's computer, as well as in this book, is probably arranged differently than your computer's Start screen.

Try the following tricks to make the Start screen feel a little more like home:

✔ Click the Desktop tile to fetch the familiar Windows desktop. Whew! If you prefer to avoid the Start screen, you can stay on the traditional Windows desktop as much as possible. (I explain the desktop in Chapter 3.)

✔ Spin the wheel on your mouse, and the Start screen moves to the left or right, accordingly. It's a handy way to move quickly across the entire Start screen, from left to right.

✔ As you move your mouse pointer, the Start screen follows along. When the pointer reaches the screen's right edge, for example, the Start screen brings the offscreen portions into view.

✔ See the little bar along the Start screen's bottom edge? That's a *scroll bar*. Drag the scroll bar's light-colored portion to the left or right: As you move that portion, the Start screen moves along with it, letting you see items living off the screen's right edge.

✔ On a touchscreen, navigate the Start screen with your finger: Pretend the Start screen is a piece of paper lying on a table. As you move your finger, the Start screen moves along with it.

✔ On a keyboard, press the right- or left-arrow keys, and the Start screen's tiles move accordingly. Press the keyboard's End key to move to the end of the Start screen; the Home key moves you back to the Start screen's front.

Windows 8 contains hidden doorways tucked away in its corners, as well as secret passages enabled by pressing certain key combinations. Here are some unlabeled ways to fetch the Start screen and switch among your apps, whether you're using a mouse, keyboard, or touchscreen.

✔ **With the mouse:** Fetch the Start screen by pointing to the screen's lower-left corner. When the Start screen icon appears, click the mouse. Switch to another currently running app by pointing to the screen's upper-left corner and then slide the mouse pointer downward. When thumbnails of your running apps appear, click the one you want to see full screen.

✔ **With the keyboard:** Fetch the Start screen by pressing the Windows key, ⊞, found near the spacebar on most keyboards. Switch to another currently running app by holding down Alt and pressing Tab to switch between currently opened apps; let go of the Alt key when you highlight your desired app.

✔ **With the touchscreen:** Fetch the Start screen by pressing the ⊞ key below your tablet's screen. Switch to another currently running app by sliding your finger inward from the screen's left edge, then back. Then tap the thumbnail of your desired app.

Launching a Start screen program or app

Windows 8 stocks your Start screen with *apps* — small programs for performing simple tasks. In fact, Windows 8 now refers to *all* Windows programs as apps. (It even refers to your once almighty desktop as the *Desktop app.*)

What's an app?

Short for *application*, apps herald from the world of *smartphones*: cell-phones powerful enough to run small programs, as well as make phone calls. The Windows 8 apps differ from traditional windows programs in several ways:

✔ Windows apps come from only one place: the Windows Store. Available as its own app, the Store app lets you download apps from Microsoft; once downloaded, they're automatically installed on your computer. Many apps are free, but others cost money.

✔ Only *Windows* apps can run on Windows. Apps found on iPhones and Android phones aren't designed to run on your Windows 8 computer. Creators of some popular apps create versions for each platform, but they sometimes differ slightly. Have you bought apps for your Android or iPhone? You'll have to pay again to buy the apps' Windows versions.

✔ Apps, by nature, fill the entire screen when running, although Windows 8 does offer an awkward way to "snap" two apps together, covered later in this chapter.

✔ Apps are usually fairly simple to use, but simplicity brings limitations. Many apps don't let you copy words, photos, or links. There's often no way to share an app's contents with a friend or to leave public comments. Most apps lack the power of traditional desktop programs.

Although Windows 8 refers to traditional desktop programs as apps, there's a big difference: Windows programs run only atop your Windows 8 desktop, whereas apps run only in the new world of the Start screen.

Each tile on the Start screen is a button for starting an app or traditional Windows program. Click the button, and the program or app jumps into action. Windows 8 complicates matters, as it offers several ways to push a button:

✔ **Mouse:** Point at the tile and click the left mouse button.

✔ **Keyboard:** Press the arrow keys until a box surrounds the desired tile. Then press the Enter key.

✔ **Touchscreens:** Tap the tile with your finger.

No matter which item you've chosen, it fills the screen, ready to inform you, entertain you, or maybe even do both. I explain the Start screen's built-in apps later in this chapter. If you feel like digging in, you can begin downloading and installing your own by clicking the Start screen's Store tile. (I explain how to download apps in Chapter 6.)

Viewing or closing your open apps

Start screen apps, by nature, consume the entire screen, with no visible menus. That makes it difficult not only to control them but also to switch among them. The same holds true when you're working in the separate world of the traditional Windows desktop.

How do you switch between recently used programs and apps? Windows 8 makes it fairly easy to switch between them by following these steps:

1. **Point the mouse pointer at the screen's bottom-most-left corner.**

   A thumbnail of your last used app appears. You can click to bring that app to the screen. Or, if you want to revisit other apps running in the background, move to the next step.

2. **When the desktop icon appears, raise your mouse pointer along the screen's left edge.**

   As you move it up the screen, shown in Figure 2-3, a bar appears alongside the screen's left edge, showing thumbnails of your open apps.

To switch to any recently used app, click its thumbnail.

Figure 2-3: Point in the bottom-left corner of the Start screen. Move the mouse pointer up the edge to see currently running Start screen apps.

3. **To return to an app, click its thumbnail.**

4. **To close an app, right-click its thumbnail and choose Close.**

These tips can help you keep track of your running apps, as well as close down the ones you no longer want open:

✔ To cycle through your currently running apps, hold down the ⊞ key and press Tab: The same bar you see in Figure 2-3 appears along the left edge. Each time you press Tab, you select another app. When you select the app you want, let go of the ⊞ key, and the app fills the screen.

✔ You can view your most recently used apps whether you're working on the Windows desktop or on the new Start screen. From the desktop, point your mouse at the screen's bottom-left corner, slide the mouse up the screen's left edge, and then click the app you want to revisit.

✔ After you close an app in Step 4, the bar listing your running apps stays onscreen. You can then close other apps by right-clicking them and choosing Close.

✔ To close an app you're currently working on, point your mouse at the screen's top edge. When the mouse pointer turns into a hand, hold down your mouse button and drag the app toward the screen's bottom. When your mouse reaches the screen's bottom edge, you've closed the app. (This trick works on the desktop as well.)

Finding a Start screen app or program

You can scroll through the Start screen until your eagle-eyes spot the tile you need, and then you can pounce on it with a quick mouse click or finger tap. But when the thrill of the hunt wanes, Windows 8 offers several short-cuts for finding apps and programs hidden inside a tile-stuffed Start screen.

When searching for a particularly elusive app or program, try these tricks:

- ✔ Mouse users can right-click on a blank portion of the Start screen. A bar rises from the screen's bottom showing an icon named All Apps. Click the All Apps icon to see an alphabetical listing of *all* your computer's apps and programs. Click the desired app or program to open it.

- ✔ While looking at the Start screen, keyboard owners can simply begin typing the name of their desired app or program, like this: **facebook**. As you type, Windows 8 lists all the apps matching what you've typed so far, eventually narrowing down the search to the runaway.

- ✔ On a touchscreen, slide your finger up from the screen's bottom. When the bottom menu appears, tap the All Apps icon to see an alphabetical list of all your apps and programs.

Adding or removing Start screen items

Removing something from the Start screen is easy, so you can begin there. To remove an unwanted or unused tile from the Start screen, right-click it and choose Unpin from Start from the pop-up menu along the screen's bottom. The unloved tile slides away without fuss.

But you'll probably want to spend more time *adding* items to the Start screen, and here's why: It's easy to escape the Start screen by clicking the Desktop app. But once you're safely on the desktop, how do you start a program without heading back to the Start screen? To escape this recursive conundrum, stock your Start screen with icons for your favorite desktop destinations, such as programs, folders, and settings. Then, instead of loading the desktop and looking lost, you can head to your final destination straight from the Start screen.

After you've stuffed your Start screen with your favorite desktop joints, head to this chapter's "Managing the Start screen" section to place them in orderly groups. When you finish, you're caught up with where you started with in previous Windows versions: a fully stocked Start screen.

To add programs or apps to the Start screen, follow these steps:

1. **Press the Start screen's All Apps button.**

   Right-click a blank portion of the Start screen (or press ⊞+Z) and then choose the All Apps button along the screen's bottom.

On a touchscreen, slide your finger upward from the screen's bottom edge and then tap the All Apps icon.

No matter which route you take, the Start screen alphabetically lists all your installed apps and programs.

2. **Right-click the item you want to appear on the Start screen and choose Pin to Start.**

3. **Repeat Step 2 for every item you want to add.**

   Unfortunately, you can't select and add several items simultaneously.

4. **Choose the Desktop app.**

   The desktop appears.

5. **Right-click desired items and choose Pin to Start.**

   Right-click a library, folder, file, or other item you want added to the Start screen; when the pop-up menu appears, choose Pin to Start.

When you're through, your Start screen will have grown considerably with all your newly added destinations.

The Charms bar and its hidden shortcuts

The Charms bar is simply a menu, one of a million in Windows 8. But the Microsoft marketing department, eager to impart a little humanity to your computer, calls it a *Charms bar.*

Shown in Figure 2-4, the Charms bar's five icons, or *charms,* list things you can do with your currently viewed screen. For example, when you're gazing at a website you want a friend to see, fetch the Charms bar, choose Share, and choose the friend who should see it. Off it goes to your friend's eyeballs.

Figure 2-4: The Charms bar in Windows 8 contains handy icons for performing common tasks.

The Charms bar can be summoned from *anywhere* within Windows 8 — from the Start screen, the Windows desktop, and even from within apps and desktop programs.

But no matter what part of Windows 8 you're working with, you can summon the Charms bar using a mouse, keyboard, or touchscreen by following these steps:

- ✔ **Mouse:** Point at the top- or bottom-right corners.
- ✔ **Keyboard:** Press ⊞+C.
- ✔ **Touchscreen:** Slide your finger inward from the screen's right edge.

When the Charms bar appears, lingering along your screen's right edge, it sports five icons, ready to be either clicked or touched. Here's what each icon does:

- ✓ **Search:** Choose this, and Windows assumes you want to search through what you're currently seeing onscreen. To expand your search, choose one of the other search locations: Apps, Settings, or Files.

- ✓ **Share:** This fetches options for sharing what's currently on your screen. When viewing a web page, for example, a click of the Share button lets you choose Mail to e-mail the page's link to a friend. (I cover e-mail in Chapter 7.)

- ✓ **Start:** This simply takes you back to the Start screen. The ⊞ key on your keyboard or tablet also whisks you back there.

- ✓ **Devices:** Choose this to send your current screen's information to another device, such as a printer, second monitor, or perhaps a phone. (The Devices option lists only devices that are currently connected with your computer and able to receive the screen's information.)

- ✓ **Settings:** This lets you quickly tweak your computer's six major settings: WiFi/Network, Volume, Screen, Notifications, Power, and Keyboard/ Language. Not enough? Then choose the words Change PC Settings along the bottom to open the Start screen's mini-Control Panel.

Tap a Charms bar icon, and Windows gives a hint as to its purpose. For example, tapping the Settings area's Screen icon on a tablet presents a sliding bar for adjusting the screen's brightness. Sitting atop the sliding bar is a lock icon that keeps the screen from rotating, which is handy for reading e-books.

Table 2-1 shows some keyboard shortcuts to bypass the Charms bar and head straight to one of its icons.

Table 2-1	The Charms Bar's Keyboard Shortcut Keys
To Do This . . .	*. . . Press This*
Open the Charms bar	⊞+C
Search for apps, files, or settings	⊞+Q
Share what you see onscreen	⊞+H
Return to the Start screen	⊞
Interact with attached devices	⊞+K
Change settings	⊞+I

Introducing your free apps

The Windows 8 Start screen comes stocked with several free apps, each living on its own square or rectangular tile. Every tile is labeled, so you know what's what. The tiles for some apps, known as *live tiles,* change constantly. The Finance app tile, for example, constantly updates with the stock market's latest swings; the Weather tile always tells you what to expect when you walk outdoors.

The Windows 8 Start screen shows only some of your apps; to see them all, right-click a blank portion of the Start screen and choose All Apps from the screen's bottom.

You may spot some or all of the following apps on the list, ready to be launched at the click of a mouse or touch of a finger:

✔ **Calendar:** This lets you add your appointments or grab them automatically from calendars already created through accounts with Google, Hotmail, or Microsoft's new Outlook.com website.

✔ **Camera:** This lets you snap photos with your computer's built-in camera or webcam.

✔ **Desktop:** Choose this to fetch the traditional Windows desktop, which runs the Windows programs you've used for the past decade. I cover the desktop in Chapter 3.

✔ **Finance:** A live tile, this shows a 30-minute delay of the Dow, NASDAQ, and S&P. Choose Finance to see the usual charts and graphs of fear and uncertainty.

✔ **Games:** Designed mostly for Xbox 360 owners, this app lets you see your friends and gaming achievements. You can explore new games, watch game trailers, and buy new games for your console.

✔ **Internet Explorer:** Covered in Chapter 8, this mini-version of Internet Explorer browses the web full-screen, with nothing to get in the way: no menus, no tabs, just you and the current page. (When you're through, press the ⊞ key on your keyboard to return to the Start screen.)

✔ **Mail:** Covered in Chapter 7, this lets you send and receive e-mail. If you enter a Hotmail, Outlook.com, or Google account, the Mail app sets itself up automatically, stocking your People list as well.

✔ **Maps:** Handy for trip planning, the Maps app brings up a version of Microsoft Bing Maps.

✔ **Messaging:** Covered in Chapter 7, this app lets you send text messages to friends through Facebook, Microsoft's Instant Messenger, and other systems.

✔ **Music:** This plays music stored on your PC. But Microsoft hopes you'll buy music from its store as well.

✔ **News:** Visit here to read the news of the day, compiled from news services.

✔ **People:** The beauty of the People app, covered in Chapter 7, comes from its openness. Once you enter your accounts — Facebook, Twitter, Google, and others — the People app grabs all your contacts, as well as their information, and stocks itself automatically.

✔ **Photos:** Covered in Chapter 8, the Photos app displays photos stored in your computer, as well as on accounts you may have on Facebook, Flickr, or SkyDrive.

✔ **Reader:** This handy app reads documents stored in the Adobe Portable Document Format (PDF). It jumps into action when you try to open any file stored in that document. (Most manuals available on websites come in PDF format; you can also find them attached to some e-mails.)

✔ **SkyDrive:** This term describes the Microsoft Internet cubbyhole where you can store your files. By storing them online in SkyDrive, covered in Chapter 5, you can access them from any Internet-connected computer.

✔ **Sports:** You can find sports news and scores here, as well as a way to add listings for your favorite sports teams.

✔ **Store:** Covered in Chapter 6, the Windows Store is the only way to add more apps on your Start screen. (Programs you install through your Windows desktop also add shortcuts to the Start screen.)

✔ **Travel:** Resembling a travel agent's billboard, this app lists travel hotspots, complete with maps, panoramic photos, reviews, and links for booking flights and hotels.

✔ **Video:** This works more like a video rental store, with a small button that lets you watch videos stored on your computer.

✔ **Weather:** This weather station forecasts a week's worth of weather in your area, but only if you grant it permission to access your location information. (Unless your computer has a GPS — Global Positioning System — the app narrows down your location by closest city rather than street address.)

The bundled Windows 8 apps work well within the confines of the Start screen. Unfortunately, Microsoft configured the Windows 8 desktop to use some of these Start screen apps rather than standard desktop programs.

Managing the Start screen

The Start screen behaves much like a grocery list, growing longer and longer as you add more items. That lack of organization comes at a cost, though. How can you find the important things inside a sprawling list of randomly colored tiles?

Give yourself a fighting chance by organizing your Start screen. The following steps begin with a small dose of organization: purging unwanted tiles and adding tiles for your favorites.

Keep following these steps, and you'll eventually reach organizational nirvana: a screen full of neatly labeled *groups* — collections of related tiles — that match *your* interests.

You can organize the tiles any way you want, into any number of groups with any names. For example, you may want to organize the Start screen tiles into four groups: Work, Play, Web, and People. (For a quick peek at what organized and labeled groups look like, page ahead to Figure 2-6.)

But no matter how organized you want to be, follow these steps to begin turning that haphazard Start screen into your *own* piles o' tiles:

1. Remove tiles you don't need.

Spot a tile you don't need? Right-click it and choose Unpin from Start. Repeat until you've removed all the tiles you don't use.

Choosing Unpin from Start doesn't *uninstall* the app or program; removing the tile merely removes that item's "start" button from the screen. In fact, if you accidentally remove the tile for a favorite app or program, you can easily put it back in Step 3.

2. Move related tiles next to each other.

As an example, you might want to keep your people-oriented apps — Mail, People, and Calendar — next to each other. To move an app to a new location, drag its tile to the desired spot. As you drag the tile, other tiles automatically move out of the way to make room for the newcomer.

When you've dragged an app's tile to the desired spot, drop the tile to set the tile into its new place.

To conserve screen real estate, shrink a wide tile from a rectangle to a square: Right-click the wide tile and click the Smaller button.

3. **Add tiles for apps, programs, folders, and files you need.**

   I explain how to add tiles for apps, programs, folders, and files earlier, in this chapter's "Adding or removing Start screen items" section.

   After you've purged any unwanted tiles, rearranged the remaining tiles, and added new tiles for items you need, your Start screen may meet your needs. If so, *stop*. You're done!

   But if your Start screen still sprawls off the screen's right edge and you can't find important items, keep reading.

   Still here? Okay. When first installed, the Windows 8 Start screen includes two unlabeled groups of tiles, with a narrow space between the two groups. Windows 8 didn't even bother to name the two groups. And, if you're like most people, you probably didn't notice the slightly wider space that separates those two groups. And that brings you to the next step.

4. **Find the gap between the Start screen's existing groups of tiles.**

Keep scrolling to the Start screen's right edge, and you'll eventually notice a place where one group of tiles breaks away from the rest, leaving a slightly wider gap between the two groups. Shown in Figure 2-5, that wider gap separates each of your Start screen's groups.

5. **To create a new group, drag and drop a tile into the gap between two existing groups.**

   Drag and hold any tile in the blank space between two groups. A vertical bar will appear, widening the space to make room for your incoming tile. Drop the tile, and the tile forms a *new* group of one lonely tile, located between the two other groups.

A gap separating the tile groups

A group of tiles   A second group of tiles

Figure 2-5: A wider gap separates tiles into groups.

6. **To add more tiles to your newly created group, drag and drop additional tiles into the group.**

   Drag and drop new tiles next to your new group's first tile. After you drop a tile into a group, you can drag the tile around to a new position within the group.

   Want to create yet another group? Then repeat Steps 4 and 5, dragging and dropping a tile between two more groups to create yet another group.

   You might find groups of related tiles to be enough organization for you. If so, stop. But if you want to label the groups or move the groups to different positions on the Start screen, go to the next step.

7. **Click in the screen's bottommost-right corner to switch to a view of your groups. Then drag the groups into your preferred order.**

   Now that you've created groups of tiles to match your interests, you can shuffle them into any order you want. For example, you can move your favorite group to the screen's far left, where it's always visible.

   To begin rearranging your groups, click the minus sign (–) icon in the Start screen's bottommost-right corner: The Start screen changes to show all your tiles as little clumps, with each clump representing one group.

   Drag and drop the groups into the order you want them to appear on your Start screen.

8. **Name the groups.**

   While still looking at your clumped groups, add the final layer of order by placing a name atop each group.

Right-click the group you want to name and click the Name Group icon that appears along the screen's bottom. When the Name box appears, type a name and then click the Name button.

9. **Return to the Start screen.**

Click any place but on the groups in the shrunken Start screen, and the shrunken groups expand to their normal size, letting you bask in your organizational prowess, as shown in Figure 2-6.

Figure 2-6: Your Start screen is easier to work with when organized into labeled groups of related tiles.

✔ As you install additional apps and desktop programs, you'll once again find a hodgepodge of tiles piling up along the Start screen's right edge. To keep things organized, drag and drop the newcomers into your existing groups or make new groups for the new tiles.

✔ Feel free to create a group for your favorite websites, as well, making it easy to visit them in the Start screen's browser.

Exiting from Windows

Ah! The most pleasant thing you'll do with Windows 8 all day could very well be to stop using it. Exiting Windows brings a new hurdle to the process, however: You must decide whether to Lock, Sign Off, Shut Down, Restart, or Sleep your computer. The answer depends on how long you're abandoning your computer.

The next two sections describe how to take either a temporary sojourn or a permanent vacation. But if you don't want to trudge through a manual in order to turn off your PC, here's the quickest way to turn it off:

1. **Move your mouse pointer to the bottom-right corner to fetch the Charms bar. (On a touchscreen, swipe inward from the right edge.)**

2. **Click the Settings icon and then click the Power icon.**

3. **Choose Shut Down.**

4. **If the computer protests, saying you'll lose unsaved work, choose Sleep instead.**

The following two sections deal with the finer points of what's become an alarmingly complex chore.

Temporarily leaving your computer

Windows 8 offers three options when you're leaving your computer temporarily. To make the right choice among the three "temporary leave" scenarios in Windows 8, follow these steps:

1. **Return to the Start screen.**

   Press the ▦ key or summon the Charms bar and click the Start icon.

2. **Click your user account picture in the Start screen's upper-right corner.**

   You can choose one of three options:

   - *Lock:* Meant to add privacy while you take short trips to the water cooler, this option locks your PC, veiling your screen with the Lock screen picture. When you return, unlock the screen and type your password; Windows quickly displays your work, just as you left it.

   - *Sign Out:* Choose this when you're through working at the PC and somebody else wants to have a go at it. Windows saves your work and your settings and then returns to the Lock screen, ready for the next person to log on.

   - *Another account:* Below your name, Windows lists names of other accounts on the computer. If one of those people wants to borrow the computer for a few minutes, let him choose his name from the list. When he types in his password, his customized screen appears, ready for him to work. When he signs out and you sign back in, all your work reappears, just as you left it.

Each of the three options lets you give up your computer for a little while, but leaves it waiting for your return. If you're finished for the day, though, you're ready for the next section.

Leaving your computer for the day

When you're done computing for the day — or perhaps you just want to shut down the laptop while on the subway or that flight to Rome — Windows 8 offers three ways to handle the situation.

You can find each option by following these steps:

1. **Summon the Charms bar.**
2. **Click the Settings icon.**

   This icon, shaped like a gear, is clearly labeled.

3. **Click the Power icon.**

   The Power icon's pop-up menu offers three settings.

   Here's the rundown on your options:

   - *Sleep:* The most popular choice, this saves your work in your PC's memory *and* on its hard drive and then lets your PC slumber in a low-power state. Later, when you return to your PC, Windows quickly presents everything — even your unsaved work — as if you'd never left.

   - *Restart:* Choose this option as a first cure when something weird happens (a program crashes, for example, or Windows seems dazed and confused). Windows turns off your computer and then starts itself anew, hopefully feeling better.

- *Shut Down:* This turns your computer off completely. It's just like Restart but without turning back on again.

That should be enough to wade through. But if you have a little more time, here are some other facts to consider:

You don't *have* to shut down your computer each night. In fact, some experts leave their computers turned on all the time, saying it's better for their computer's health. Other experts say that their computers are healthier if they're turned *off* each day. Still others say the Sleep mode gives them the best of both worlds. However, *everybody* says to turn off your monitor when you're done working. Monitors definitely enjoy cooling down when not in use.

Don't just press your PC's Off button to turn off your PC, or you might lose unsaved work. Instead, be sure to shut down through one of its official options: Sleep or Shut Down. Otherwise, your computer can't properly prepare itself for the dramatic event, which can lead to future troubles.

Want your laptop or tablet to wake up in Airplane mode, cut off from wireless access? Then switch to Airplane mode and use Sleep rather than Shut Down. When your laptop or tablet wakes back up, it stays in Airplane mode, disconnected from the Internet.

Chapter 3

The Traditional Desktop

● ●

In This Chapter

▶ Finding the desktop

▶ Finding the Start screen

▶ Touching the desktop on a touchscreen

▶ Working on the desktop

▶ Retrieving deleted items from the Recycle Bin

▶ Understanding the taskbar

▶ Customizing the desktop

▶ Making programs easier to find

● ●

*T*he app-filled world of Windows 8 works fine for
couch-top computing. Without leaving your Start
screen, you can listen to music, check your e-mail, watch
the latest funny cat videos, and see whether anything
particularly embarrassing has surfaced on Facebook.

But when Monday morning inevitably rolls around, it's
time to switch gears. Working usually requires ditching
the Start screen simple apps and firing up more full-
featured programs. Employers prefer that you work with
spreadsheets and word processors rather than play
Angry Birds.

That's when the second half of Windows 8, the *desktop,* comes into play. The desktop works like a *real* desktop, a place where you arrange your work and make things happen.

Thankfully, the desktop lives on in Windows 8, ready for those inevitable Monday mornings. This chapter shows you how to transform your computer from an entertainment device into a workhorse.

Finding the Desktop and the Start Screen

The Windows 8 Start screen treats the desktop as just another *app:* a small, single-purpose program. So, you open the desktop just as you'd open any other app: Click the Start screen's Desktop tile.

The Desktop tile looks like a miniature version of your *real* desktop, complete with your current desktop background. When summoned, the desktop pushes aside the Start screen and fills the screen, ready to run your traditional Windows programs.

The Windows 8 desktop works much like the desktop found in previous Windows versions. Shown in Figure 3-1, the Windows 8 desktop is almost indistinguishable from the one in the previous version, Windows 7.

Point and click here to return to your last-used app.

Recycle Bin

Hover the mouse in either of these two corners to see the Charms bar and click its icons.

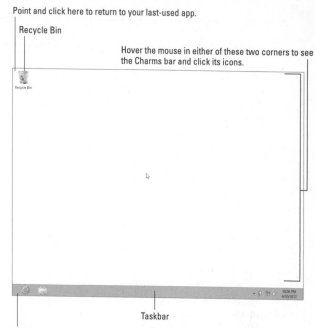

Taskbar

Point and click here to return to the Start screen.

Figure 3-1: The Windows 8 desktop lacks a Start button but otherwise looks identical to Windows 7.

The desktop, with its tiny buttons and thin bars, works best with a keyboard and mouse. If you're using Windows on a touchscreen tablet, you'll probably want to buy a portable mouse and keyboard for desktop work.

Touching the desktop on a touchscreen

Fingers work well for tapping the Start screen's extra-large tiles. And if you grimace enough, your touchscreen's touch controls will still work on the desktop's tiny buttons and thin borders. Here's how to control the desktop with your fingers:

✔ **Select:** To select something on the desktop, tap it with a fingertip; the pad of your finger may be too large.

✔ **Double-click:** To double-click something, tap it twice. Again, your fingertip works best.

✔ **Right-click:** To right-click an item, press your fingertip gently on it and wait for a small square to appear onscreen. When the square appears, remove your finger, and the pop-up menu stays on the screen. Then you can tap your desired option on the menu.

If your fingertip seems too wide for delicate desktop window maneuvers, buy a Bluetooth mouse and keyboard to use with your tablet. They turn it into two computers: the lightweight Start screen apps for casual computing and the full Windows desktop for doing some *real* work.

The Windows 8 desktop will run nearly all the Windows programs that ran on your old Windows XP, Windows Vista, or Windows 7 computer. Exceptions are antivirus programs, security suites, and some utility programs. Those don't usually transfer well from one Windows version to another.

Still addicted to apps? You can "snap" an app to the right or left side of your desktop, which gives you the best of both worlds. I describe how in this chapter's "Snapping an app alongside the desktop" section.

Working with the Desktop

Start screen apps hog the entire screen, making it difficult to multitask. The desktop, by contrast, lets you run several programs simultaneously, each living within its own little *window.* That lets you spread several programs across the screen, easily sharing bits of information between them.

Windows 8 starts with the freshly scrubbed, nearly empty desktop shown earlier in Figure 3-1. After you've been working for a while, your desktop will fill up with *icons* — little buttons that load your files with a quick double-click. Many people leave their desktops strewn with icons for easy access. Others organize their work: When they finish working on something, they store their files in a *folder,* a task covered in Chapter 5.

But no matter how you use the desktop, it comes with four main parts, labeled earlier in Figure 3-1:

- ✔ **Start screen:** Although hidden, you can fetch the Start screen by pointing your mouse at the very bottom-left corner and clicking the Start screen thumbnail. (A press of the ⊞ key returns you to the Start screen, as well.) When summoned, the Start screen still lets you choose programs to run on your desktop.

- ✔ **Taskbar:** Resting lazily along the desktop's bottom edge, the taskbar lists the desktop programs and files you currently have open, as well as icons for a few favored programs. (Point at a program's icon on the taskbar to see the program's name or perhaps a thumbnail photo of that program in action.)

✔ **Recycle Bin:** The desktop's *Recycle Bin,* that waste-basket-shaped icon, stores your recently deleted files for easy retrieval. Whew!

✔ **Charms bar:** Technically, the shortcut-filled Charms bar isn't part of the desktop; it lives *everywhere* in Windows 8, hidden beyond every screen's right edge. To summon the Charms bar with a mouse, point at your desktop's top- or bottom-right corners.

I cover those items later in this chapter and throughout the book, but these tricks will help you until you page ahead:

✔ You can start new projects directly from your desk-top: Right-click a blank part of the desktop, choose New, and choose the project of your dreams from the pop-up menu, be it loading a favorite program or creating a folder to store new files. (The New menu lists most of your computer's programs, allowing you to avoid a laborious journey back to the Start screen.)

✔ Are you befuddled about some desktop object's reason for being? Timidly rest the pointer over the mysterious doodad, and Windows pops up a little box explaining what that thing is or does. Right-click the object, and the ever-helpful Windows 8 usually tosses up a menu listing nearly everything you can do with that particular object. This trick works on most icons and buttons found on your desktop and its programs.

✔ All the icons on your desktop may suddenly disap-pear, leaving it completely empty. Chances are good that Windows 8 hid them in a misguided attempt to be helpful. To bring your work back to life, right-click your empty desktop and choose View from the pop-up menu. Finally, make sure the Show Desktop Icons menu option has a check mark so everything stays visible.

Summoning the Start screen and open apps

The Start button no longer lives in the desktop's bottom-left corner. Now, simply pointing and clicking at that little corner of desktop real estate fetches the new Windows 8 Start *screen.* When the Start screen appears, you click the app or program you'd like to run. To visit the Start screen from the desktop, as well as to revisit any recently opened apps, follow these steps:

1. **Point the mouse cursor at your screen's bottom-left corner.**

   A tiny thumbnail-sized Start screen icon rears its head. Click it to return to the Start screen.

   Or, if you want to return to any currently running apps, move to the next step.

2. **When the Start screen icon appears, slowly raise your mouse pointer along the screen's left edge.**

   As you move the pointer up the screen's edge, thumbnails of your open apps appear, leaving you with several choices:

   - To return to an open app, click its thumbnail. The desktop disappears, and the app fills the screen, looking just as you last left it.

   - To return to the desktop from any app, head for the Start screen and click the Desktop tile. Or, if you spot a Desktop thumbnail among the list of recently used apps, click the Desktop thumbnail to return to the desktop.

   - To close an open app, right-click its thumbnail and choose Close. The app disappears from the screen, leaving you at the desktop.

You can also fetch the Start screen by pressing the ⊞ key on your keyboard or tablet.

Cleaning up a messy desktop

When icons cover your desktop like a year's worth of sticky notes, Windows 8 offers several ways to clean up the mess. If you simply want your desktop clutter to look more organized — lined up straight or in organized piles, for example — then do this: Right-click the desktop and choose Sort By from the pop-up menu. The submenu offers these choices:

- ✔ **Name:** Arrange all icons in alphabetical order using neat, vertical rows.

- ✔ **Size:** Arrange icons according to their size, placing the smallest ones at the top of the rows.

- ✔ **Item Type:** This lines up icons by their *type*. All photographs are grouped together, for example, as are all links to websites.

- ✔ **Date Modified:** Arrange icons by the date you or your PC last changed them.

Right-clicking the desktop and choosing the View option lets you change the desktop icons' size, as well as play with these desk-organizing options:

- ✔ **Auto Arrange Icons:** Automatically arrange everything in vertical rows — even newly positioned icons are swept into tidy rows.

- ✔ **Align Icons to Grid:** Turned on by default, this option places an invisible grid on the screen and aligns all icons within the grid's borders to keep them nice and tidy — no matter how hard you try to mess them up.

✔ **Show Desktop Icons:** Always keep this option turned on. When turned off, Windows hides every icon on your desktop. If you can remember in your frustration, click this option again to toggle your icons back on.

✔ **Show Desktop Gadgets:** Gadgets are little things like clocks and weather forecasters you can add to your desktop. Introduced in Windows Vista and Windows 7 but rarely used, they've been replaced by apps.

Most View options are also available within any of your folders. To find them, click any folder's View tab that lives along its top edge.

Jazzing up the desktop's background

To jazz up your desktop, Windows 8 covers it with a pretty picture known as a *background.* (Many people refer to the background simply as *wallpaper.*) When you tire of the built-in scenery, feel free to replace it with a picture stored on your computer:

1. **Right-click a blank part of the desktop, choose Personalize, and click the Desktop Background option in the window's bottom-left corner.**

2. **Click any one of the pictures, and Windows 8 quickly places it onto your desktop's background.**

   Found a keeper? Click the Save Changes button to keep it on your desktop. Or, if you're still searching, move to the next step.

3. **Click the Browse button to see photos inside your Pictures library or My Pictures folder.**

Most people store their digital photos in their Pictures library or My Pictures folder.

4. **Click different pictures to see how they look as your desktop's background.**

When you find a background you like, you're done. Exit the program with a click in its upper-right corner, and your chosen photo drapes across your desktop.

Here are some tips on changing your desktop's background:

- Options listed in the Picture Position section let you choose whether the image should be *tiled* repeatedly across the screen, *centered* directly in the middle, or *stretched* to fill the entire screen. The Tile, Fill, and Fit options work best with small photos, such as those taken with cellphones, by repeating or enlarging them to fit the screen's borders.

- The desktop's Internet Explorer web browser can easily borrow any picture found on the Internet for a background. Right-click on the website's picture and choose Set as Background from the pop-up menu. Microsoft sneakily copies the image onto your desktop as its new background.

- If a background photograph makes your desktop icons too difficult to see, splash your desktop with a single color instead: After Step 1 of the preceding list, click the Picture Location box's down arrow. When the drop-down list appears, select Solid Colors. Choose your favorite color to have it fill your desktop.

- To change the entire *look* of Windows 8, right-click on the desktop, choose Personalize, and select a theme. Aimed at heavy-duty procrastinators, different themes splash different colors across the various Windows buttons, borders, and boxes.

Snapping an app alongside the desktop

Windows 8 normally keeps the Start screen and the desktop separated into two distinct worlds. You can work within the Start screen or within the desktop, but not both. Sometimes, though, that's not good enough.

For example, you may want to see the Start screen's Calendar app resting alongside your desktop to remind you of your day's commitments. Or perhaps you need your Messenger app open while you work, so you can consult a friend on a name for your latest jazz band. The solution is to *snap* your app alongside the desktop: The app consumes less than one quarter of the screen, while the desktop fills the rest, as shown in Figure 3-2. Or, you can give your app the larger screen portion, shrinking the desktop.

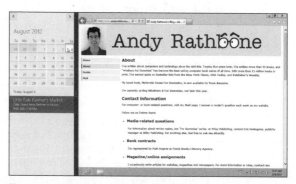

Figure 3-2: Snapping an app (placing it alongside your desktop) lets you view an app from the desktop.

To snap an app on your desktop, follow these steps:

1. **Open any Start screen app.**

   To reach the Start screen, press the ⊞ key. Or, using a mouse, point at the bottom-left corner of your desktop and click when the Start screen icon appears. Then open an app you want to snap alongside the desktop.

   If you're using a mouse or touchscreen, jump ahead to Step 3.

2. **If you're using a keyboard, hold down the ⊞ key and press the period key.**

   The app snaps to the left of your screen. (Press ⊞+. [period] again to snap the app to the screen's *right* edge, instead.) If you don't see the desktop along the app's side, move to Step 3; the desktop will open alongside the docked app.

3. **Switch back to the desktop.**

   To return to the desktop, hold down the ⊞ key and press D, or click the Start screen's Desktop tile.

4. **Snap the app of your choosing against your desktop.**

   These steps are much simpler to *do* than read. But here goes:

   - **Mouse:** Point at the screen's top- or bottom-left corner until a thumbnail of your most recently used app appears. Right-click the desired app and, from the pop-up menu, choose Snap Left or Snap Right to snap the app to the screen side of your choosing.

   - **Touchscreen:** Slowly drag your finger from the left edge of the screen inward; your most recently opened app appears, following along with the motion of your finger. When a vertical strip appears onscreen, lift your finger, and the app snaps itself to the screen's left edge.

When the app snaps against the desktop's edge, it leaves a vertical bar separating it from your desktop. When the app snaps against the desktop's edge, it stays there, even if you switch to the Start screen or load other apps.

Although app snapping works well for a few tasks, it comes with more rules than a librarian:

- ✔ To *unsnap* the app, drag that vertical bar toward the screen's edge. Or press ⊞+. (period) until the app disappears.

- ✔ When the app sticks to the side, you can drag the vertical bar inward, making the app fill most of the screen and turning the desktop into a rather useless little strip.

- ✔ To toggle the app from one edge to another, press ⊞+. (period); the app switches sides. Press ⊞+. (period) again, and the app unsnaps from the edge.

- ✔ You can't snap an app to the side of the Start screen. The Start screen *always* consumes the entire screen. But when you switch away from the Start screen, the previously snapped app will still be in place, clinging to its same edge.

- ✔ You can only snap *one* app at a time. For example, you can't snap an app onto each side of your desktop.

- ✔ You can snap apps only on a screen with a resolution of at least 1366 x 768. In human language, that means an *extra-wide* computer screen, which you won't find on most netbooks or older laptops. You *will* find that resolution, however, on all Windows 8 tablets.

✔ To see your screen's resolution, open the desktop by pressing ⊞+D. Right-click a blank part of your desktop and choose Screen Resolution from the pop-up menu. You can select your resolution from the Resolution drop-down scroll bar. (You should usually choose the highest resolution offered.)

Dumpster diving in the Recycle Bin

The Recycle Bin, that glass wastebasket icon in the corner of your desktop, works much like a *real* recycle bin. It lets you retrieve the discarded coupons you thought you'd never need. You can dump something from the desktop — a file or folder, for example — into the Windows 8 Recycle Bin in either of these ways:

✔ Simply right-click on the unwanted item and choose Delete from the menu. Windows 8 asks cautiously if you're *sure* that you want to delete the item. Click Yes, and Windows 8 dumps it into the Recycle Bin, just as if you'd dragged it there. Whoosh!

✔ For a quick deletion rush, click the unwanted object and poke your Delete key.

Want something back? Double-click the Recycle Bin icon to see your recently deleted items. Right-click the item you want and choose Restore. The handy little Recycle Bin returns your precious item to the same spot where you deleted it. (You can also resuscitate deleted items by dragging them to your desktop or any other folder; drag 'em back into the Recycle Bin to delete them again.)

The Recycle Bin can get pretty crowded. If you're searching frantically for a recently deleted file, tell the Recycle Bin to sort everything by the date and time you deleted it: Right-click an empty area inside the Recycle Bin and

choose Sort By. Then choose Date Deleted from the
pop-up menu.

To delete something *permanently,* just delete it from
inside the Recycle Bin: Click it and press the Delete key.
To delete *everything* in the Recycle Bin, right-click the
Recycle Bin icon and choose Empty Recycle Bin.

To bypass the Recycle Bin completely when deleting files,
hold down Shift while pressing Delete. Poof! The deleted
object disappears, ne'er to be seen again — a handy trick
when dealing with sensitive items.

✔ The Recycle Bin icon changes from an empty waste-
paper basket to a full one as soon as it's holding any
deleted file or files.

✔ Your Recycle Bin keeps your deleted files until the
garbage consumes about 5 percent of your hard
drive space. Then it purges your oldest deleted files
to make room for the new. If you're low on hard
drive space, shrink the bin's size by right-clicking
the Recycle Bin and choosing Properties. Decrease
the Custom Size number to purge the bin more
quickly; increase the number, and the Recycle Bin
hangs onto files a little longer.

✔ The Recycle Bin saves only items deleted from your
own computer's drives. That means it won't save
anything deleted from a CD, memory card, MP3
player, flash drive, or digital camera.

✔ If you delete something from somebody else's
computer over a network, it can't be retrieved. The
Recycle Bin holds only items deleted from your *own*
computer, not somebody else's computer. (For some
awful reason, the Recycle Bin on the other person's
computer doesn't save the item, either.) Be careful.

Bellying Up to the Taskbar

Whenever more than one window sits across your desktop, you face a logistics problem: Programs and windows tend to overlap, making them difficult to spot. To make matters worse, programs such as Internet Explorer and Microsoft Word can each contain several windows apiece. How do you keep track of all the windows?

The Windows 8 solution is the *taskbar* — a special area that keeps track of your currently running programs and their windows. Shown in Figure 3-3, the taskbar lives along the bottom of your desktop, constantly updating itself to show an icon for every currently running program.

Figure 3-3: Click buttons for currently running programs on the taskbar.

Not sure what a taskbar icon does? Rest your mouse pointer over any of the taskbar's icons to see either the program's name or a thumbnail image of the program's contents, as shown in Figure 3-3. In that figure, for example, you can see that Internet Explorer contains two web pages.

From the taskbar, you can perform powerful magic, as described in the following list:

✔ **To play with a program listed on the taskbar, click its icon.** Whenever you load a program on the desktop, its icon automatically appears on the taskbar. If one of your open windows ever gets lost on your desktop, click its icon on the taskbar to bring it to the forefront. Clicking the taskbar icon yet again minimizes that same window.

✔ **To close a window listed on the taskbar, *right-click* its icon and choose Close from the pop-up menu.** The program quits, just as if you'd chosen its Exit command from within its own window.

✔ **Traditionally, the taskbar lives along your desktop's bottom edge, but you can move it to any edge you want, a handy space saver on extra-wide monitors.** (*Hint:* Try dragging it to your screen's side. If it doesn't move, right-click the taskbar and click Lock the Taskbar to remove the check mark by that option.)

✔ **If the taskbar keeps hiding below the screen's bottom edge, point the mouse at the screen's bottom edge until the taskbar surfaces.** Then right-click the taskbar, choose Properties, and remove the check mark from Auto-Hide the Taskbar.

✔ **You can add your favorite programs directly to the taskbar.** From the Start screen, right-click the favored program's tile and choose Pin to Taskbar. The program's icon then lives on the taskbar for easy access, just as if it were running. Tired of the program hogging space on your taskbar? Right-click it and choose Unpin This Program from Taskbar.

Shrinking windows to the taskbar and retrieving them

Windows spawn windows. You start with one window to write a letter of praise to your local taco shop. You open another window to check an address, for example, and then yet another to ogle online reviews. Before you know it, four more windows are crowded across the desktop. To combat the clutter, Windows 8 provides a simple means of window control: You can transform a window from a screen-cluttering square into a tiny button on the taskbar, which sits along the bottom of the screen. The solution is the Minimize button.

See the three buttons lurking in just about every window's top-right corner? Click the *Minimize button* — the button with the little line in it, shown in the margin. Whoosh! The window disappears, represented by its little button on the taskbar at your screen's bottom.

To make a minimized program on the taskbar revert to a regular, onscreen window, just click its icon on the taskbar. Pretty simple, huh?

Switching to different tasks from the taskbar's Jump Lists

The Windows 8 taskbar doesn't limit you to opening programs and switching between windows. You can jump to other tasks, as well, by right-clicking the taskbar's icons. As shown in Figure 3-4, right-clicking the Internet Explorer icon brings up a quick list of your recently visited websites. Click any site on the list to make a quick return visit.

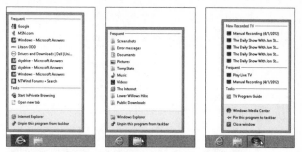

Figure 3-4: Jump Lists, from left to right: Internet Explorer, File Explorer, and Windows Media Center.

Called *Jump Lists,* these pop-up menus add a new trick to the taskbar: They let you jump to previously visited locations, letting you work more quickly.

Clicking the taskbar's sensitive areas

Like a crafty card player, the taskbar comes with a few tips and tricks. For example, here's the lowdown on the icons near the taskbar's right edge, shown in Figure 3-5, known as the *notification area.* Different items appear in the notification area depending on your PC and programs, but you'll probably encounter some of these:

✔ **Minimize Windows:** This small strip hidden against the taskbar's far-right edge instantly minimizes all open windows when you click it. (Click it again to put the windows back in place.)

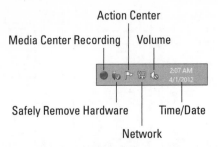

Action Center

Media Center Recording | Volume

Safely Remove Hardware | Time/Date

Network

Figure 3-5: The taskbar's tiny icons along the right edge mostly show items running in the background on your PC.

✔ **Time/Date:** Click the time and date to fetch a handy monthly calendar and clock. If you want to change the time or date, or even add a second time zone, click the Time/Date area and choose Change Date and Time Settings.

✔ **Windows Media Center Recording:** The glowing red circle means Windows Media Center, available separately as an add-on, is currently recording something off the television.

✔ **Media Center Guide Listings:** Media Center is downloading the latest TV listings.

✔ **Safely Remove Hardware:** Before unplugging a storage device, click here. That tells Windows to prepare the gadget for unplugging.

✔ **Action Center:** Windows wants you to do something, be it to click a permission window, install an antivirus program, check your last backup, or perform some other important task.

✔ **Wired Network:** This appears when you're connected to the Internet or other PCs through a wired network. Not connected? A red X appears over the icon.

✔ **Wireless Network:** Your PC is wirelessly connected to the Internet or other network. When all five bars show, you have a very strong signal.

✔ **Volume:** Click or tap this ever-so-handy little speaker icon to adjust your PC's volume.

✔ **Windows Problem Reporting:** When Windows runs into trouble, this icon appears; click it to see possible solutions.

✔ **Windows Automatic Updates:** This icon appears when Windows downloads *updates,* usually small programs designed to fix your PC, from Microsoft's website at Windows Update.

✔ **Task Manager:** This little program can end misbehaving programs, monitor background tasks, monitor performance, and do other stuff of techie dreams.

✔ **Windows Host Process:** This dismally named icon delivers an even worse message: Your newly plugged-in gadget won't work, be it your printer, scanner, music player, or other item. Try unplugging the device, running its installation software again, and plugging it back in.

✔ **Explorer:** Older PCs come with two types of USB ports: fast and slow. This icon means you've plugged a speedy gadget into your slow port. Try unplugging it and plugging it into a different port. (The USB ports on a desktop computer's back side are often the faster ones.)

✔ **Power, Outlet:** This shows that your laptop is plugged into an electrical outlet and is charging its battery.

✔ **Power, Battery:** Your laptop or tablet is running on batteries only. (Rest your mouse pointer over the icon to see how much power remains.)

✔ **Arrow:** Sometimes the taskbar hides things. If you see a tiny upward-pointing arrow at the start of the taskbar's notification area, click it to see a few hidden icons slide out.

Customizing the taskbar

Windows 8 brings a whirlwind of options for the lowly taskbar, letting you play with it in more ways than a strand of spaghetti and a fork. And that's especially important in Windows 8: By stocking the taskbar with icons for oft-used programs, you can avoid unnecessary trips to the Start screen.

First, the taskbar comes preloaded with two icons on its far left: Internet Explorer (your full-featured web browser) and File Explorer (your file browser). Like all your taskbar icons, they're movable, so feel free to drag them to any order you want.

If you spot a favored program's icon on your Start screen, right-click the icon and choose Pin to Taskbar from the pop-up menu. You can drag and drop a desktop program's icon directly onto the taskbar, as well.

For even more customization, right-click a blank part of the taskbar and choose Properties to make Taskbar Properties dialog box appear.

Feel free to experiment with the taskbar until it looks right for you. After you've changed an option, see the changes immediately by clicking the Apply button. Don't like the change? Reverse your decision and click Apply to return to normal. After you set up the taskbar just the way you want it, select the Lock the Taskbar check box to keep it that way.

The Jump Lists tab of the Taskbar Properties dialog box placates privacy seekers. It lets you prevent Jump Lists (described earlier in this chapter) from remembering where you've been, so others don't see those places in your Jump Lists.

The taskbar's crazy toolbars

Your taskbar won't always be a steadfast, unchanging friend. Microsoft lets you customize it even further, often beyond the point of recognition. Some people enjoy adding *toolbars,* which tack extra buttons and menus onto their taskbar. Others accidentally turn on a toolbar and can't figure out how to get rid of the darn thing.

To turn a toolbar on or off, right-click on a blank part of the taskbar (even the clock will do) and choose Toolbars from the pop-up menu. A menu leaps out, offering these five toolbar options:

✔ **Address:** Choose this toolbar, and part of your task-bar becomes a place for typing websites to visit.

✔ **Links:** This toolbar adds quick access to your favor-ite websites.

✔ **Touch Keyboard:** A perk for tablet owners, this adds a button that brings a keyboard to the forefront for touch-typing on the glass.

✔ **Desktop:** The real gem, this toolbar adds quick access to *all* your PC's resources, often saving a trip to the Start screen.

    ✔ **New Toolbar:** This lets you create a toolbar from
any folder's contents, which is handy for people
who always store special projects in one particular
folder.

Making Programs Easier to Find

After you've found your way to the desktop on a desktop PC, you'll probably want to stay there and avoid the
Start screen's over-stretching conglomeration of clunky
tiles. Avoid that time-wasting trip to the Start screen by
stocking your desktop with shortcuts to your favorite
programs and places. This section explains how to set up
camp on the desktop and stay there as long as possible.

Add five helpful icons to your desktop

When first opened, the desktop contains only three icons:
the Recycle Bin lives in the top corner; the taskbar's left
corner offers File Explorer (for browsing your own files)
and Internet Explorer (for browsing the world's offerings
on the web). Everything else requires a trip to the Start
screen. Until you follow these steps, that is:

   1. **Right-click a blank portion of your desktop and
choose Personalize.**

     The Personalization window appears.

   2. **On the Personalization window's left side, click
the Change Desktop Icons link.**

     The Desktop Icon Settings window appears.

3. **Put a check mark in the top five boxes: Computer, User's Files, Network, Recycle Bin, and Control Panel. Then click Apply.**

   Shortcuts for those five icons appear on your desktop for quick and easy access.

4. **Remove the check mark from the option labeled Allow Themes to Change Desktop Icons.**

   That ensures that those icons will stay put, even if you drape your desktop with a decorative theme.

After those icons appear on your desktop, feel free to drag and drop them any place you'd like. Chances are good that they'll save you quite a few trips to the Start screen.

Creating taskbar shortcuts for your favorite programs

Whenever you install a new program on your computer, the program usually asks way too many obtuse questions. But perk up your ears when you see this question: "Would you like a shortcut icon placed on your desktop or taskbar?" Say yes, please, as that will save you from dashing out to the Start screen to find the program's tile.

But if your favorite programs don't yet have icons on the desktop or taskbar, put them there by following these steps:

1. **Head to the Start screen and open its menu bar.**

   Right-click a blank portion of the Start screen (or press ⊞+Z) to reveal the Start screen's menu bar along the screen's bottom edge. (Or, if you're a touchscreen owner, reveal the bar by sliding your finger up from the Start screen's bottom edge.) Chapter 2 covers the Start screen and its menus.

2. **From the bottom menu, click the All Apps icon to see a list of all your available apps and programs.**

3. **On the Start screen, right-click any app or program you want to appear on the desktop and choose Pin to Taskbar.**

   In an odd break in protocol, touchscreens can't right-click on the Start screen. Instead, *select* a Start screen tile: Hold your finger down on the tile and slide your finger down a fraction of an inch. When a check mark appears in the tile's upper-right corner, lift your finger. The menu bar appears below, letting you tap the Pin to Taskbar option.

   To *deselect* the tile, slide your finger down on it, just as before. This time, though, the check mark disappears.

4. **Repeat Step 3 for every app or program you want to add.**

   Unfortunately, you can't select several simultaneously.

When you're through, your taskbar will have sprouted new icons for your favorite programs. Now, instead of heading to the Start screen, you can launch them straight from the taskbar.

After you've stocked your taskbar with icons, pretend they're numbered, from left to right. Pressing ⊞+1 from the desktop opens the first program; ⊞+2 opens the second, and so on. You've created automatic shortcuts!

Chapter 4

Basic Desktop Window Mechanics

● ●

In This Chapter

▶ Understanding a window's parts

▶ Manipulating buttons, bars, and boxes

▶ Finding commands on the Ribbon

▶ Understanding the Navigation Pane

▶ Moving windows and changing their size

● ●

*T*he simplistic Windows 8 Start screen comes with bold, oversized buttons, large letters, and bright colors that shout from the screen. The Windows desktop, by contrast, comes with miniscule, monochrome buttons, tiny lettering, and windows with pencil-thin borders.

And in another contrast, every Start screen app fills the entire screen for easy viewing. On the crowded desktop, though, dozens of windows can overlap. To help you maneuver through this messy maze of desktop windows, this chapter provides a windows anatomy and navigation lesson.

Dissecting a Typical Desktop Window

Figure 4-1 places a typical window on the slab, with all its parts labeled. You might recognize the window as your Documents library, that storage tank for most of your work.

Windows behave differently depending on where they've been clicked. The next few sections describe the main parts of the Documents library window in Figure 4-1, how to click them, and how Windows reacts in response.

✔ Windows XP veterans remember their My Documents folder — that stash for all their files. Windows Vista dropped the word *My* to create the Documents folder; Windows 7 and Windows 8 put the word *My* back in place. (No matter what it's called, you're still supposed to stash your files inside it.)

✔ In a break from the past, Windows 8 places a thick, control-filled panel called the *Ribbon* to the top of your folders.

✔ Windows 8 places your My Documents folder inside your Documents *library* — a type of super folder described in Chapter 5. The Documents library displays both your My Documents folder and the Public Documents folder. (Everybody who uses your PC sees the same Public Documents folder, making it a handy folder for sharing files.)

✔ Windows 8 is full of little oddly shaped buttons, borders, and boxes. You don't need to remember all their names, although that would give you a leg up on figuring out the scholarly Windows Help menus.

Ribbon menu

Ribbon menu tabs

Quick Access toolbar

Backward

Forward

Home tab

Maximize

Share tab   Manage tab   Minimize Close

View tab   Title bar

Help

Minimize the Ribbon menu

Search box

Refresh view

Up one folder

Folder history

Scroll box   Preview pane

Vertical scroll bar

Navigation pane

Address bar

Figure 4-1: Here's how the ever-precise computer nerds address the parts of a window.

✔ You can deal with most things in Windows by clicking, double-clicking, or right-clicking. ***Hint:*** When in doubt, always right-click.

✔ Navigating the desktop on a touchscreen computer? For some touching tips, drop by Chapter 3 for information on touching the desktop on a Windows 8 tablet.

✔ After you click a few windows a few times, you realize how easy it is to boss them around. The hard part is finding the right controls for the *first* time, like figuring out the dashboard on that rental car.

Tugging on a window's title bar

Found atop nearly every window, the title bar usually lists the program name and the file it's currently working on.

Although mild-mannered, the mundane title bar holds hidden powers, described in the following tips:

✔ Title bars make convenient handles for moving windows around your desktop. Point at a blank part of the title bar, hold down the mouse button, and move the mouse around: The window follows along as you move your mouse. Let go of the mouse button, and the window sets up camp in its new spot.

✔ Double-click a blank portion of the title bar, and the window leaps to fill the entire screen. Double-click it again, and the window retreats to its original size.

✔ The cluster of little icons in a program's top-left corner form the Quick Access Toolbar, and it's part of what Microsoft calls a *Ribbon interface.* The icons offer one-click access to common tasks such as saving a file.

✔ The right end of the title bar contains three square buttons. From left to right, they let you Minimize, Restore (or Maximize), or Close a window.

✔ To find the window you're currently working on, look for a darker title bar sporting a red Close button in its top-right corner. By glancing at all the title bars on the screen, you can tell which window is awake and accepting anything you type.

Dragging, dropping, and running

Although the phrase *drag and drop* sounds as if it's straight out of a Mafia guidebook, it's really a nonviolent mouse trick used throughout Windows. Dragging and dropping is a way of moving something — say, an icon on your desktop — from one place to another.

To *drag,* put the mouse pointer over the icon and *hold down* the left or right mouse button. (I prefer the right mouse button.) As you move the mouse across your desk, the pointer drags the icon across the screen. Place the pointer/icon where you want it and release the mouse button. The icon *drops,* unharmed.

Holding down the *right* mouse button while dragging and dropping makes Windows toss up a helpful little menu, asking whether you want to *copy* or *move* the icon.

Helpful Tip Department: Did you start dragging something and real-ize midstream that you're dragging the wrong item? Don't let go of the mouse button — instead, press Esc to cancel the action. Whew! (If you've dragged with your right mouse button and already let go of the button, there's another exit: Choose Cancel from the pop-up menu.)

Navigating folders with a window's Address Bar

Directly beneath every folder's title bar lives the *Address Bar,* shown atop the Documents library in Figure 4-2. Internet Explorer veterans will experience déjà vu: The Windows 8 Address Bar is lifted straight from the top of Internet Explorer and glued atop every folder.

Figure 4-2: An Address Bar.

The Address Bar's four main parts, described from left to right in the following list, perform four different duties:

- ✔ **Backward and Forward buttons:** These two arrows keep track as you forage through your PC's folders. The Backward button backtracks to the folder you just visited. The Forward button brings you back. (Click the miniscule arrow to the right of the Forward arrow to see a list of places you've visited previously; click any entry to zoom right there.)

- ✔ **Up Arrow button:** Click the Up Arrow button to move up one folder from your current folder.

- ✔ **Address Bar:** The Windows 8 Address Bar displays your current folder's address — its location inside your PC.

- ✔ **Search box:** As in Internet Explorer, every Windows 8 folder sports a Search box. Instead of searching the Internet, though, it rummages through your folder's contents.

In the Address Bar, notice the little arrows between the words *Libraries, Documents,* and *Stuff.* The arrows offer quick trips to other folders. Click any arrow — the one to the right of the word *Documents,* for example. A little menu drops down from the arrow, letting you jump to any other folder inside your Documents library.

Finding commands on the Ribbon

The Windows desktop has more menu items than an Asian restaurant. To keep everybody's minds on computer commands instead of seaweed salad, Windows 8 places menus inside a new tab-filled *Ribbon* that lives atop every folder and library. (See Figure 4-3.)

Figure 4-3: The Ribbon's tabs.

The Ribbon's tabs each offer different options. To reveal the secret options, click any tab — Share, for example. The Ribbon quickly changes, as shown in Figure 4-4, presenting all your options related to *sharing* a file.

Figure 4-4: Click any Ribbon tab to see its associated commands.

Sometimes a window isn't capable of offering all its menu items. Any unavailable options are *grayed out,* like the Print option in Figure 4-4. If a button's meaning isn't immediately obvious, hover your mouse pointer over it; a little message explains the button's *raison d'être*. My own translations for the most common tabs and buttons are in the following list:

- ✔ **File:** Found along every Ribbon's left edge, this handy shortcut offers little in rewards: basically, opening new windows.

- ✔ **Home:** Found on every folder's Ribbon, the Home tab offers tools to select, cut, copy, paste, move, delete, or rename a folder's items.

- ✔ **Share:** As the name implies, this offers ways to let you share a folder's contents with other people using your computer. More important, by clicking a name and clicking the Stop Sharing button, you can cut off access to mistakenly shared documents.

- ✔ **View:** Click here to change how files appear in the window. In your Pictures library, for example, choose Extra Large Icons to see larger thumbnails of your photos.

- ✔ **Manage:** This general-purpose tab shows customized ways to handle your folder's items. Atop the Pictures library, for example, it offers a Slide Show button, as well as buttons to rotate skewed photos or turn them into desktop backgrounds.

Don't like that thick Ribbon hogging an inch of space atop your window? If you're pressed for space, axe the ribbon by clicking the little upward-pointing arrow next to the blue question mark icon in the upper-right corner. Click it again to bring back the Ribbon. (Or hold down the Ctrl key and press F1 to toggle it on and off again, which is often more fun than doing something productive.)

Quick shortcuts with the Navigation Pane

Look at most "real" desktops, and you'll see the most-used items sitting within arm's reach. Similarly, Windows 8 gathers your PC's most frequently used items and places them in the Navigation Pane.

Found along the left edge of every folder, the Navigation Pane contains five main sections: Favorites, Libraries, Homegroup, Computer, and Network. Click any of those sections, and the window's right side shows you the contents of what you've clicked. Here's a description of each part of the Navigation Pane:

✓ **Favorites:** Not to be confused with your favorite websites in Internet Explorer, the Favorites in the Navigation Pane are words serving as clickable shortcuts to your most frequently accessed locations in Windows: Desktop, Downloads, Recent Places, and Recorded TV (if you've ponied up the extra cash to buy the Windows 8 Media Pack for recording TV shows).

✓ **Libraries:** Unlike normal folders, libraries show you the contents of several folders, all collected in one place for easy viewing. Windows' libraries (Documents, Music, Pictures, and Videos) begin by showing the contents of two folders: your _own_ folder and its _public_ equivalent, which is available to anyone with an account on your PC.

✓ **Homegroup:** A convenient way of sharing information between several household computers, Homegroups are two or more PCs that share information through a simple network.

✔ **Computer:** Opened mainly by PC techies, this button lets you browse through your PC's folders and disks.

✔ **Network:** Although Homegroups simplify file sharing, old-school networks still work in Windows 8, and any networked PCs — including your Homegroup buddies — appear here.

To avoid treks back to the Start screen, add your own favorite places to the Navigation Pane's Favorites area: Drag and drop folders onto the word Favorites, and they turn into clickable shortcuts.

Messed up your Favorites or Libraries area? Tell Windows 8 to repair the damage by right-clicking the problem child and choosing Restore Favorite Links or Restore Default Libraries.

Moving inside a window with its scroll bar

The scroll bar rests along the edge of all overstuffed windows. You can even find a scroll bar along the bottom of the Start screen. Inside the scroll bar the *scroll box* rides along as you move through the window's contents. In fact, by glancing at the box's position in the scroll bar, you can tell whether you're viewing items in the window's beginning, middle, or end.

By clicking in various places on the scroll bar, you can quickly view different parts of things. Here's the dirt:

✔ Click inside the scroll bar in the direction you want to view. On a *vertical* scroll bar, for example, click above the scroll box to move your view up one page; similarly, click below the scroll box to move your view down a page.

✔ Clicking the scroll bar along the bottom of the Start screen lets you view any shy apps hiding beyond the screen's right edge.

✔ Don't see a scroll box in the bar? Then you're already seeing all that the window has to offer; there's nothing to scroll.

✔ To move around in a hurry, drag the scroll box inside the scroll bar. As you drag, you see the window's contents race past. When you see the spot you want, let go of the mouse button to stay at that viewing position.

✔ Spin your mouse wheel, and the scroll box moves quickly inside the scroll bar, shifting your view accordingly. It's a handy way to explore the Start screen, long documents, and file-filled folders.

Boring borders

A *border* is that thin edge surrounding a window. Compared with a bar, it's really tiny.

To change a window's size, drag the border in or out. (Dragging by a corner gives the best results.) Some windows, oddly enough, don't have borders. Stuck in limbo, their size can't be changed — even if they're an awkward size.

Maneuvering Windows Around the Desktop

A terrible dealer at the poker table, Windows 8 tosses windows around your desktop in a seemingly random way. Programs cover each other or sometimes dangle off the desktop. This section shows you how to gather all your windows into a neat pile, placing your favorite window on the top of the stack. If you prefer, lay them all down like a poker hand. As an added bonus, you can change their size, making them open to any size you want, automatically.

Moving a window to the top of the pile

Windows 8 says the window atop the pile that gets all the attention is called the *active* window. Being the active window means that it receives any keystrokes you or your cat happen to type. You can move a window to the top of the pile so that it's active in any of several ways:

- ✔ Move the mouse pointer until it hovers over any portion of your desired window; then click the mouse button. Windows 8 immediately brings the window to the top of the pile.

- ✔ On the taskbar along the desktop's bottom, click the button for the window you want.

- ✔ Hold down the Alt key and keep tapping the Tab key. A small window pops up, displaying a thumbnail of each open window on your desktop. When your press of the Tab key highlights your favorite window, let go of the Alt key: Your window leaps to the forefront.

✔ Hold down the Windows key (⊞) and keep tapping the Tab key. A bar appears along your screen's left edge, showing thumbnails of all your running apps and programs. When your tap of the Tab key highlights your desired window, let go of the ⊞ key.

Is your desktop too cluttered for you to work comfortably in your current window? Then hold down your mouse pointer on the window's title bar and give it a few quick shakes; Windows 8 drops the other windows down to the taskbar, leaving your main window resting alone on an empty desktop.

Moving a window from here to there

Sometimes you want to move a window to a different place on the desktop. You can move a window by dragging and dropping its *title bar,* that thick bar along its top. When you *drop* the window in place, the window not only remains where you've dragged and dropped it, but it also stays on top of the pile — until you click another window, that is, which brings *that* window to the pile's top.

Making a window fill the whole screen

Sooner or later, you'll grow tired of all this multiwindow mumbo jumbo. To make any desktop window grow as large as possible, double-click its *title bar,* that bar along the window's topmost edge. The window leaps up to fill the screen, covering up all the other windows. To bring the pumped-up window back to its former size, double-click its title bar once again. The window quickly shrinks to its former size, and you can see things that it covered.

- ✔ If you're morally opposed to double-clicking a window's title bar to expand it, you can click the little Maximize button. It's the middle of the three buttons in the upper-right corner of every window.

- ✔ When a window is maximized to fill the screen, the Maximize button turns into a Restore button. Click the Restore button, and the window returns to its smaller size.

- ✔ Need a brute force method? Then drag a window's top edge until it butts against the top edge of your desktop. The shadow of the window's borders expands to fill the screen; let go of the mouse button, and the window's borders fill the screen. (Yes, simply double-clicking the title bar is faster, but this method impresses any onlookers from neighboring cubicles.)

- ✔ Too busy to reach for the mouse? Maximize the current window by holding down the ⊞ key and pressing the Up Arrow key.

Closing a window

When you're through working in a window, close it: Click the little X in its upper-right corner. Zap! You're back to an empty desktop.

If you try to close your window before finishing your work, be it a game of Solitaire or a report for the boss, Windows cautiously asks whether you'd like to save your work. Take it up on its offer by clicking Yes and, if necessary, typing in a filename so that you can find your work later.

Making a window bigger or smaller

Like big, lazy dogs, windows tend to flop on top of one another. To space your windows more evenly, you can resize them by *dragging and dropping* their edges inward or outward. It works like this:

1. **Point at any corner with the mouse arrow. When the arrow turns into a two-headed arrow, pointing in the two directions, you can hold down the mouse button and drag the corner in or out to change the window's size.**

2. **When you're happy with the window's new size, release the mouse button.**

   As the yoga master says, the window assumes the new position.

Placing two windows side by side

The longer you use Windows, the more likely you are to want to see two windows side by side. For example, you may want to copy things from one window into another, or compare two versions of the same file. By spending a few hours with the mouse, you can drag and drop the windows' corners until they're in perfect juxtaposition. If you're impatient, Windows lets you speed up this handy side-by-side placement several ways:

✔ For the quickest solution, drag a window's title bar against one side of your screen; when your mouse pointer touches the screen's edge, let go of the mouse button. Repeat these same steps with the second window, dragging it to the opposite side of the monitor.

✔ Right-click on a blank part of the taskbar (even the clock will do) and choose Show Windows Side by Side. The windows align next to each other, like pillars. To align them in horizontal rows, choose Show Windows Stacked. (If you have more than three open windows, Show Windows Stacked tiles them across your screen, handy for seeing just a bit of each one.)

✔ If you have more than two windows open, click the Minimize button (the leftmost icon in every window's top-right corner) to minimize the windows you *don't* want tiled. Then use the Show Windows Side by Side from the preceding bullet to align the two remaining windows.

✔ To make the current window fill the screen's right half, hold the ▦ key and press the → key. To fill the screen's left half, hold the ▦ key and press the ← key.

Making windows open to the same darn size

Sometimes a window opens to a small square; other times, it opens to fill the entire screen. But windows rarely open to the exact size you want. Until you discover this trick, that is: When you *manually* adjust the size and placement of a window, Windows memorizes that size and always reopens the window to that same size. (Be sure to resize the window *manually* by dragging its corners or edges with the mouse. Simply clicking the Maximize button won't work.)

Follow these three steps to see how it works:

1. **Open your window.**

   The window opens to its usual unwanted size.

2. **Drag the window's corners until the window is the exact size and in the exact location you want; then let go of the mouse.**

3. **Immediately close the window.**

   Windows memorizes the size and placement of a window at the time it was last closed. When you open that window again, it should open to the same size you last left it. But the changes you make apply only to the program you made them in. For example, changes made to the Internet Explorer window will be remembered only for *Internet Explorer,* not for other programs you open.

Most windows follow these sizing rules, but a few renegades from other programs may misbehave, unfortunately.

Storage: Internal, Exton...
and in the Sky

••

In This Chapter

▶ Managing files with the desktop's File Explorer

▶ Navigating drives, folders, and flash drives

▶ Understanding libraries

▶ Creating and naming folders

▶ Selecting and deselecting items

▶ Duplicating and relocating files and folders

▶ Writing to CDs and memory cards

▶ Understanding Windows SkyDrive

••

*E*verybody hoped the new Start screen would
their work, finally transcending the complica
world of files and folders. Unfortunately, that's r
case. Insert a flash drive or plug your digital car
your Windows 8 computer, and the Start scree
you onto the Windows desktop. There, File Ex
Windows' age-old digital filing cabinet — rear

Because the Start screen lacks a file manager, you're stuck with File Explorer whenever you need to find folders inside your computer, *outside* your computer on plug-in drives, and even in storage spots on the Internet. This chapter explains how to use the Windows 8 filing program, called *File Explorer.* Along the way, you ingest a big enough dose of Windows file management for you to get your work done.

Browsing the File Explorer File Cabinets

To keep your programs and files neatly arranged, Windows cleaned up the squeaky old file cabinet metaphor with whisper-quiet Windows icons. Inside File Explorer, the icons represent your computer's storage areas, allowing you to copy, move, rename, or delete your files before the investigators arrive.

To see your computer's file cabinets — called *drives* or *disks* in computer lingo — open the Start screen's File Explorer tile. The Start screen vanishes, and the Windows desktop appears, with your files and folders listed in File Explorer. File Explorer can display its contents in many ways. To see your computer's storage areas, click the word Computer from the pane along the left edge.

The File Explorer image shown in Figure 5-1 will look slightly different from the one on your PC, but you'll still see the same basic sections, each described in the upcoming list.

Figure 5-1: The File Explorer window displays your computer's storage areas.

The File Explorer window comes with these main parts:

- ✔ **Navigation Pane:** The handy Navigation Pane, that strip along the left edge, lists shortcuts to special folders called *libraries* that hold your most valuable computerized possessions: your Documents, Music, Pictures, and Videos. (It tosses in a few other convenient items, covered in Chapter 4.)

- ✔ **Hard Disk Drives:** Shown in Figure 5-1, this area lists your PC's *hard drives* — your biggest storage areas. Every computer has at least one hard drive. Double-clicking a hard drive icon displays its files and folders, but you'll rarely find much useful information when probing that way. No, your most important files live in your Documents, Music, Pictures, and Videos libraries, which live one click away on the Navigation Pane.

Notice the hard drive bearing the little Windows icon? That means Windows 8 lives on that drive. The more colored space you see in the line next to each hard drive's icon, the more files you've stuffed onto your drive. When the line turns red, your drive is almost full, and you should think about upgrading to a larger drive.

✔ **Devices with Removable Storage:** This area shows detachable storage gadgetry attached to your computer. Some of the more common ones include CD, DVD, and Blu-ray drives; memory card readers and flash drives; MP3 players; and digital cameras.

✔ **Network Location:** This icon is seen only by people who've linked groups of PCs into a *network*; it represents the Media Player library living on another PC. Click one of these icons to access the music, photos, and video stored on those other PCs.

If you plug a digital camcorder, cellphone, or other gadget into your PC, the File Explorer window will often sprout a new icon representing your gadget. If Windows neglects to ask what you'd like to do with your newly plugged-in gadget, right-click the icon; you see a list of everything you can do with that item. No icon? Then you need to install a *driver* for your gadget.

Getting the Lowdown on Folders and Libraries

A *folder* is a storage area on a drive, just like a real folder in a file cabinet. Windows 8 divides your computer's hard drives into many folders to separate your many projects.

For example, you store all your music in your My Music folder and your pictures in your My Pictures folder.

A *library,* by contrast, is a super folder. Instead of showing the contents of a single folder, it shows the contents of *several* folders. For example, your Music library shows the tunes living in your *My* Music folder, as well as the tunes in your *Public* Music folder. (The Public Music folder contains music available to everyone who uses your PC.)

Windows 8 gives you four libraries for storing your files and folders. For easy access, they live in the Navigation Pane along the left side of every folder.

Peering into Your Drives, Folders, and Libraries

Knowing all this folder stuff not only impresses computer store employees but also helps you find the files you want. Put on your hard hat; go spelunking among your computer's drives, folders, and libraries; and use this section as your guide.

Seeing the files on a disk drive

Like everything else in Windows 8, disk drives are represented by buttons, or icons. The File Explorer program also shows information stored in other areas, such as MP3 players, digital cameras, or scanners. Opening an icon usually lets you access the device's contents and move files back and forth, just as with any other folders in Windows 8.

When you double-click a hard drive icon in File Explorer, Windows 8 promptly opens the drive to show you the folders packed inside. But how should Windows react when you insert something new into your computer, such as a CD, DVD, or flash drive?

Earlier versions of Windows tried to second-guess you. When you inserted a music CD, for example, Windows automatically began playing the music. The more polite Windows 8, by contrast, asks how you prefer it to handle the situation.

When you the message asking you what you want to do, click it; a second message appears, shown in Figure 5-2, listing everything you can do with that item. Choose an option, and Windows 8 behaves the same way the next time you insert a similar item.

Figure 5-2: Choose how Windows 8 should react the next time you insert that item.

But what if you change your mind about how Windows 8 should treat a newly inserted item? Then you just need to change the Windows 8 reaction: In File Explorer, right-click the inserted item's icon and choose Open AutoPlay. Once again, Windows 8 asks you to plot the future course.

When in doubt as to what you can do with an icon in File Explorer, right-click it. Windows 8 presents a menu of all the things you can do to that object. (You can choose Open, for example, to see the files on a flash drive, making it simpler to copy them to your computer.)

Seeing what's inside a folder

Because folders are really little storage compartments, Windows 8 uses a picture of a little folder to represent a place for storing files. To see what's inside a folder, either in File Explorer or on the Windows 8 desktop, just double-click that folder's picture. A new window pops up, showing that folder's contents. Spot another folder inside that folder? Double-click that one to see what's inside. Keep clicking until you find what you want or reach a dead end.

Reached a dead end? If you mistakenly end up in the wrong folder, back your way out as if you're browsing the web. Click the Back arrow at the window's top-left corner. That closes the wrong folder and shows you the folder you just left. If you keep clicking the Back arrow, you end up right where you started.

The Address Bar provides another quick way to jump to different places in your PC. As you move from folder to folder, the folder's Address Bar — that little word-filled box at the folder's top — constantly keeps track of your trek.

Notice the little arrows between the folder names. Those little arrows provide quick shortcuts to other folders and windows. Try clicking any of the arrows; menus appear, listing the places you can jump to from that point.

Here are some more tips for finding your way in and out of folders:

- ✔ While burrowing deeply into folders, the Forward arrow provides yet another quick way to jump immediately to any folder you've plowed through: Click the downward-pointing arrow next to the Forward arrow in the window's top-left corner. A menu drops down listing the folders you've plowed past on your journey. Click any name to jump quickly to that folder.

- ✔ Removed from Windows 7 and Windows Vista, the Up Arrow button reappears in Windows 8. Click the Up Arrow button, located just to the right of the Address Bar, to move your view up one folder. Keep clicking it, and you'll eventually wind up at someplace recognizable: your desktop.

- ✔ When faced with a long list of alphabetically sorted files, click anywhere on the list. Then quickly type the first letter or two of the desired file's name. Windows immediately jumps up or down the list to the first name beginning with those letters.

Managing a library's folders

The Windows 8 library system may seem confusing, but you can safely ignore the mechanics behind it. Just treat a library like any other folder: a handy spot to store and grab similar types of files. But if you want to know the inner workings behind a library, hang around for this section.

To find out which folders are appearing in the Documents library, for example, double-click the Navigation Pane's Documents library, and you see that library's two folders: My Documents and Public Documents.

If you keep files in another location, perhaps a portable hard drive or even a networked PC, feel free to add them to the library of your choice by following these steps:

1. **Right-click the library you want to expand and choose Properties.**

   If you choose the Documents library, for example, the Documents Properties dialog box appears, as shown in Figure 5-3.

Figure 5-3: The Documents Properties dialog box lists the library's visible folders.

2. **Click the Add button.**

   The Include Folder in Documents window appears.

3. **Navigate to the folder you want to add, click the folder, click the Include Folder button, and click OK.**

   The library automatically updates itself to display that folder's contents, sorting the contents into groups.

✔ You may add as many folders to a library as you want, which is handy when your music files are spread out across many places. The library automatically updates to show the folders' latest contents.

✔ To remove a folder from a library, follow the first step but click the folder to be removed and click the Remove button.

✔ You can create additional libraries to meet your own needs: Right-click Libraries in the Navigation Pane, choose New, and choose Library from the pop-up menu. A new Library icon appears, ready for you to type in a name. Then begin stocking your new library with folders by following Steps 1–3 in the preceding step list.

Creating a New Folder

To store new information in a file cabinet, you grab a manila folder, scrawl a name across the top, and start stuffing it with information. To store new information in Windows 8, you create a new folder, think up a name for the new folder, and start stuffing it with files.

To create a new folder quickly, click Home from the folder's toolbar buttons and choose New Folder from the Ribbon menu. If you can't find the right menus, though, here's a quick and foolproof method:

1. **Right-click inside your folder (or on the desktop) and choose New.**

2. **From the resulting side menu, select Folder.**

   When you choose Folder, a new folder quickly appears, waiting for you to type a new name.

3. Type a new name for the folder.

A newly created folder bears the boring name of New Folder. When you begin typing, Windows 8 quickly erases the old name and fills in your new name. Done? Save the new name by either pressing Enter or clicking somewhere away from the name you've just typed.

If you mess up the name and want to try again, right-click the folder, choose Rename, and start over.

Certain symbols are banned from folder (and file) names. The "Using legal folder names and filenames" sidebar spells out the details, but you never have trouble when using plain old letters and numbers for names.

Using legal folder names and filenames

Windows is pretty picky about what you can and can't name a file or folder. If you stick to plain old letters and numbers, you're fine. But don't try to stick any of the following characters in there:

    : / \ * | < > ? "

If you try to use any of those characters, Windows 8 bounces an error message to the screen, and you have to try again. Here are a couple illegal filenames:

    1/2 of my Homework

    He's no "Gentleman"

These names are legal:

    Half of my Term Paper

    A #@$%) Scoundrel

Renaming a File or Folder

Sick of a filename or folder name? Then change it. Just right-click the offending icon and choose Rename from the menu that pops up. Windows highlights the file's old name, which disappears as you begin typing the new one. Press Enter or click the desktop when you're through, and you're off. Or you can click the filename or folder name to select it, wait a second, and click the name again to change it. Some people click the name and press F2; Windows automatically lets you rename the file or folder.

When you rename a file, only its name changes. The contents are still the same, the file is still the same size, and the file is still in the same place. Renaming certain folders confuses Windows, especially if those folders contain programs. And please don't rename these folders: My Documents, My Pictures, My Music, or My Videos.

To rename large groups of files simultaneously, select them all, right-click the first one, and choose Rename. Type in the new name and press Enter; Windows 8 renames that file. However, it also renames all your *other* selected files to the new name, adding a number as it goes: `cat`, `cat (2)`, `cat (3)`, `cat (4)`, and so on. It's a handy way to rename photographs.

Selecting Bunches of Files or Folders

Although selecting a file, folder, or other object may seem particularly boring, it swings the doors wide open for further tasks: deleting, renaming, moving, and copying, for example. To select a single item, just click it. To select several files and folders, hold down the Ctrl key when you click the names or icons. Each name or icon stays highlighted when you click the next one.

To gather several files or folders sitting next to each other in a list, click the first one. Then hold down the Shift key as you click the last one. Those two items are highlighted, along with every file and folder sitting between them.

 Windows 8 lets you *lasso* files and folders as well. Point slightly above the first file or folder you want; then, while holding down the mouse button, point at the last file or folder. The mouse creates a colored lasso to surround your files. Let go of the mouse button, and the lasso disappears, leaving all the surrounded files highlighted.

 To quickly select all the files in a folder, choose Select All from the folder's Edit menu. (No menu? Then select them by pressing Ctrl+A.) Here's another nifty trick: To grab all but a few files, press Ctrl+A and, while still holding down Ctrl, click the ones you don't want.

Getting Rid of a File or Folder

Sooner or later, you'll want to delete a file that's no longer important. To delete a file, folder, shortcut, or just about anything else in Windows, right-click its name or icon. Then choose Delete from the pop-up menu. To delete in a hurry, click the offending object and press the Delete key. Dragging and dropping a file or folder to the Recycle Bin does the same thing.

The Delete option deletes entire folders, including any files or folders stuffed *inside* those folders. Make sure that you select the correct folder before you choose Delete.

After you choose Delete, Windows tosses a box in your face, asking whether you're *sure.* If you're sure, click Yes. If you're tired of Windows' cautious questioning, right-click the Recycle Bin, choose Properties, and remove the check mark next to Display Delete Confirmation Dialog. Windows now deletes any highlighted items whenever you — or an inadvertent brush of your shirt sleeve — press the Delete key.

Be extra sure that you know what you're doing when deleting any file that has pictures of little gears in its icon. These files are usually sensitive hidden files, and the computer wants you to leave them alone. (Other than that, they're not particularly exciting, despite the action-oriented gears.)

Icons with little arrows in their corner are *shortcuts* — push buttons that merely load files. Deleting shortcuts deletes only a *button* that loads a file or program. The file or program itself remains undamaged and still lives inside your computer.

Copying or Moving Files and Folders

To copy or move files to different folders on your hard drive, it's sometimes easiest to use your mouse to *drag* them there. For example, here's how to move a file to a different folder on your desktop. In this case, I'm moving the Traveler file from the House folder to the Morocco folder.

1. **Align the two windows next to each other.**

   I explain aligning windows in Chapter 4.

2. **Aim the mouse pointer at the file or folder you want to move.**

   In this case, point at the Traveler file.

3. **While holding down the right mouse button, move the mouse until it points at the destination folder.**

   Moving the mouse drags the file along with it, and Windows 8 explains that you're moving the file. As shown in Figure 5-4, the Traveler file is being dragged from the House folder to the Morocco folder.

Figure 5-4: To move an item, drag it while holding down the right mouse button.

Always drag icons while holding down the *right* mouse button. Windows 8 is then gracious enough to give you a menu of options when you position the icon, and you can choose to copy, move, or create a shortcut. If you hold down the *left* mouse button, Windows 8 sometimes doesn't know whether you want to copy or move.

4. **Release the mouse button and choose Copy Here, Move Here, or Create Shortcuts Here from the pop-up menu.**

When dragging and dropping takes too much work, Windows offers a few other ways to copy or move files. Depending on your screen's current layout, some of the following onscreen tools may work more easily:

- **Right-click menus:** Right-click a file or folder and choose Cut or Copy, depending on whether you want to move or copy it. Then right-click your destination folder and choose Paste.

- **Ribbon commands:** In File Explorer, click your file or folder; then click the Ribbon's Home tab and choose Copy To (or Move To). A menu drops down, listing some common locations. Don't spot the right spot? Then click Choose Location, click through the drive and folders to reach the destination folder, and Windows transports the file accordingly.

  I explain more about the new Windows 8 Ribbon menus in Chapter 4.

- **Navigation Pane:** Described in Chapter 4, this panel along File Explorer's left edge lists popular locations: libraries, drives, and oft-used folders. That lets you drag and drop a file into a spot on the Navigation Pane, sparing you the hassle of opening a destination folder.

After you install a program on your computer, don't ever move that program's folder. Programs wedge themselves into Windows. Moving the program may break it, and you'll have to reinstall it. Feel free to move a program's *shortcut* (shortcut icons contain a little arrow), though.

Writing to CDs and DVDs

Most computers today write information to CDs and DVDs using a flameless approach known as *burning*. To see whether you're stuck with an older drive that can't burn discs, remove any discs from inside the drive; then open File Explorer from the Start screen and look at the icon for your CD or DVD drive.

Because computers always speak in secret code, here's what you can do with the disc drives in your computer:

- **DVD-RW:** Read and write to CDs *and* DVDs.

- **BD-ROM:** Read and write to CDs and DVDs, plus read Blu-ray discs.

- **BD-RE:** These can read and write to CDs, DVDs, *and* Blu-ray discs.

If your PC has two CD or DVD burners, tell Windows 8 which drive you want to handle your disc-burning chores: Right-click the drive, choose Properties, and click the Recording tab. Then choose your favorite drive in the top box.

Buying the right kind of blank CDs and DVDs for burning

Stores sell two types of CDs: CD-R (short for CD-Recordable) and CD-RW (short for CD-ReWritable). Here's the difference:

- **CD-R:** Most people buy CD-R discs because they're very cheap and they work fine for storing music or files. You can write to them until they fill up; then you can't write to them anymore.

- **CD-RW:** Techies sometimes buy CD-RW discs for making temporary backups of data. You can write information to them, just like CD-Rs. But when a CD-RW disc fills up, you can erase it and start over with a clean slate.

DVDs come in both R and RW formats, just like CDs, so the preceding R and RW rules apply to them, as well. Most DVD burners sold in the past few years can write to any type of blank CD or DVD.

Copying files to or from a CD or DVD

CDs and DVDs once hailed from the school of simplicity: You simply slid them into your CD player or DVD player. But as soon as those discs graduated to PCs, the problems grew. When you create a CD or DVD, you must tell your PC *what* you're copying and *where* you intend to play it: Music for a CD player? Photo slideshows for a TV's DVD player? Or files to store on your computer?

If you choose the wrong answer, your disc won't work, and you've created yet another coaster.

Here are the Disc Creation rules:

✔ **Music:** To create a CD that plays music in your CD player or car stereo, you need to fire up the Windows 8 Media Player program and burn an *audio CD*.

✔ **Photo slide shows:** Windows 8 no longer includes the Windows DVD Maker bundled with Windows Vista and Windows 7. To create photo slideshows, you now need a third-party program.

If you just want to copy *files* to a CD or DVD, perhaps to save as a backup or to give to a friend, stick around.

Follow these steps to write files to a new, blank CD or DVD. (If you're writing files to a CD or DVD that you've written to before, jump ahead to Step 4.)

1. **Insert the blank disc into your disc burner. Then click or tap the Notification box that appears in the screen's upper-right corner.**

2. **When the Notification box asks how you'd like to proceed, click the box's Burn Files to Disc option.**

3. **In the resulting Burn a Disc dialog box, type a name for the disc, describe how you want to use the disc, and click Next.**

   Windows can burn the files to the disc two different ways:

   - **Like a USB flash drive:** This method lets you read and write files to the disc many times, a handy way to use discs as portable file carriers.

   - **With a CD/DVD player:** If you plan to play your disc on a fairly new home stereo disc player that's smart enough to read files stored in several different formats, select this method.

   Armed with the disc's name, Windows 8 prepares the disc for incoming files.

4. **Tell Windows 8 which files to write to disc.**

   Now that your disc is ready to accept the files, tell Windows 8 what information to send its way. You can do this in any of several ways:

   - Right-click the item you want to copy, be it a single file, folder, or selected files and folders. When the pop-up menu appears, choose Send To and select your disc burner from the menu.

   - Drag and drop files and/or folders on top of the burner's icon in File Explorer.

   - From your My Music, My Pictures, or My Documents folder, click the Share tab and then click Burn to Disc. This button copies all of that folder's files (or just the files you've selected) to the disc as files.

- Tell your current program to save the information to the disc rather than to your hard drive.

No matter which method you choose, a progress window appears, showing the disc burner's progress. When the progress window disappears, Windows has finished burning the disc.

5. **Close your disc-burning session by ejecting the disc.**

When you're through copying files to the disc, push your drive's Eject button (or right-click the drive's icon in File Explorer and choose Eject).

If you try to copy a large batch of files to a disc — more than will fit — Windows 8 complains immediately. Copy fewer files at a time, perhaps spacing them out over two discs.

Most programs let you save files directly to disc. Choose Save from the File menu and select your CD burner. Put a disc (preferably one that's not already filled) into your disc drive to start the process.

Working with Flash Drives and Memory Cards

Digital camera owners eventually become acquainted with *memory cards* — those little plastic squares that replaced the awkward rolls of film. Windows 8 can read digital photos directly from the camera after you find its cable and plug it into your PC. But Windows 8 can also grab photos straight off the memory card, a method praised by those who've lost their camera's cables.

Duplicating a CD or DVD

Windows 8 doesn't have a command to duplicate a CD, DVD, or Blu-ray disc. It can't even make a copy of a music CD. (That's why so many people buy CD-burning programs.)

But it can copy all of a CD's or DVD's files to a blank disc using this two-step process:

1. **Copy the files and folders from the CD or DVD to a folder on your PC.**

2. **Copy those same files and folders back to a blank CD or DVD.**

That gives you a duplicate CD or DVD, which is handy when you need a second copy of an essential backup disc.

You can try this process on a music CD or DVD movie, but it won't work. (I tried.) It works only when you're duplicating a disc containing computer programs or data files.

The secret is a *memory card reader:* a little slot-filled box that stays plugged into your PC. Slide your memory card into the slot, and your PC can read the card's files, just like reading files from any other folder. Most office supply and electronics stores sell memory card readers that accept most popular memory card formats, and some computers even come with built-in card readers.

The beauty of card readers is that there's nothing new to figure out: Windows 8 treats your inserted card just like an ordinary folder. Insert your card, and a folder appears on your screen to show your digital camera photos. The same drag-and-drop and cut-and-paste rules covered earlier in this chapter still apply, letting you move the pictures or other files off the card and into a folder in your Pictures library.

Flash drives — also known as thumbdrives — work just like memory card readers. Plug the flash drive into one of your PC's USB ports, and the drive appears as an icon in File Explorer, ready to be opened with a double-click.

✔ First, the warning: Formatting a card or disk wipes out all its information. Never format a card or disk unless you don't care about the information it currently holds.

✔ Now, the procedure: If Windows complains that a newly inserted card or floppy isn't formatted, right-click its drive and choose Format. (This problem happens most often with brand-new or damaged cards.) Sometimes formatting also helps one gadget use a card designed for a different gadget — your digital camera may be able to use your MP3 player's card, for example.

SkyDrive: Your Cubbyhole in the Clouds

Storing files inside your computer works fine while you're at home or work. And when leaving your computer, you can tote files on flash drives, CDs, DVDs, and portable hard drives — if you remember to grab them on the way out. But how can you access your files from *anywhere,* even if you've forgotten to pack them?

Microsoft's solution to that problem is called *SkyDrive.* Basically, it's your own private storage space on the Internet where you can dump your files and then retrieve them whenever you find an Internet connection.

Romantic engineers refer to Internet-stashed files as *cloud storage.*

The Windows 8 Start screen comes with the free SkyDrive app, but you need a few extra things in order to use it:

- ✔ **Microsoft account:** You need a Microsoft account in order to upload or retrieve files to SkyDrive. Chances are, you created a Microsoft account when you first created your account on your Windows 8 PC. (I describe Microsoft accounts in Chapter 2.)

- ✔ **An Internet connection:** Without an Internet signal, either wireless or wired, your files stay floating in the clouds, away from you and your computer.

- ✔ **Patience:** Uploading files always takes longer than downloading files. Although you can upload small files fairly quickly, larger files like digital photos can take several minutes to upload.

For some people, SkyDrive offers a safe haven where they'll always find their most important files. For others, though, SkyDrive brings yet another possible hiding place for that file they were working on last night. If you don't care for SkyDrive, buy a flash drive, store your files there, and keep the flash drive in your pocket.

Accessing files with the SkyDrive app

To add, view, or download files you've stored on SkyDrive from the Start screen's SkyDrive app, as well as to add your own, follow these steps:

1. From the Start screen, open the SkyDrive app.

When opened, the SkyDrive app may react any of several different ways depending on whether you've used SkyDrive before, and how.

When opened, SkyDrive lists your stored folders along the left edge and your files along the right.

2. To copy files from your computer to SkyDrive, choose Upload and locate the desired files on your computer.

To add files, right-click a blank part of the SkyDrive program; when the app's menu appears along the screen's bottom edge, choose Upload. The Start screen's File Picker appears, shown in Figure 5-5, ready for you to choose the files you'd like to store in the clouds.

When you spot the folder containing the files you want, click it to open it and see its files.

3. Choose the files you'd like to upload to SkyDrive.

Click the files you'd like to upload; if you click one by mistake, click it again to remove it from the upload list. Each time you click a file, SkyDrive adds the file to its upload list, shown along the app's bottom edge in Figure 5-5.

Jump to another folder and click more files; SkyDrive adds those file to the list along the bottom as well.

4. Click the Add to SkyDrive button.

SkyDrive begins uploading your selected files to the sky. Documents float up there pretty quickly, but digital music and photos can take a lot of time.

Folders in currently viewed Library

Move view up one folder

View files in other libraries and folders

Files in currently viewed folder

Sort files by name or date

Currently viewed Library on your computer

Clear or select all files

Currently selected files

Upload currently selected rive

Figure 5-5: Click the files to be sent to SkyDrive.

The SkyDrive app makes it fairly easy to open files you've already uploaded to the cloud, but it offers little control. For more features, visit SkyDrive from your desktop's web browser, a chore described in the next section.

Accessing SkyDrive from the desktop

If the Start screen's SkyDrive app is too simple for your needs, head for the Windows desktop and visit the SkyDrive website at `http://skydrive.live.com`.

The SkyDrive website offers much more control when shuttling files between your computer and the cloud. From the SkyDrive website, you can add, delete, move, and rename files, as well as create folders and move files between folders.

For best results, use the SkyDrive website to upload and manage your files. After you've stocked SkyDrive with your favorite files, use the Start screen's SkyDrive app to access the particular files you need.

For even more control over SkyDrive and your files, download the SkyDrive for Windows program from `http://apps.live.com/skydrive`. The desktop program creates a special folder on your computer that mirrors what's stored on SkyDrive. That makes SkyDrive particularly easy to use: Whenever you change the contents of that special folder on your computer, Windows automatically updates SkyDrive, as well.

Chapter 6

Working with Apps

● ●

In This Chapter

▶ Opening a program, app, or document

▶ Installing, uninstalling, and updating apps

▶ Seeing the apps you're currently running

▶ Finding what you lost

● ●

*I*n Windows, *programs* and *apps* are your tools: Load a program or app, and you can add numbers, arrange words, and shoot spaceships.

Documents, by contrast, are the things you create with apps and programs: tax forms, heartfelt apologies, and lists of high scores.

This chapter explains the basics of opening programs and apps from the new, tile-filled Start screen in Windows 8. It explains how to find and download a new app from the Start screen's Store app. It also tells you how to update or uninstall an app, and how to find any missing app or file.

Starting a Program or App

Windows 8 banished the Start button from its oft-clicked spot on the desktop's bottom-left corner. Microsoft prefers to say, however, that it has *expanded* the Start button, turning it into a full-screen launching pad for your programs.

I explain the giant new Start screen in Chapter 2, as well as how to customize it, adding or removing tiles to ensure you find things more easily.

But even though the Start screen lives in a new place, it still lets you launch programs or apps by following these steps:

1. **Open the Start screen.**

   Because there's no longer a Start button, you can summon the Start screen any of these ways:

   • **Mouse:** Point your mouse in the screen's bot-tom-left corner and then click when the Start icon appears.

   • **Keyboard:** Press the Windows key (⊞).

   • **Touchscreen:** Slide your finger inward from your screen's right edge and then tap the Start icon.

   The Start screen appears, bringing a screen full of tiles representing many of your apps and programs. (I explain how to add or remove tiles to the Start screen in Chapter 2.)

2. **If you spot the tile for your program or app, choose it with a mouse click or, on a touchscreen, a tap of a finger.**

   Don't see a tile for your sought-after program on the Start screen's list? Move to the next step.

3. **Scroll to the screen's right to see more tiles.**

   The Start screen always opens to display the tiles on its farthest left edge. To see the apps and programs hiding from view, point at the screen's right edge with your mouse cursor; the rest of the Start screen's tiles begin scrolling into view.

   If you're a touchscreen owner, you can view the tiles by sliding your finger across the screen to the left.

   Still don't see your program or app listed? Head for Step 4.

4. **View *all* your apps.**

   The Start screen shows apps first, followed by desktop programs. But to keep the list from stretching down the hallway, the Start screen doesn't list everything.

   To reveal them *all*, right-click a blank part of the Start screen and then choose All Apps. All your apps appear listed by name and icon, followed by alphabetical lists of desktop programs, organized by categories. (Your most recently installed desktop programs always appear on the farthest right edge.)

   To see all your apps on a touchscreen, slide your finger upward from the screen's bottom edge and click the All Apps icon.

If you *still* can't find your program on the admittedly crowded Start screen, follow these tips for other ways to open an app or program:

- ✔ While you view the Start screen, begin typing the missing program's name. As you type the first letter, the Start screen clears, presenting a list of names beginning with that letter. Type a second or third letter, and the list of matches shrinks accordingly. When you spot the app or program you want, open it with a double-click (or a touch on a touchscreen).

- ✔ Open File Explorer from the Start screen, choose Documents from the Navigation Pane along the window's left edge, and double-click the file you want to open. The correct program automatically opens with that file in tow.

- ✔ Double-click a *shortcut* to the program. Shortcuts, which often sit on your desktop, are handy, disposable buttons for launching files and folders.

- ✔ While you're on the desktop, you may spot the program's icon on the *taskbar* — a handy strip of icons lazily lounging along your desktop's bottom edge. If so, click the taskbar icon, and the program leaps into action.

- ✔ Right-click on the Windows desktop, choose New, and select the type of document you want to create. Windows 8 loads the right program for the job.

Windows offers other ways to open a program, but the preceding methods usually get the job done.

Adding and Deleting Apps

Apps, which are mini-programs specialized for single tasks, come from the world of *smartphones*: computerized cellphones.

Apps differ from traditional desktop programs in several ways:

- ✔ **Apps consume the entire screen;** programs run within windows on the desktop.

- ✔ **Apps are tied to your Microsoft account.** That means you need a Microsoft account to download a free or paid app from the Store app.

- ✔ **When you download an app from the Windows 8 Store app, you can run it on up to five PCs or devices** — as long as you're signed in to those PCs or devices with your Windows account.

- ✔ **Apps consume just one tile on the Start screen, thereby reducing Start screen bloat.** When installed, programs tend to sprinkle several tiles onto your Start screen.

Apps and programs can be created and sold by large companies as well as by basement-dwelling hobbyists working in their spare time.

Although desktop programs and Start screen apps look and behave differently, Microsoft unfortunately refers to both as *apps* in Windows 8. You'll run across this terminology quirk when dealing with older programs as well as newer programs created by companies not hip to Microsoft's new lingo.

Adding new apps from the Store app

When you're tired of the apps bundled with Windows 8 or you need a new app to fill a special need, follow these steps to bring one into your computer.

1. **Open the Store app from the Start screen.**

   Don't see the Start screen? Press your keyboard's ⊞ key to whisk your way there.

   The Store app fills the screen, as shown in Figure 6-1.

Figure 6-1: The Store apps lets you download apps to run from your Start screen.

The Store opens to show the Spotlight category, but scrolling to the right reveals many more categories, such as Games, Books and Reference, News and Weather, and others.

2. To narrow your search, choose a category by clicking its name.

As you see more of the Store, you see several more ways to sort the available apps, as shown in Figure 6-2.

Figure 6-2: Narrow your search by subcategory, price, and rating.

3. Sort by subcategory, price, and noteworthiness, and choose apps that look interesting.

For example, you can sort by subcategory, limiting the Games category to show only Card games.

Some categories also let you sort by price, and you can choose Free, Paid, or Trial. And if you sort by noteworthiness, Microsoft shows you which apps are either Newest, have the Highest Rating, or Lowest Price.

4. Choose any app to read a more detailed description.

A page opens to show more detailed information, including its price tag, pictures of the app, and reviews left by previous customers.

5. Click the Install, Buy, or Try button.

When you find a free app that you can't live with-out, click the Install button. Paid apps let you click either Buy or Try (a limited trial run). If you choose to install, try, or buy an app, its tile appears on your Start screen as quickly as your Internet connection speed allows.

Newly downloaded apps appear in a group on the Start screen's far-right edge.

Uninstalling apps

Downloaded a dud app? To uninstall any app from the Start screen, right-click its tile. When the menu bar rises up from the screen's bottom edge, click Uninstall.

Uninstalling an app only removes that app from *your* account's Start screen. Your action won't affect other account holders who may have installed the app.

Updating Your Apps

Programmers constantly tweak their apps, smoothing over rough spots, adding new features, and plugging security holes. When the program releases an update for your app, the Store tells you about it by putting a number on the Store app's tile.

To grab any waiting updates, visit the Start screen's Store app. Then click the word Update(s) in the top-right corner. The Store lists all the apps requiring updates; click Update All to bring them all up-to-date.

Note: When you update an app, it's not updated for every account holder on the computer. That holds true for apps that came preinstalled on your computer, as well as ones you've chosen to install afterward.

Finding Currently Running Start Screen Apps

By nature, Start screen apps fill the screen. Switch to another app, and *it* fills the screen, shoving away the previous app. Because the Start screen shows only one app at a time, your other running apps remain hidden beneath an invisibility cloak.

When you switch to the desktop, you're in yet another world, away from the land of apps. How do you return to an app you just used?

To solve that problem, Windows 8 can reveal a list of your recently used apps, complete with thumbnail photos, as shown in Figure 6-3. The list conveniently includes your desktop, letting you shuffle easily between apps and the desktop.

The thumbnail-filled strip pops up along the screen's left edge, and it's available whether you're on the Start screen *or* the desktop.

Figure 6-3: Find recently used apps in a strip along the screen's left edge.

To see that list of your recently used apps (and to close unwanted apps, if desired), employ any of these tricks:

✔ **Mouse:** Point in the screen's top-right corner; when a thumbnail of your last-used app appears, slide the mouse down the screen: The list of your most-recently used apps sticks to the screen's left side. To switch to an app, click it. To close an app, right-click its thumbnail and choose Close.

✔ **Keyboard:** Press ⊞+Tab to see the list of your most recently used apps, as shown in Figure 6-3. While still holding down the ⊞ key, press the Tab key; each press of the Tab key highlights a different app on the list. When you've highlighted your desired app, release the ⊞ key, and the app fills the screen. (Highlighted an app you want to close? Then press the Delete key.)

✔ **Touchscreen:** Slide your finger gently inward from the screen's left edge. When the last-used app begins to appear, slide back toward the left edge; the list of recently used apps sticks to the left edge. Tap any app on the strip to make it fill the screen. To close an unwanted app, slide your finger from the screen's top to the screen's bottom until the app vanishes, like water off a cliff.

This trick reveals currently running *apps,* but not desktop *programs.* That's because Windows 8 treats your desktop as a single app: No matter how many desktop programs you may have running, the left strip shows only a single app for the desktop.

Locating a Missing App, Program, Setting, or File

The preceding section explains how to find *currently running* apps. But what about things that you haven't looked at for a while?

To help you find lost apps, wandering files, hidden settings, or even things like missing e-mail, Windows 8 offers an easily searchable index. To begin searching, fetch the Charms bar's Search icon. You can do that any of three ways:

✔ **Mouse:** Move the mouse pointer to the screen's top- or bottom-right corner; when the Charms bar appears, click the Search icon.

✔ **Keyboard:** Press ⊞+Q to both summon the Charms bar *and* open the Charm bar's Search pane.

✔ **Touchscreen:** Slide your finger inward from the screen's right edge; when the Charms bar appears, tap the Search icon.

After you've summoned the Windows 8 Search pane using one of these methods, search for missing things by following these steps:

1. Click the category you'd like to search.

Unlike Windows 7, Windows 8 doesn't search your entire computer, subsequently listing every match. Instead, Windows 8 first makes you specify what *category* you want to search. Route your search to any category by clicking its name:

- **Apps:** The default choice in Windows 8, this searches for both Start screen apps and desktop programs. Should you begin typing letters directly onto the Start screen, Windows 8 quickly chooses this option automatically and begins listing matching apps and programs.

- **Settings:** This lets you search through the zillions of settings in both the desktop's Control Panel and the Start screen's PC Settings area. It's a handy way to find settings dealing with only fonts, for example, keyboards, backups, or other technicalities.

- **Files:** An oft-chosen option, choose this to locate a specific file on your computer's hard drive.

- **A Particular App:** Below the three main categories — Apps, Settings, and Files — the Search pane lists names of apps. To route a search to your mailbox, for example, choose the Mail app. The Mail app opens, and the

Search pane continues to hug the screen's right edge, waiting for you to type in your search.

2. **Type your search term into the white text box.**

Type a word or phrase that appears somewhere inside your chosen category.

As soon as you begin typing, the Start screen begins listing matches. With each letter you type, Windows 8 whittles down the list. After you type enough letters, your lost item floats alone to the top of the list.

No matches? Then Windows didn't find your lost item, unfortunately. Try searching for fewer words, or even portions of words.

3. **Click a match or press Enter after typing your word or phrase, and Windows shows all the matching files, settings, or apps.**

Windows 8 lists detailed information about all the matching items. Click a match, and Windows brings it to the screen.

4. **Choose a matching item to open it, bringing it to the screen.**

Click a song, for example, and it begins playing. Click a Setting, and the Control Panel or PC Settings window appears, open to your setting's contents. Click a letter, and it opens in your word processor.

The Windows 8 index includes every file in your Documents, Music, Pictures, and Videos libraries, which makes storing your files in those folders more important than ever. (Windows 8 doesn't let you search through private files stored in accounts of *other* people who may be using your PC.)

Keyboard hounds can search only Files by pressing ⊞+F; search for *Settings* by pressing ⊞+W; and search through your *Apps* and programs by pressing ⊞+Q.

Chapter 7

Engaging the Social Apps

. . . .

In This Chapter

▶ Adding your accounts

▶ Setting up e-mail

▶ Sending and receiving files and photos

▶ Managing your contacts

▶ Managing your calendar

▶ Sending and receiving instant messages

. . . .

*T*hanks to the Internet's never-fading memory, your friends and acquaintances never disappear. Old college chums, business pals, and even those elementary school bullies are all waiting for you online. Toss in a few strangers you may have swapped messages with on websites, and the Internet has created a huge social network.

Windows 8 helps you stay in touch with friends you enjoy and avoid those you don't. To manage your online social life, Windows 8 includes a suite of intertwined social apps: Mail, People, Calendar, and Messaging. You can pretty much guess which app handles what job.

This chapter describes the Windows 8 suite of social apps and how they work with Facebook, Google, Twitter, LinkedIn, and other accounts. It explains how to set them up, keep the communications flowing, and when necessary, turn them off when you're feeling information overload.

Adding Your Social Accounts to Windows 8

For years, you've heard people say, "Never tell *anybody* your user account name and password." Now, it seems Windows 8 wants you to break that rule.

When you first open your People, Mail, or Messaging apps, Windows 8 asks you to enter your account names and passwords from Facebook, Google, Twitter, LinkedIn, Hotmail, and other services.

It's not as scary as you think, though. Microsoft and the other networks have agreed to share your information, *only if you approve it.* And should you approve it, Windows connects to your social network — Facebook, for example — where you can tell Facebook it's okay to share your information with the People app in Windows 8.

And, frankly, approving the information swap is a huge time-saver. When you link those accounts to Windows 8, your computer signs in to each service, imports your friends' contact information, and stocks your apps.

To fill in Windows 8 about your online social life, follow these steps:

1. **From the Start screen, open the Mail app.**

   The tile-filled Start screen appears when you first turn on your computer. If it's not onscreen, and you need a refresher on how to fetch it, refer to Chapter 2.

   Click the Mail tile, and the app opens. If you haven't yet signed up for a Microsoft account, a prompt appears, reminding you that you need one. (I explain how to sign up for a Microsoft account in Chapter 2.)

   When the Mail app first appears, it usually contains at least one e-mail: a welcoming message from Microsoft. (Mail also asks you to Allow or Decline the sending of error messages to Microsoft, so the company can improve its products.)

2. **Enter your accounts into the Mail app.**

   To add accounts, summon the Charms bar, click the Settings icon, click Accounts, and click Add an Account. Mail lists the accounts you can add: Hotmail, Google, Outlook, or Exchange.

   To add a Google account, for example, click the word Google. Windows 8 takes you to a secure area on Google's website where you can authorize the transaction by entering your Gmail e-mail address and password and then clicking Connect.

   Repeat these steps for other listed accounts, authorizing each of them to share information with your Windows account.

   I explain how to add e-mail addresses besides Hotmail, Outlook, and Google in this chapter's "Adding other e-mail accounts to Mail" sidebar.

3. Return to the Start screen, click the People tile, and enter your other accounts.

Now's your chance to tell Windows about your friends: Click the People tile on the Start screen. When it appears, you may spot friends listed in the address books associated with the e-mail accounts you entered in Step 1.

Continue adding contacts by entering your usernames and passwords from accounts from Facebook, Twitter, LinkedIn, and others.

For example, choose Facebook, click Connect, and a window appears for you to enter your Facebook name and password.

After you've entered your accounts, Windows 8 automatically fetches your e-mail through your Mail app, fills the People app with your friends' contact information, and adds any appointments in your Calendar app.

Although it might seem frightening to give Windows 8 your coveted usernames and passwords, it enriches Windows 8 in many ways:

✔ Instead of typing in your contacts by hand, they're waiting for you automatically, whether they're from Facebook, Twitter, or LinkedIn or they're connected with your Google, Hotmail, Outlook, or Windows Live account.

✔ Windows 8 apps work well with apps and programs from other companies. For example, if a friend wants to chat with you from Facebook, the Windows 8 Messaging program opens, letting you swap messages.

✔ You can view your friends' Facebook, Twitter, and LinkedIn messages and photos directly from the People app. You no longer need to make the rounds of all your social networks to see what everybody's doing.

✔ Don't like these new-fangled Windows 8 apps? Then ignore them and spend your time on the Windows 8 desktop. There, you can visit Facebook and your other accounts from your web browser, the same way you've always done.

Understanding the Mail App

Unlike Windows 7, Windows 8 comes with a built-in app for sending and receiving your e-mail. Not only is the Mail app free, but it also comes with a spell checker.

Considered a *live* app, the Mail app automatically updates its Start screen's tile. A glance at the Start screen's Mail tile quickly shows you the senders' names and subjects of your latest e-mails.

However, like many free things, the Mail app carries a cost in convenience, as described by these limitations:

✔ You need a Microsoft account to use the Mail app, as well as to use the bundled People, Calendar, and Messaging apps. I describe how to sign up for a free Microsoft account in Chapter 2.

✔ The Mail app works only with Hotmail accounts, Windows Live accounts (including Outlook), and Google's Gmail accounts. (It also works with Exchange accounts, but those require special equipment usually found only in larger businesses, not homes.)

Adding other e-mail accounts to Mail

The Mail app can fetch e-mail only from Hotmail, Outlook, or Gmail accounts. So, to add other accounts, you need to visit the Windows desktop, open Internet Explorer, and visit either Hotmail (www. hotmail.com), Outlook (www.outlook.com/), or Gmail (www. google.com/mail).

From there, open the Options menu and look for an area where you can add other accounts. You'll need to enter your account's username and password.

When your Hotmail, Outlook, or Google accounts begin importing your mail from your other accounts, that mail will be waiting for you in your Mail app.

If you need to add a different type of e-mail account, you need to do it through Internet Explorer on the Windows desktop. There you can visit your Microsoft or Google account and add your other e-mail accounts, should you need them. I explain more about that process in this chapter's "Adding other e-mail accounts to Mail" sidebar.

Navigating the Mail app's views, menus, and accounts

To load Windows' Mail app, open the Start screen with a press of your Windows key (⊞) and then click the Mail app tile. The Mail app quickly fills the screen, shown in Figure 7-1.

Mail app folders

Currently viewed e-mail account

Number of unread messages

Latest e-mail from currently viewed e-mail account

E-mail accounts

Folders on other accounts like Gmail will appear here

Figure 7-1: The selected e-mail's contents appear on the right.

The Mail app lists your e-mail accounts in its bottom-left corner. Figure 7-1, for example, shows a Hotmail account at the top and a Google account beneath it. (If you've only set up one account, you see only one account listed.)

To see the mail sent to your account, click the account's name. For example, see how the name Hotmail is listed in the top-left corner in Figure 7-1? That's because it's the currently viewed account; accordingly, the Mail app shows the Hotmail account's newest e-mail on the screen's right side.

Beneath the names of your e-mail accounts, the Mail app lists its main folders:

- ✔ **Inbox:** Shown when you first load the Mail app, the Inbox folder lists your waiting e-mail. Mail automatically checks for new e-mail, but if you tire of waiting, click Sync. That immediately grabs any waiting Mail. (Right-click a blank portion of the Mail app to reveal its menu — including the Sync icon — along the bottom edge.)

- ✔ **Drafts:** When you're midway through writing an e-mail and want to finish it later, click the Close icon and choose Save Draft from the drop-down menu. The e-mail then waits in this folder for retrieval later.

- ✔ **Sent Items:** *Every* piece of e-mail you've sent lingers in this folder, leaving a permanent record. (To kill any embarrassing e-mail from any folder, select the offending e-mail with a click and click the Delete icon.)

- ✔ **Junk:** The Mail app sniffs out potential junk mail and drops suspects into this folder. Peek in here every once in a while to make sure nothing falls in by mistake.

- ✔ **Deleted Items:** The Deleted Items folder serves as the Mail app's Recycle Bin, letting you retrieve mistakenly deleted e-mail. To delete something permanently from this folder, select it and choose the Delete icon.

> ✔ **Outbox:** When you send or reply to a message, the Mail app immediately tries to connect to the Internet and send it. If Mail can't find the Internet, your message lingers here. When you connect to the Internet again, click the Sync button, if necessary, to send it on its way.

To see the contents of any folder, click it. Click any e-mail inside the folder, and its contents appear in the pane to the far right.

Created folders in your Gmail account? When you click your Google account, the Mail app lists those folders beneath the Map app's own folders, as shown in Figure 7-1.

But where are the Mail app's menus? Like *all* Start screen apps, the Mail app hides its menus on an App bar along the screen's bottom edge. You can reveal the App bar in Mail and *any* Windows app with a few tricks.

To summon the App bar along the bottom of any app, choose one of these options:

> ✔ **Mouse:** Right-click on a blank portion inside the app.
>
> ✔ **Keyboard:** Press ⊞+Z.
>
> ✔ **Touchscreen:** From the screen's bottom, slide your finger upward.

When the App bar rises from the screen's bottom edge, shown in Figure 7-2, it reveals icons to help you maneuver through the Mail app.

Delete currently viewed e-mail

Respond to currently viewed e-mail

Create new e-mail

Return to folder view

Currently viewed e-mail account

Currently viewed e-mail

App bar

Move currently viewed e-mail to a folder

Mark currently viewed e-mail as unread

Pin the current e-mail account as a Start screen tile

Send and recieve new messages

Figure 7-2: As in all Start screen apps, the App bar rises from the screen bottom.

Composing and sending an e-mail

When you're ready to send an e-mail, follow these steps to compose your letter and drop it in the electronic mailbox, sending it through virtual space to the recipient's computer:

1. **From the Start screen, open the Mail app's tile and click the New icon in the program's top-right corner.**

   A New Message window appears, empty and awaiting your words.

   If you've added more than one e-mail account to the Mail app, choose your return address by clicking the downward-pointing arrow in the From box — the box currently listing your e-mail address. Then select the account you want to use for sending that particular mail.

2. **Type your friend's e-mail address into the To box.**

   As you begin typing, the Mail app scans your People app's list for both names and e-mail addresses, listing potential matches below the To box. Spot a match on the list? Click it, and the Mail app automatically fills in the rest of the e-mail address.

   To send an e-mail to several people, click the plus sign to the right of the To box. The People app appears, listing your contacts' names and e-mail addresses. Click the name — or names — of the people you want to receive your e-mail and then click the Add button. The Mail app addresses your e-mail, just as if you'd typed it in manually.

3. **Click in the Subject line and type in a subject.**

   Click the words Add a Subject at the top of the message and type in your own subject.

4. **Type your message into the large box beneath the Subject line.**

   Type as many words as you want. As you type, the Mail app underlines potentially misspelled words in red. To correct them, right-click the underlined word and choose the correct spelling from the pop-up menu.

You can also change formatting by fetching the App bar along the app's bottom edge by right-clicking, by pressing ⊞+Z, or by swiping upward on a tablet. The App bar along the bottom lets you add bulleted lists, change fonts, add italics, and more.

5. **If you want, attach any files or photos to your e-mail.**

I describe how to attach files in the "Sending and Receiving Files through E-Mail" section, but if you're feeling savvy, you can attach them by clicking the Attachments icon on the Mail app's App bar.

6. **Click the Send button along the top-right corner.**

Whoosh! The Mail app whisks your message through the Internet to your friend's mailbox. Depending on the speed of your Internet connection, mail can arrive anywhere from five seconds later to a few days later, with a few minutes being the average.

Don't want to send the message? Then click the Close button. When a drop-down menu appears, choose Delete to delete the message or choose Save Draft to keep a copy in your Drafts folder for later polishing.

Reading a received e-mail

When your computer is connected to the Internet, the Windows Start screen tells you as soon as a new e-mail arrives. The Mail app's tile automatically updates itself to show the sender and subject of your latest unread e-mails.

To see more information than that — or to respond to the message — follow these steps:

1. **Click the Start screen's Mail tile.**

   Mail opens to show the messages in your Inbox, shown earlier in Figure 7-1. Each subject is listed, one by one, with the newest one at the top.

2. **Click the subject of any message you want to read.**

   The Mail app spills that message's contents into the pane along the window's right side.

3. **From here, the Mail app leaves you with several options, each accessed from the buttons along the e-mail's top edge:**

   - **Nothing:** Undecided? Don't do anything, and the message simply sets up camp in your Inbox folder.

   - **Respond:** Click the Respond button in the top-right corner and choose Reply from the drop-down menu. A new window appears, ready for you to type in your response. The window is just like the one that appears when you first compose a message but with a handy difference: This window is pre-addressed with the recipient's name and the subject. Also, the original message usually appears at the bottom of your reply for reference.

   - **Reply All:** Some people address e-mails to several people simultaneously. If you see several other people listed on an e-mail's To line, you can reply to all of them by clicking Respond and choosing Reply All from the drop-down menu.

- **Forward:** Received something that a friend simply must see? Click Respond and choose Forward from the drop-down menu to kick a copy of the e-mail to your friend's Inbox.

- **Delete:** Click the Delete button to toss the message into your Deleted Items folder. Your deleted messages sit inside that folder until you open the Deleted Items folder, click all the messages, and click the Delete button again.

To print your currently viewed e-mail, summon the Charms bar, click the Devices icon, choose your printer from the list of devices, and click the Print button.

The Mail app works for basic e-mail needs. If you need more, you can find a more full-featured e-mail program, or you can open Internet Explorer, go online to Hotmail (www.hotmail.com), Outlook (www.outlook.com), or Google (www.google.com/gmail), and manage your e-mail from there.

Sending and Receiving Files through E-Mail

Like a pair of movie tickets slipped into the envelope of a thank-you note, an *attachment* is a file that piggybacks onto an e-mail message. You can send or receive any type of file as an attachment.

Saving a received attachment

When an attachment arrives in an e-mail, you'll recognize it: It's a large rectangle at the top of your e-mail; the rectangle lists the file's name with the word *Download* listed directly beneath it.

Saving the attached file or files takes just a few steps.

1. **Click the word *Download* next to the attached file.**

   This tells the Mail app to actually download the file.

2. **When the file downloads to the Mail app, click the attached file's icon and choose Save.**

   That tells the Mail app to copy the file from your e-mail and save it to a folder in your computer.

3. **Choose a folder to receive the saved file.**

   The Windows 8 File Picker appears, letting you navigate to a folder.

4. **Click the word Files in the File Picker's top-left corner and then choose which library to receive the incoming file: Documents, Pictures, Music, or Videos.**

   Saving the file inside one of your four libraries is the easiest way to ensure you'll find it later.

5. **Click the Save button in the File Picker's bottom-right corner.**

   The Mail app saves the file in the library of your choosing.

After you've saved the file, the Mail app returns to the screen. And, if you notice, the attachment still remains inside the e-mail. That's because saving attachments always saves a *copy* of the sent file. That's handy because, if you accidentally delete your saved file, you can return to the original e-mail and save the file yet again.

The built-in virus checker in Windows 8, Windows Defender, automatically scans your incoming e-mail for any evil file attachments.

Sending a file as an attachment

Sending a file through the Mail app works much like saving an attached file, although in reverse: Instead of grabbing a file from an e-mail and saving it into a folder or library, you're grabbing a file from a folder or library and saving it in an e-mail.

To send a file as an attachment in the Mail app, follow these steps:

1. **Open the Mail app and create a new e-mail, as described earlier in this chapter's "Composing and sending an e-mail" section.**

2. **Open the Mail app's App bar and click the Attachments icon.**

   Open the App bar by right-clicking on a blank part of the e-mail. When you click the Attachments icon, the Windows 8 File Picker window appears.

3. **Navigate to the file you'd like to send.**

   For easy browsing, click the word Files. That fetches a drop-down menu that lists your computer's major storage areas. Most files are stored in your Documents, Pictures, Music, and Videos libraries.

   Click a folder's name to see the files it contains. Not the right folder? Click the File Picker's Go Up link to move back out of the folder and try again.

4. **Click the filenames you want to send and click the Attach button.**

   Selected too many files? Deselect unwanted files by clicking their names yet again. When you click the Attach button, the Mail app adds the file or files to your e-mail.

5. **Click the Send button.**

   The Mail app whisks off your mail and its attachment to the recipient.

Managing Your Contacts in the People App

When you let Windows 8 eavesdrop on your online social networks, as described in this chapter's first section, you've conveniently stocked the People app with your online friends from Facebook, Twitter, and other networks.

To see everybody in your People app, click the Start screen's People tile. The People app appears, listing all your online friends, as shown in Figure 7-3.

The People app handles much of its upkeep automatically, axing people you've unfriended on Facebook, for example, and slyly removing contacts who've unfriended *you,* as well.

Figure 7-3: The People app stocks itself with friends from social networks.

But friends who don't share their lives online through social networks won't appear in the People app. And some privacy-concerned Facebook friends may have told Facebook to withhold their information from other programs — and that includes Windows 8.

That means you'll need to edit some People entries manually. This section explains the occasional pruning needed to keep up with our constantly evolving social networks.

Adding contacts

Although the People app loves to reach its fingers into any online crevice you toss its way, you can easily add people the old-fashioned way, typing them in by hand.

To add somebody to the People app, which makes those names available in your Mail and Messaging apps, follow these steps:

1. **Click the People tile on the Start screen.**

2. **Right-click on a blank part of the People app, and the App bar rises from the program's bottom edge. Then click the New icon.**

   A blank New Contact form makes its appearance.

3. **Fill out the New Contact form.**

   Most of the choices are self-explanatory fields such as Name, Address, Email, and Phone. Click the Other Info button on the right to add items such as a job title, website, significant other, or notes.

   The biggest challenge comes with the Account field, an option seen only by people who've entered more than one e-mail account into the Mail app. Which e-mail *account* should receive the new contact?

   The answer hinges mainly on which cellphone you own. Choose your Google account if you use an Android phone, so your newly added account will appear on your Android phone's contacts list.

   Choose the Microsoft account if you use a Microsoft phone, so the contact will appear there.

4. **Click the Save button.**

The People app dutifully saves your new contact. If you spot a mistake, however, you may need to go back and edit the information, described in the next section.

Deleting or editing contacts

Has somebody fallen from your social graces? Or perhaps just changed a phone number? Either way, it's easy to delete or edit a contact by following these steps:

1. **Click the People tile on the Start screen.**

   The People app appears.

2. **Click a contact.**

   The contact's page appears full-screen.

3. **Right-click a blank part of the contact's page to summon the App bar.**

4. **Click Delete to delete the contact or click Edit to update a contact's information. Then click Save.**

   Clicking Delete removes the person completely. However, the Delete button appears only for contacts you've added *by hand*. If they've been added through Facebook or another online social media site, you have to delete them by removing them from your contacts on that site.

   Clicking Edit fetches the Contact form, where you can update or delete any information before clicking Save to save your changes.

   Designed for best friends, the Pin to Start button turns that person into a Start screen tile, giving you easy access to her contact information and latest status updates.

To send a quick message to a contact in your People app, click her name. When her contact information appears, click the Send Email button. The Mail app calls up a handy, pre-addressed New Message window, ready for you to type your message and click Send. (This trick works only if you have that contact's e-mail address.)

Managing Appointments in Calendar

After you enter your social networking accounts such as Facebook and Google, as described in this chapter's first section, you've already stocked the Calendar app with appointments entered by both you and your online friends.

The Calendar displays your Facebook friends' birthdays, for example — if your Facebook friends have chosen to share that information. You can also find any appointments you've made in Google's calendar, a handy perk for owners of Android phones.

To see your appointments, click the Start screen's Calendar tile. The Calendar app appears, listing all your online appointments, as shown in Figure 7-4.

Figure 7-4: The Calendar app gets appointments from your online social networks.

Very few people keep all their appointments online, though, so you'll occasionally need to edit some entries, add new ones, or delete those you can no longer attend. This section explains how to keep your appointments up-to-date.

The Calendar opens to show a monthly view, shown earlier in Figure 7-4. To switch to other views, right-click the calendar app to fetch the App bar; then click the Day, Week, or Month button.

No matter which view the Calendar app displays, you can flip through the appointments by clicking the little arrows near the screen's top corners. Click the right arrow to move forward in time; click the left arrow to move backward.

The Calendar app grabs whatever appointments it can find from your online social networks. But you can still add or edit appointments manually when needed.

To add an appointment to your Calendar app, follow these steps:

1. **Click the Calendar tile on the Start screen.**

   The Calendar appears (refer to Figure 7-4).

2. **Load the Apps bar and click the New icon.**

   I explain how to load any app's menu bar earlier in this chapter. (*Hint:* Right-click anywhere on the Calendar.)

3. **Fill out the Details form.**

   Most of the choices are self-explanatory fields.

The biggest challenge comes with the Calendar field, an option available only if you've entered more than one e-mail account into your Mail app. Which e-mail *account* should receive the new calendar appointment?

Chatting through Messaging

A computing staple for decades, instant messaging apps let you exchange messages with other online friends. Unlike e-mail, instant messaging takes place, well, *instantly*: The screen displays two boxes, and you type messages back and forth at each other.

Messaging apps spawn a love/hate relationship. Some people love the convenience and intimacy of keeping in touch with faraway friends. Others hate feeling trapped in an elevator and forced to make small talk. But love it or hate it, the Windows Messaging app handles both heartfelt conversations and idle chatter. And even if your online friends use different messaging services and programs, Windows Messaging can swap messages with them all.

To begin swapping small talk, er, philosophical conversations with your online friends, follow these steps:

1. **From the Start screen, click the Messaging tile.**

   The Messaging app appears, shown in Figure 7-5.

2. **Click the New Message link.**

   Shown in the top-left corner of Figure 7-5, the New Message link lets you see which of your friends are currently online in their own messaging programs. If a friend doesn't appear here, she's either not online or she's not listed in your People app.

Figure 7-5: The Messaging app lists previous conversations on the left edge; click a conversation to see its contents on the right.

3. **Click the person you'd like to chat with.**

   When the messaging window appears, begin typing. Your friend will see a notice from his or her own messaging program, whether it's on Facebook, a cellphone, or a different system.

   When you press Enter, your message appears in their messaging program. And that's it. When you're done typing messages at each other, just say goodbye. The next time you visit the Messaging app, your conversation will still be there, waiting to be continued, if you wish.

Which brings this section to the finer points of instant messaging:

- ✔ To delete a conversation, right-click inside the Messaging app to fetch the App bar and then click the Delete icon.

- ✔ Clicking the App bar's Status icon and choosing Invisible keeps you from showing up as available in your friends' messaging programs. To reappear to your circle of friends, click the Status icon and choose Online.

↳ Messaging usually works best if you send a message and then wait for a response before sending another message. Too many quick messages make for a disjointed conversation, sort of like a press conference where everybody calls out questions at once.

Chapter 8

Entertaining Yourself through the Start Screen

. . . .

In This Chapter

▶ Connecting to the Internet wirelessly

▶ Navigating the web from the Start screen

▶ Playing music from the Start screen

▶ Taking photos with your computer's camera

▶ Viewing photos in your Pictures library

. . . .

*I*n keeping with the two-headed persona of Windows 8, your computer comes with dual versions of various apps and programs. For example, Windows 8 is quite web-dependent, and its two web browser versions are both confusingly named Internet Explorer. One runs on the Start screen, naturally; the other hugs its traditional window on the desktop. In this chapter, find out how to connect with the Internet, visit websites, and find all the good stuff online from your Start screen.

Similarly, Windows 8 gives you two media players: One is bound to the Start screen, and the other is the desktop's Windows Media Player, a Windows staple for years. This chapter explains how to get the most from using the Start screen player.

And you may already be familiar with working with digital pictures on your computer. In this chapter, find out how to take pictures with the Start screen's Camera app (using the digital camera that's built-in to your computer), as well as how to view and share your photos.

What's an ISP, and Why Do I Need One?

Everybody needs three things to connect with the Internet: a computer, web browser software, and an Internet service provider (ISP).

You already have the computer, be it a tablet, laptop, or desktop PC. And Windows 8 comes with a pair of web browsers. The Start screen's Internet Explorer browser works for full-screen, quick information grabs; the desktop's Internet Explorer browser offers more in-depth features.

That means most people need to find only an ISP. Although music wafts through the air to your car radio for free, you must pay an ISP for the privilege of surfing the web. When your computer connects to your ISP's computers, Internet Explorer automatically finds the Internet, and you're ready to surf the web.

Choosing an ISP is fairly easy because you're often stuck with whichever ISPs serve your particular geographical area. Ask your friends and neighbors how they connect and whether they recommend their ISP. Call several ISPs serving your area for a rate quote and then compare rates. Most bill on a monthly basis, so if you're not happy, you can always switch.

✔ Although ISPs charge for Internet access, *you* don't always have to pay. Some places share their Internet access for free, usually through a wireless connection. If your laptop or tablet includes wireless support, and most do, you can browse the Internet whenever you're within range of a free wireless signal. (I cover wireless in the next section.)

✔ Although a few ISPs charge for each minute you're connected, most charge from $30 to $100 a month for unlimited service. Make sure that you know your rate before hopping aboard, or you may be unpleasantly surprised at the month's end.

✔ ISPs let you connect to the Internet in a variety of ways. The slowest ISPs require a dialup modem and an ordinary phone line. Faster still are *broadband* connections: special DSL or ISDN lines provided by some phone companies, and the even faster cable modems, supplied by your cable television company. When shopping for broadband ISPs, your geographic location usually determines your options.

✔ You need to pay an ISP for only *one* Internet connection. By setting up a network, you can share that single connection with any other computers, cellphones, TVs, and other Internet-aware gadgetry in your home or office.

Connecting Wirelessly to the Internet

Windows *constantly* searches for a working Internet connection. If it finds one that you've used previously, you're set: Windows passes the news along to Internet Explorer, and you're ready to visit the web.

When you're traveling, however, the wireless networks around you will often be new, so you'll have to authorize these new connections. Whenever you want to connect with a new network, you need to tell Windows that you want to connect, please.

To connect to a nearby wireless network for the first time, either one in your own home or in a public place, follow these steps:

1. **Summon the Charms bar and click or tap the Settings icon.**

   Any of these three tricks summons the Charms bar and its Settings screen, which I cover in Chapter 2:

   - **Mouse:** Point at the screen's top- or bottom-right edge; when the Charms bar appears, click the Settings icon.

   - **Keyboard:** Press ⊞+I to head straight for the Charms bar's Settings screen.

   - **Touchscreen:** Slide your finger inward from the screen's right edge; when the Charms bar appears, tap the Settings icon.

2. Click or tap the wireless network icon.

Among the Settings screen's six bottom icons, the one in the top left represents wireless networks. The icon changes shape, depending on your surroundings:

- **Available:** When the icon says Available, you're within range of a wireless network. Start salivating and move to the next step.

- **Unavailable:** When the icon says Unavailable, you're out of range. Time to head for a different seat in the coffee shop or perhaps a different coffee shop altogether. Then return to Step 1.

3. Click or tap the Available icon if it's present.

Windows lists all the wireless networks within range of your PC. Don't be surprised to see several networks listed; if you're at home, your neighbors probably see your network listed, too.

4. Choose to connect to the desired network by clicking its name and clicking the Connect button.

If you select the adjacent Connect Automatically check box before clicking the Connect button, Windows automatically connects to that network the next time you're within range, sparing you from connecting manually each time.

If you're connecting to an *unsecured network* — a network that doesn't require a password — you've finished. Windows warns you about connecting to an unsecured network, but a click or tap of the Connect button lets you connect anyway. (Don't do any shopping or banking on an unsecured connection.)

5. Enter a password if needed.

If you try to connect to a *security-enabled* wireless connection, Windows asks you to enter a *network security key* — technospeak for *password.* If you're at home, here's where you type in the same password you entered into your router when setting up your wireless network.

If you're connecting to somebody *else's* password-protected wireless network, ask the network's owner for the password. If you're in a hotel, pull out your credit card. You probably need to buy some connection time from the people behind the front desk.

6. Choose whether you want to share your files with other people on the network.

If you're connecting on your own home or office network, choose "Yes, turn on sharing and connect to devices." That lets you share files with others and use handy devices, like printers.

If you're connecting in a public area, by contrast, choose "No, don't turn on sharing or connect to devices." That keeps out snoops.

If you're still having problems connecting, try the following tips:

✔ When Windows says that it can't connect to your wireless network, it offers to bring up the Network Troubleshooter. The Network Troubleshooter mulls over the problem and then says something about the signal being weak. It's really telling you this: "Move closer to the wireless transmitter."

✔ If you can't connect to the secured network you want, try connecting to one of the unsecured networks. Unsecured networks work fine for casual browsing on the Internet.

- ✔ Cordless phones and microwave ovens, oddly enough, interfere with wireless networks. Try to keep your cordless phone out of the same room as your wireless PC, and don't heat up that sandwich when web browsing.

- ✔ If your desktop's taskbar contains a wireless network icon, click it to jump to Step 3. While you're working on the Windows 8 desktop, that wireless network icon provides a handy way to connect wirelessly in new locations.

Browsing Quickly from the Start Screen

Built for quick, on-the-fly browsing, the Start screen's browser works quickly. Part of its speed comes from its limitations, though. Every site fills the screen, making it easy to read. But the browser shows the sites in their full glory only by hiding its own menus, making navigation challenging.

To open the Internet Explorer app from the Start screen, click its tile. The browser opens, filling the screen with your last-viewed site.

When you want to visit someplace else, fetch the browser's hidden menus with any of these commands:

- ✔ **Mouse:** Right-click a blank portion of the web page, away from any words or pictures.

- ✔ **Keyboard:** Press ⊞+Z.

- ✔ **Touchscreen:** From the screen's top or bottom edge, slide your finger toward the screen's center.

What's the difference between the two web browsers?

Windows 8 comes with *two* web browsers. Adding to the confusion, each bears the name Internet Explorer. Although they look completely different, the Start screen's browser is really just a stripped-down version of the desktop's browser.

Because they're basically the same beast, they share your browsing history, cookies, saved passwords, and temporary files. Deleting those items from one browser also deletes them from the other.

The browsers differ in a few other ways, but most obviously through the limitations of the Start screen's browser. The Start screen's browser shows sites only in full-screen view; you can't place two sites side by side to compare them. It also won't let you save a Home screen; instead, the browser always opens to the last site you visited.

The Start screen's browser can only display Flash on a list of Microsoft-approved websites, so on some sites, you'll miss out on not only some movies but some advertisements. (Not that you'll miss those.)

If you find yourself needing a more powerful browser while in the Start screen, perhaps to watch something in Flash, right-click a blank portion of the currently viewed website. (On a tablet, swipe your finger inward from the top or bottom.) When the app's menu rises up from the screen's bottom edge, click the wrench icon and choose View in Desktop.

The browser's top and bottom menus appear, shown and neatly labeled in Figure 8-1.

> ✔ **Currently open sites:** Your last-visited sites appear here, letting you revisit them with a click. (Or, you can close them by clicking the X in their upper-right corners.)

New InPrivate tab/Close tabs

Open new blank tab

Currently open websites

How do I right-click on a touch-screen tablet?

Address bar

Reload web page

Revisit previous web page

Pin to Start menu

Search page/View on desktop browser

Currently viewed web page

Move forward one web page

Figure 8-1: The Start screen's browser offers hidden menus along the top and bottom.

✔ **New Tab:** Clicking this icon fetches a blank screen with an Address Bar along the bottom. Type in the address of the website you'd like to visit.

✔ **Tab Tools:** Clicking this icon brings a drop-down list with two options: New InPrivate Tab and Close Tabs. Select the New InPrivate Tab option to open a new tab for visiting a website *privately;* the browser will conveniently forget you've visited that site. The other menu option, Close Tabs, removes the thumb-nails of all your previously viewed sites from along the browser's top.

✔ **Back:** This icon on the bottom left lets you revisit the page you just visited.

✔ **Address Bar:** Type in the address of a website you'd like to visit in this box. Or, just type in a subject, and your browser will search for it, displaying possible matches. *Tip:* Click inside the Address Bar to see a list of your frequently visited sites, as well as sites you've pinned to the Start screen.

✔ **Refresh:** Handy for viewing news sites, this icon reloads the currently viewed page, gathering the latest material available.

✔ **Pin to Start:** Take note of this one: When you find a website you like, click this icon to add the page to your Start screen as a tile. That gives you one-click access for a return visit.

✔ **Page Tools:** This icon fetches a menu with two main options: Find On Page lets you search for text on the current page, whereas View on the Desktop lets you view that page on your desktop's Internet Explorer, which is handy when the Start screen's browser can't display something correctly. A third option, Get App for this Site, only appears when the site offers an app for direct access. (Accessing some sites is easier with an app than the browser.)

✔ **Forward:** Just as in the desktop browser, this icon lets you return to the page you just left.

You can also search for items through the Charms bar's Search icon. I cover the Charms bar in Chapter 2, but here's a hint: Point your mouse at the screen's right-top or -bottom corner to fetch the Charms bar, then click the Search icon, and type a name for what you're hankering.

When you're on the go and looking for quick information, the Start screen's speedy browser and its simple menus might be all you need. When you need more control, though, or if a website doesn't seem to display properly, head for the desktop browser, described next.

On many sites, the Start screen's browser doesn't support *Flash,* a popular technology for displaying web videos. If you find a site that says you need a Flash plug-in, ignore it. Instead, click the Page Tools icon and choose View on the Desktop. That loads the desktop's browser, which shows the site properly.

Moving among Web Pages

Web pages come with specific addresses, just like homes do. *Any* web browser lets you move between those addresses. You can use Internet Explorer from the Start screen or desktop, or even use a competing browser such as Firefox (www.getfirefox.com) or Chrome (www.google.com/chrome).

No matter which browser you use, they all let you move from one page to another in any of three different ways:

✔ By pointing and clicking a button or link that automatically whisks you away to another page

✔ By typing a complicated string of code words (the web address) into the Address Bar of the web browser and pressing Enter

✔ By clicking the navigation buttons on the browser's toolbar, which is usually at the top of the screen

Clicking links

The first way is by far the easiest. Look for *links* — highlighted words or pictures on a page — and click them.

For example, see how the mouse pointer turned into a hand as it pointed at the word *Books* in Figure 8-2? Click that word to see a web page with more information about that subject. The mouse pointer morphs into a hand whenever it's over a link. Click any linked word to see pages dealing with that link's particular subject.

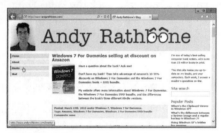

Figure 8-2: When the mouse pointer becomes a hand, click that word or picture.

Typing web addresses in the Address Bar

The second method is more difficult. If a friend gives you a napkin with a cool web page's address written on it, you need to type the website's address into your browser's *Address Bar* — the text-filled bar across the top. You'll do fine, as long as you don't misspell anything.

Internet Explorer's secret history of your web visits

Internet Explorer keeps a record of every website you visit. Although Internet Explorer's History list provides a handy record of your computing activities, it's a spy's dream.

To keep tabs on what Internet Explorer is recording, click your Favorites button and click the History icon on the drop-down menu. Internet Explorer lists every website you've visited in the past 20 days. Feel free to sort the entries by clicking the little arrow to the right of the word History. You can sort them by date, alphabetically, most visited, or by the order you've visited on that particular day — a handy way to jump back to that site you found interesting this morning.

To delete a single entry from the history, right-click it and choose Delete from the menu. To delete the entire list, exit the Favorites area. Then choose Internet Options from the Tools menu and click the Delete button in the Browsing History section. A menu appears, letting you delete your History and other items.

To turn off the History, click the Settings button instead of the Delete button. Then in the History section, change the Days to Keep Pages in History option to 0.

Deleting your History in the Internet Explorer's desktop version also deletes it in the Start screen's version of Internet Explorer.

See the address for my website along the top of Figure 8-2? I typed **www.andyrathbone.com** into the Address Bar. When I pressed Enter, Internet Explorer scooted me to my web page. (You don't need to type the `http://` part, thank goodness.)

Using Internet Explorer's toolbar

Finally, you can maneuver through the Internet by clicking various buttons on Internet Explorer's newly stripped-down toolbar, which sits at the top of the screen.

If you're not sure what each button does, hover your mouse pointer over a button to see a tooltip that describes its purpose in life.

Playing Music from the Start Screen

The Start screen's Music app isn't as much of a music player as it is an online storefront. The program devotes most of its onscreen real estate to advertising: Billboard-like tiles promote the latest releases by the latest artists.

And your *own* music? Scroll to the left, and you'll find tiles dedicated to music already on your computer. There's another surprise in the app's name. Although it's called Music, it calls itself *Xbox Music* once opened.

To launch the Music app and begin playing (or buying) music, follow these steps:

1. **Click the Start screen's Music tile.**

   The Start screen appears when you first turn on your computer. To find it from the desktop, press your keyboard's Windows key (🔲) or point your mouse cursor to the screen's bottom-left corner and click.

On a touchscreen, slide your finger inward from any screen's right edge to summon the Charms bar; then tap the Start icon to return to the Start screen.

2. Sign in with your Microsoft account or your Xbox LIVE account, if desired, or click Cancel.

Each time you open the Music app, Microsoft tries to link the Music app with your Microsoft account or Xbox LIVE account. Because those accounts can be linked to a credit card, you need one of those accounts to buy music.

Don't want to buy music? The app still lets you listen to your own music, but you'll see the words Can't Sign In located in the screen's upper-right corner. If you change your mind and want to buy music, click the words Can't Sign In, and the app offers you a chance to sign in with a Microsoft account.

3. Scroll to the right to sample or buy new music.

The Music app contains several screens, which you navigate by pressing the right-arrow key or pointing your mouse to the screen's right or left edges.

The opening screen shows either pictures of popular artists or a collage of the music stored on your computer. In the bottom-left corner, the opening screen lists the last song you heard. Click the Play button to hear it again.

The second screen to the right, called Xbox Music Store, lets you hear song previews from the latest CDs, and purchase the songs, if you wish.

One more screen to the right reveals Most Popular, yet another storefront for the latest popular tunes.

Click any tile to explore its category.

4. Scroll to the far left to see and play music stored on your computer.

To head straight for your own music, scroll to the far left; there, the My Music screen lists music stored on your own computer. Click an album's tile to see its songs.

To see *all* your stored music, click the words My Music at the screen's top; a list of your music appears, letting you sort it alphabetically by songs, albums, artists, or playlists.

5. To play an album or song, click its tile and then click Play.

Click a tile for an album or song, and the mini-player finally appears. Depending on the licensing agreements and your own equipment, you can choose to play it on your computer, play it on your Xbox, or add it to a playlist.

6. Adjust the music while it plays.

Right-click the screen (or tap it with a touchscreen) to bring up the controls on the App bar. The App bar offers you five icons to control your music: Shuffle, Repeat, Previous (to move to the previous song), Pause, and Next (to move to the next song).

As the music plays, the Music app shows a collage of your music's cover art, but it tosses in art from other artists in the hopes that it will inspire you to make an impulse purchase.

To adjust the volume, summon the Charms bar by pressing ⊞+C or pointing your mouse cursor at the screen's bottom-right corner. Click the Settings icon, click the Sound icon, and slide the volume indicator up or down.

Most touchscreen tablets include a volume toggle switch built in to one of their edges.

The Music app keeps playing music even if you begin working with other apps or switch to the desktop. To pause or move between tracks, you must return to the Music app and fetch its App bar, described in Step 6.

Taking Photos with the Camera App

Most tablets, laptops, and some desktop computers come with built-in cameras, sometimes called *webcams*. Their tiny cameras can't take high-resolution close-ups of that rare bird in the neighbor's tree, but they work fine for their main purpose: Taking a quick photo to e-mail to friends or post on Facebook.

To take a photo through your computer's camera with the Camera app, follow these steps:

1. **From the Start screen, click the Camera tile to open the app.**

2. **If the app asks to use your camera and micro-phone, choose Allow.**

   As a security precaution, Windows asks permission to turn on your camera. That helps prevent sneaky apps from spying on you without your knowing.

   After you grant approval, the computer screen turns into a giant viewfinder, showing you exactly what the camera sees: your face.

3. Adjust the settings, if desired.

Depending on your type of camera, the Camera app's App bar offers different icons:

- **Change camera:** Meant for laptops and tablets with front- and back-facing cameras, this button lets you toggle between the two.

- **Camera Options:** Clicking this icon brings up a pop-up menu that enables you to choose your camera's resolution and toggle between different microphones attached to your computer. If you see More Options at the pop-up menu's bottom edge, choose it to tweak even more options offered by your particular camera.

- **Timer:** Helpful for setting up shots, this tells the camera to snap the photo three seconds *after* you click the screen. (When you click the icon, it turns white, letting you know it's turned on.)

- **Video mode:** Click this icon to shoot videos rather than still shots. Clicking the screen toggles the video on and off. (The video icon turns white when activated, so you know the camera's in video mode.) While recording, a small timer appears in the screen's bottom-right corner, letting you know the video's current length.

4. To snap a photo, click anywhere on the screen.

To see the photo you just snapped, click the arrow on the left edge of the screen; to return to the Camera app, click the arrow to the right of the screen.

The Camera app saves all your snapped photos and videos in a folder called Camera Roll in your Pictures library.

Viewing Photos from the Start Screen

The two-headed beast of Windows 8 naturally includes *two* ways to view your digital photos on your computer: the Start screen's Photos app and the Desktop app's Photo Viewer.

The Start screen's Photos app works best for quickly showing off photos. It pulls in photos from your social networks such as Facebook and Flickr, making it easy to display *all* your photos from within one program.

What the Photos app lacks, however, are options. It won't rotate a sideways photo so it's right-side-up. You can't see the date you snapped a photo, or which camera snapped it. It's awkward for managing photos. It can't print, nor can it crop.

But when you want to show off your photos without a lot of fuss, follow these steps:

1. **From the Start screen, click the Photos tile.**

   The Photos app quickly appears, showing tiles representing your main photo storage areas:

   • **Pictures Library:** These photos live in your *own* computer, inside your Pictures library. You can see these photos even if you're not connected to the Internet. Photos stored in the other areas, by contrast, can't usually be seen without an Internet connection.

- **SkyDrive:** These photos live on Microsoft's huge Internet-connected computers. You can access them from any Internet-connected computer after you enter your Microsoft account and password. (I cover Microsoft accounts in Chapter 2, and SkyDrive in Chapter 5.)

- **Facebook:** This area shows all the photos you've uploaded to your Facebook account (www.facebook.com).

- **Flickr:** These photos come from your account on Flickr (www.flickr.com), one of many photo-sharing sites.

Depending on the social media accounts you've added to Windows 8, you may see other areas listed here, including photos stored on other Windows 8 computers connected to your network. (I explain how to add social media accounts to Windows in Chapter 7.)

2. **Click a storage area to see its photos; while inside any storage area, right-click the screen to see its App bar, which offers that screen's particular menus.**

Click or tap a storage area to see the photos and folders hidden inside. The Photos app shows photos in a long, horizontal strip across your screen, as shown in Figure 8-3. The folder's name appears across the top.

Return to previous folder

Location of current folder   Number of files in current folder

Name of current folder

Click any photo to view full-screen

View slide show

Select all photos in folder

Import photos from camera

Figure 8-3: Scroll to the left or right to see the photos.

On a touchscreen, slide your finger up from the screen's bottom edge to see the App bar, shown in Figure 8-3. Depending on what you're viewing, you'll see icons to Delete, Select All, Browse by Date, or see a Slide Show.

To navigate between folders, click the left-pointing arrow in the screen's top-left corner. (Click or tap the photo to bring a missing arrow into view.)

To delete a photo, right-click it and then click the Delete icon (shown in the margin) from the App bar along the screen's bottom edge.

3. Click a photo to see it full-screen.

When a photo fills the screen, an arrow appears on its left and right edges; click the arrow to move from photo to photo.

On a touchscreen, tap a photo to view it full-screen and then tap the side arrows to navigate between photos.

When viewing a photo full-screen, right-click to see the App bar. From the App bar, choose the Set As icon for options to set the current photo as the background for your Lock Screen, the Photo app's Start screen tile, or the background for the Photo app itself.

Viewing a photo that a friend *has* to see? E-mail it to him. I describe the details in Chapter 7, but here's the quick-and-dirty version: Fetch the Charms bar, click the Share icon (or press ⊞+H), and click Mail.

To return to the strip view of your photos, click the left-pointing arrow at the top-left corner. (You may need to click the photo to see the arrow.)

4. To view a slide show of the current folder, right-click any photo and then click the Slide Show icon on the App bar.

The slide show lacks any options for timing.

5. To exit the slide show, click any photo.

To exit the Photos app, head for the Start screen: Press the ⊞ key or fetch the Charms bar and click the Start icon.

Chapter 9

Customizing Windows 8 and Computing Safely

● ●

In This Chapter

▶ Understanding the two Windows control panels

▶ Assessing your safety in Action Center

▶ Setting Family Safety controls

▶ Staying safe on the Internet

▶ Altering the appearance of Windows 8

▶ Adjusting your hardware

▶ Automatically setting the computer's time and date

▶ Installing or removing apps and programs

▶ Adjusting for special needs

● ●

*M*ost science fiction movies include a close-up of a smoking control panel, ready to burst into flames. If that happens in Windows, grab an extra fire extinguisher: Windows 8 contains *two* switch-packed control panels.

The Start screen's control panel, the PC Settings screen, which is full of oversized buttons, helps mostly with simple chores, such as changing your account photo or turning on the spell checker's autocorrect option. The desktop's mammoth set of switches, called simply *Control Panel,* carries the more powerful settings found in earlier Windows versions.

But no matter which bank of switches you face, both control panels let you customize the look, feel, behavior, and vibe of Windows 8. This chapter explains the switches and sliders you'll want to tweak, and it steers you away from the ones that are prone to causing fires.

This chapter also tells you about staying safe in the world of Windows and the Internet. Because there's no easy way to recognize potentially bad stuff online, something that looks innocent — a friend's e-mail or a program found on the Internet — may be a virus that infects your computer. In this chapter, you find some steps to take to protect yourself from harm and minimize any damage.

Finding the Right Switch

Windows 8 comes with hundreds of settings, sprinkled between two completely different control panels. You'll rarely stumble randomly across the setting you need. So, instead of clicking aimlessly at menus, let Windows do the hunting.

Follow these steps to find the setting you need:

1. **From the Start screen, summon the Charms bar's Search pane.**

   You can summon the Charms bar's Search pane in any of three ways:

• **Mouse:** Point the cursor at the screen's top- or bottom-right corner; when the Charms bar appears, click the Search icon.

• **Keyboard:** Press ⊞+Q.

• **Touchscreen:** Slide your finger from the screen's right edge inward and then tap the Search icon.

2. **In the Search pane, click the word *Settings*.**

   That tells Windows to search through its *settings,* rather than your apps or files.

3. **In the search box, type a word describing your desired setting.**

   When you type the first letter, every setting containing that letter appears in a list. If you don't know the exact name of your setting, begin typing a keyword: **display**, **mouse**, **user**, **privacy**, or something similar.

   Don't see the right setting? Press the Backspace key to delete the letters you've typed and then try again with a different word.

4. **Click your desired setting on the list.**

   Windows takes you directly to that setting on the appropriate control panel.

When searching for a setting, always try the Search pane first. A few minutes spent at the Search pane yields better results than scouring the hundreds of settings stuffed in the two Windows 8 control panels.

The Start Screen's PC Settings Screen

The Start screen's mini control panel — the PC Settings screen — would make more sense if it simply offered mini tweaks, such as changing colors or other cosmetic fluff. But oddly enough, Microsoft stuffed it with some of the most powerful commands in Windows 8. To open the Start screen's PC Settings screen, follow these steps:

1. **Summon the Charms bar's Settings pane.**

2. **Choose the words *Change PC Settings* with a mouse click or tap of a finger.**

The PC Settings screen appears.

Like the desktop's large Control Panel, the PC Settings screen breaks its settings down into categories, each described here:

✔ **Personalize:** This lets you choose a new picture for your Start screen and lock screen. The Account Picture area lets you change the thumbnail photo assigned to your user account.

Don't overlook the Lock Screen Apps section, found at the bottom of the Lock Screen page of the PC Settings screen. This section lets you choose which tiles should automatically update on your lock screen. Click the Calendar app, for example, and the lock screen displays your next appointment's time and date.

✔ **Users:** This category lets you change your password or authorize another person to use your computer.

✔ **Notifications:** Sometimes called *toast notifications,* these little strips of text appear on your screen's top-right corner. If you find them informative, you needn't visit here. But if they're distracting, head here to choose which programs, if any, are allowed to display onscreen notifications.

✔ **Search:** You can safely ignore this settings category, unless you want to prevent an app or its contents from being indexed. You usually want Windows to index *everything,* making everything easier to find.

✔ **Share:** Designed for social networkers who enjoy sharing what they see on their computer screens, this lets you choose apps that can share information. Windows 8 starts with your Mail and People apps for e-mailing items to friends. As you install other apps, they may appear as options here, as well.

✔ **General:** This catch-all category offers a way to turn off the spell checker and to make Windows ignore Daylight Savings Time. Don't ignore the General category completely, though, because three important troubleshooting tools live here: Refresh Your PC, Remove Everything, and Advanced Startup.

✔ **Privacy:** The Privacy category lets you prevent apps from knowing your geographic location and from sharing your name and account picture. If you're concerned about privacy, though, look for the Delete History buttons sprinkled in the General, Share, and Search categories.

✔ **Devices:** This simply lists all your computer's *devices* — things you've plugged into your computer. That usually includes things like a mouse, monitor, printer, camera, speakers, and other gadgetry.

✔ **Ease of Access:** This includes settings to make Windows more navigable by people with challenges in vision and hearing.

✔ **Sync Your Settings:** If you've signed in to Windows 8 with a Microsoft account, this category lets you pick which settings should link to your account. Then, when you sign in to a different Windows 8 computer, that computer automatically changes to reflect the settings you chose.

✔ **Homegroup:** This lets you choose which libraries to share with other computers in your *Homegroup* — a simplified way to share files between connected computers.

✔ **Windows Update:** This settings category lets you know at a glance if Windows Update isn't working. Click the Check for Updates Now button to see whether Microsoft has released any fixes for your computer today.

The Big Guns: The Desktop's Control Panel

When the Start screen's PC Settings screen isn't enough, head for the big guns: The desktop's Control Panel lets you while away an entire workweek opening icons and flipping switches to fine-tune Windows 8. Part of the attraction comes from the Control Panel's magnitude: It houses nearly *50* icons, and some icons summon menus with dozens of settings and tasks.

Don't be surprised, though, when you flip one of the desktop Control Panel's switches and wind up in the Start screen's PC Settings screen to finish the job. The two control panels can't seem to leave each other alone.

To open the desktop's Control Panel, point your mouse cursor in the screen's bottom-left corner and right-click. (Or press ⊞+X.) When the text menu pops up in the bottom-left corner, choose Control Panel.

To save you from searching aimlessly for the right switch, the Control Panel lumps similar items together in its Category view, as shown in Figure 9-1.

Figure 9-1: The desktop's Control Panel settings grouped into eight categories.

Below each category's name, shortcuts list that category's most popular offerings. The System and Security category icon in Figure 9-1, for example, offers shortcuts to review your computer's maintenance and security status, turn on the File History backup, and access troubleshooting tools.

Some controls don't fall neatly into categories, and others merely serve as shortcuts to settings found elsewhere. To see these and every other icon the Control Panel offers, choose either Large Icons or Small Icons from the View By drop-down list, in the top-right corner.

Rest your mouse pointer over any confusing icon or category in the Control Panel, and Windows 8 thoughtfully explains its meaning in life. (Add this perk to the list of reasons why touchscreen owners will want a mouse when visiting the Windows desktop.)

System and Security

Like an old car or a new friendship, Windows 8 needs occasional maintenance. In fact, a little bit of maintenance can make Windows 8 run so much more smoothly. For example, you can speed up Windows, free up hard drive space, back up your data, and create a safety net called a restore point.

This category's security section contains a full brigade of soldiers, including the Action Center. Part of the Control Panel, the Action Center displays any problems it notices with the Windows 8 main defenses, and it provides handy, one-button fixes for the situations. Its taskbar icon, the white flag, always shows the Action Center's current status.

Assessing your safety in the Action Center

The Action Center window color codes problems by their severity; a blood red band shows critical problems requiring immediate action, and a yellow band means the problem needs attention soon.

Every defense in the Security category should be up and running for maximum safety because each protects you against different things.

If any of your computer's big cannons aren't loaded and pointing in the right direction, the Action Center's tiny taskbar icon appears with a red X across the flag. When you spot that red-flagged icon on your taskbar, follow these steps to visit the Action Center and fix the problem:

1. **Click the taskbar's red-flagged Action Center icon and choose Open Action Center from the pop-up menu.**

   The Action Center hops onscreen to display your computer's status in both security and maintenance. Normally, it doesn't list anything. But if you see an item listed in either category, something's wrong.

2. **Click the button next to flagged items to fix any potential security problems.**

   Whenever you notice that one of the Windows 8 defenses is turned off in the Action Center, click the button next to the item.

Avoiding viruses with Windows Defender

When it comes to viruses, *everything* is suspect. Viruses travel not only through e-mail messages, programs, files, networks, and flash drives, but also in screen savers, themes, toolbars, and other Windows add-ons. To combat the problem, Windows 8 includes a new version of Windows Defender that incorporates Microsoft Security Essentials, a security and antivirus program Microsoft formerly offered as a free download.

Windows Defender scans everything that enters your computer from anywhere. If Windows Defender notices something evil trying to enter your computer, it lets you know with a message on either the Start screen or the desktop (see Figure 9-2). Then Windows Defender quarantines the virus, rendering it unable to infect your computer.

Figure 9-2: Windows Defender warns you of an intruder and takes action.

Windows Defender constantly scans your PC in the background. But if your PC acts strangely, tell Windows Defender to scan your PC immediately by following these steps:

1. **While you're viewing the Start screen, type** Windows Defender **and press Enter.**

2. **Click the Scan Now button.**

   Windows Defender immediately performs a quick scan of your PC.

Windows Defender normally doesn't scan flash drives and portable hard drives. To include them, click the program's Settings tab, click Advanced, and put a check mark in the box called Scan Removable Drives. Click Save Changes to save the changes. The program's scans will take slightly longer, but the results are worth it.

Avoiding phishing scams

Eventually, you'll receive an e-mail from your bank, eBay, PayPal, or a similar website announcing a problem with your account. Invariably, the e-mail offers a handy link to click, saying that you must enter your username and password to set things in order.

Don't do it, no matter how realistic the e-mail and website may appear. You're seeing an ugly industry called *phishing:* Fraudsters send millions of these messages worldwide, hoping to convince a few frightened souls into typing their precious account name and password.

How do you tell the real e-mails from the fake ones? It's easy, actually, because *all* these e-mails are fake. Finance-related sites may send you legitimate history statements, receipts, or confirmation notices, but they will *never, ever* e-mail you a link for you to click and enter your password.

If you're suspicious, visit the company's *real* website — by typing the web address by hand into Internet Explorer's Address Bar. Chances are good that the real site won't list anything as being wrong with your account.

Windows 8 employs several safeguards to thwart phishing scams:

✔ When you first run Internet Explorer, make sure its SmartScreen filter is turned on by clicking the Tools icon and choosing Safety from the top menu. When the Safety menu appears, look for an entry called Turn *on* SmartScreen Filter. If you spot it, select it. That turns the important filter back on.

✔ Internet Explorer compares a website's address with a list of known phishing sites. If it finds a match, the SmartScreen filter keeps you from entering, as shown in Figure 9-3. Should you ever spot that screen, close the web page.

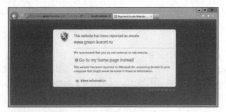

Figure 9-3: Internet Explorer warns you when you visit a known phishing site.

So, why can't the authorities simply arrest those people responsible? Because Internet thieves are notoriously difficult to track down and prosecute. The reach of the Internet lets them work from any place in the world.

✔ If you've already entered your name and password into a phishing site, take action immediately: Visit the *real* website and change your password. Then contact the company involved and ask it for help. It may be able to stop the thieves before they wrap their electronic fingers around your account.

✔ If you've entered credit card information, call the card's issuer immediately. You'll almost always find a toll-free, 24-hour phone number on the back of your credit card.

User Accounts and Family Safety

Windows 8 lets you create separate accounts for other people to use your PC. This lets them use your PC but limits the amount of damage they can do to Windows and your files. If you want to create a user account for a visitor, simply fetch the Charms bar, click the Settings icon, and click Change PC Settings. Choose Users and then choose Add a User.

The Control Panel's User Accounts and Family Safety category also includes a link to the Security section's Family Safety area, where you can place limits on how and when your kids access your PC. In fact, people who share their PC with roommates should drop by Family Safety, as well.

Family Safety controls work best with these conditions:

✔ You must hold an Administrator account. If everybody shares one PC, make sure that the other account holders — especially children or your roommates — have Standard accounts.

✔ If your children have their own PCs, create an Administrator account on their PCs for yourself. Then change their accounts to Standard.

To set up Family Safety, follow these steps:

1. **Right-click the bottommost-left corner of the screen and choose Control Panel from the pop-up text menu.**

   From the Start screen, tap the Desktop tile. Then slide a finger inward from a screen's right edge to summon the Charms bar. Touch the Settings icon, and touch the word Control Panel from the top of the Settings pane.

2. **From the User Accounts and Family Safety section, click the Set Up Family Safety For Any User link.**

3. **In the resulting window, click the user account you want to restrict; the Family Safety screen appears.**

4. **Turn the Family Safety settings on or off to enforce or suspend the rules you'll be setting up.**

5. **Choose the categories you'd like to enforce and set the limits.**

   Click any of these four categories — Web Filtering, Time Limits, Windows Store and Game Restrictions, and App Restrictions — and make your changes.

6. **When you're through, close the Family Safety window.**

   Your changes take place immediately.

Although the Family Safety controls work well, few things in the computer world are foolproof. If you're worried about your children's computer use, cast an occasional eye their way.

Network and Internet

Plug an Internet connection into your PC, and Windows 8 quickly starts slurping information from the web. Connect it with another PC, and Windows 8 wants to connect the two with a Homegroup or another type of network.

But should Windows 8 botch the job, the Control Panel's Network and Internet category has some troubleshooting tools.

Changing the Windows 8 Appearance and Personalization

One of the most popular categories, Appearance and Personalization lets you change the look, feel, and behavior of Windows 8 in a variety of ways. Inside the category await these six icons:

- ✔ **Personalization:** This area lets you stamp your own look and feel across Windows, including the desktop, screen saver, window colors, and so on.

- ✔ **Display:** Whereas personalization lets you fiddle with colors, the Display area lets you fiddle with your computer's screen. For example, it lets you enlarge the text to soothe tired eyes, adjust the screen resolution, and adjust the connection of an additional computer screen.

✔ **Taskbar:** Head here to add program shortcuts to your taskbar, the strip living along your desktop's bottom edge.

✔ **Ease of Access:** Designed to help people with special needs, this shortcut contains settings to make Windows more navigable by people with physical challenges. Because Ease of Access exists as its own category, I describe it in its own section later in this chapter.

✔ **Folder Options:** Visited mainly by experienced users, this area lets you tweak how folders look and behave.

✔ **Fonts:** Here's where you preview, delete, or examine fonts that spruce up your printed work.

Changing the desktop background

A *background,* also known as wallpaper, is simply the picture covering your desktop. To change it, follow these steps:

1. **Right-click your desktop and choose Personalize.**

2. **From the Personalization window, select Desktop Background from the windows' bottom left.**

3. **In the resulting window, click a new picture for the background.**

   Be sure to click the drop-down list to see all the available photos and colors that Windows offers. Feel free to click the adjacent Browse button and search your own Pictures library for potential backgrounds.

When you click a new picture, Windows immediately places it across your desktop. If you're pleased, jump to Step 5.

4. **Decide whether to fill, fit, stretch, tile, or center the picture.**

   You can automatically switch between images by choosing more than one photo. (Hold down Ctrl while clicking each one.) The picture then changes every 30 minutes unless you change the time in the Change Picture Every drop-down list.

5. **Click the Save Changes button to save your new background.**

   Windows saves your new background across your screen.

Choosing a screen saver

In the dinosaur days of computing, computer monitors suffered from *burn-in:* permanent damage when an oft-used program burned its image onto the screen. Today's computer screens no longer suffer from burn-in problems, but people still use screen savers because they look cool. Windows comes with several built-in screen savers. To try one out, follow these steps:

1. **Right-click your desktop and choose Personalize to open the Personalization window. Then select the Screen Saver link from the window's bottom-right corner.**

2. **In the Screen Saver Settings dialog box, click the downward-pointing arrow in the Screen Saver box and select a screen saver.**

   After choosing a screen saver, click the Preview button for an audition. And be sure to click the Settings button because some screen savers offer options.

3. **If desired, add security by selecting the On Resume, Display Logon Screen check box.**

   This safeguard keeps people from sneaking into your computer while you're fetching coffee. It makes Windows ask for a password after waking up from screen saver mode.

4. **When you're done setting up your screen saver, click OK. Windows saves your changes.**

Changing the computer's theme

Themes are simply collections of settings to spruce up your computer's appearance: You can save your favorite screen saver and desktop background as a *theme,* for example. Then, by switching between themes, you can change your computer's clothes more quickly.

To try one of the built-in themes in Windows 8, right-click your desktop and choose Personalize. Windows 8 lists its token bundled themes, as well as an option to create your own. Click any theme, and Windows 8 tries it on immediately.

The window offers these themes, with options listed along the window's bottom.

✔ **My Themes:** Themes you've personally created appear here. If you have a Microsoft account, you'll see a Synced Theme, which is the theme you'll see on every PC you sign in to with that account.

✔ **Windows Default Themes:** This category includes the bundled themes in Windows 8, including its original one called simply Windows.

✔ **Basic and High Contrast Themes:** This features high-contrast themes for the visually impaired.

Instead of choosing from the built-in themes, feel free to make your own by clicking the buttons for changing the Desktop Background, Window Color, Sounds, and Screen Saver. After creating the perfect look for your computer, save your work by clicking Save Theme and typing a name.

Changing the screen resolution

One of Windows' many change-it-once-and-forget-about-it options, *screen resolution* determines how much information Windows 8 can cram onto your computer screen. Changing the resolution either shrinks everything to pack more stuff onscreen or enlarges everything at the expense of desktop real estate.

To find your most comfortable resolution — or if a program or game mutters something about you having to change your *screen resolution* or *video mode* — follow these steps:

1. **Right-click a blank part of your desktop and choose Screen Resolution.**

   The Screen Resolution window appears.

2. **To change the screen resolution, click the Resolution drop-down list and use your mouse to drag the little bar between High and Low.**

   Watch the little preview screen near the window's top change as you move the mouse. The more you slide the bar upward, the larger your computer screen grows. Unfortunately, the more information Windows 8 can pack onto your computer screen, the smaller that information appears.

   There's no right or wrong choice here, but choosing Windows' recommended setting makes for the clearest text and images.

3. **View your display changes by clicking the Apply button. Then click the Keep Changes button to authorize the change.**

   When Windows 8 makes a drastic change to your display, it gives you 15 seconds to approve the change by clicking a Keep Changes button. If a technical glitch renders your screen unreadable, you won't be able to see or click the onscreen button. After a few seconds, Windows notices that you didn't approve, and it reverts to your original, viewable display settings.

4. **Click OK when you're done tweaking the display.**

   After you change your video resolution once, you'll probably never return here unless you buy a new, larger monitor. You'll also want to revisit here if you plug a second computer screen into your PC, which I describe in the sidebar.

Hardware and Sound

The Windows 8 Hardware and Sound category shows some familiar faces. The Display icon, for example, also appears in the Appearance and Personalization category, described in this chapter's previous section.

This category controls the parts of your PC you can touch or plug in. You can adjust the settings of your display here, as well as your mouse, speakers, keyboard, printer, telephone, scanner, digital camera, game controllers, and, for you graphic artists out there, digital pen.

Adjusting volume and sounds

The Sound area lets you adjust your PC's volume, a handy commodity when trying to sneak in a computer game on a Windows tablet during a boring business meeting.

Most Windows 8 tablets come with toggle-switch volume controls mounted along their left or right edge. The top button turns up the volume; the lower button decreases the volume. Experiment with them a bit before playing Angry Birds in the boardroom.

To turn down your PC's volume from the desktop, click the little speaker by your clock and slide down the volume. No speaker on your taskbar? Restore it by right-clicking the taskbar's clock, choosing Properties, and turning the Volume switch to On.

To mute your PC, click the little speaker icon at the bottom of the sliding control. Clicking that icon again lets your computer blare music again.

Click the word *Mixer* at the bottom of the sliding volume bar to set different volumes for different desktop programs. You can quietly detonate explosives in your favorite game while still allowing your desktop's e-mail program to loudly announce any new messages. (*Note:* The volume levels for Start screen apps won't appear here, unfortunately.)

To adjust the sound quickly from the Start menu on a touchscreen, summon the Charms bar by sliding a finger inward from the screen's right edge. When the Charms bar appears, tap the Settings icon and then tap the Sound icon. A sliding control appears, letting you slide it up or down to adjust the volume. (Slide the control to the bottom to mute the speakers.)

Installing or setting up speakers

Most PCs come with only two speakers. Others come with four, and PCs that double as home theaters or gaming rigs sometimes have up to eight. To accommodate the variety of setups, Windows 8 includes a speaker setup area, complete with a speaker test.

If you're installing new speakers, or you're not sure your old ones are working, follow these steps to introduce them properly to Windows 8:

1. **From the desktop, right-click your taskbar's Speaker icon and choose Playback Devices.**

2. **Click your speaker or speakers icon and then click the Configure button.**

The Speaker Setup dialog box appears.

3. Click the Test button, adjust your speaker's settings, and click Next.

Windows 8 walks you through selecting your number of speakers and their placement and then plays each one in turn so that you can hear whether they're in the correct locations.

4. Click the tabs for any other sound devices you want to adjust. When you're through adjusting, click the OK button.

While you're here, check your microphone volume by clicking the Recording tab, as well as tabs for any other sound gadgetry you've been able to afford.

If your speakers and microphone don't show up as devices, Windows 8 doesn't know they're plugged into your computer. That usually means you need to install a new *driver*.

Adding a Bluetooth gadget

Bluetooth technology lets you connect gadgets wirelessly to your computer, removing clutter from your desktop. On a tablet, it lets you add a mouse and keyboard without hogging one of your coveted USB ports.

Bluetooth can also connect your computer, laptop, or tablet with some cellphones for wireless Internet access — if your wireless provider allows it, of course.

To add a Bluetooth item to a computer, laptop, or tablet, follow these steps:

1. Make sure your Bluetooth device is turned on.

Sometimes you can simply flip a switch. Other devices make you hold down a button until its little light begins flashing.

2. **From the Start screen, fetch the Charms bar, click the Settings icon, and click the Change PC Settings button.**

You can summon the Charms bar's Settings pane in any of three ways:

- **Mouse:** Point the cursor at the screen's top- or bottom-right corner; when the Charms bar appears, click the Settings icon, and then click the Change PC Settings button.

- **Keyboard:** Press ⊞+I and press Enter.

- **Touchscreen:** Slide your finger from the screen's right edge inward, tap the Settings icon, and then tap Change PC Settings.

3. **From the Devices category, click the Add a Device icon.**

The PC Settings' Devices pane appears, listing all your connected devices. Your computer quickly begins searching for any nearby Bluetooth devices that want to connect.

If your device doesn't appear, head back to Step 1 and make sure your Bluetooth gadget is still turned on. (Many give up and turn off after 30 seconds of waiting to connect.)

4. **When your computer lists your device's name in the Devices pane, choose the name with a tap or mouse-click.**

5. **Type in your device's code if necessary and, if asked, click the Pair button.**

   Here's where things get sticky. For security reasons, you need to prove that you're sitting in front of your *own* computer and that you're not an adjacent stranger trying to break in. Unfortunately, devices employ slightly different tactics when making you prove your innocence.

   Sometimes you need to type a secret string of numbers called a *passcode* into both the device and your computer. (The secret code is usually hidden somewhere in your device's manual.) But you need to type quickly before the other gadget stops waiting.

   On some gadgets, particularly Bluetooth mice, you hold in a little push button on the mouse's belly at this step.

   Cellphones sometimes make you click a Pair button if you see matching passcodes on both your computer and phone.

   When in doubt, type **0000** on your keyboard. That's often recognized as a universal passcode for frustrated Bluetooth devices owners who are trying to connect their gadgets.

   After a gadget successfully pairs with your computer, its name and icon appear in the Devices category of the PC Settings screen.

To add a Bluetooth device from the Windows 8 desktop, click the taskbar's Bluetooth icon, choose Add a Bluetooth Device, and then jump to Step 3 in the preceding list. Don't see the taskbar's Bluetooth icon? Then click the upward-pointing arrow that lives a few icons to the left of the taskbar's clock. The Bluetooth icon appears in the pop-up menu, ready for your click.

Adding an Xbox 360 game console

The Control Panel lets you add or tweak most computer accessories, but the Xbox 360 game console begs for an exception. If you own one of Microsoft's game machines, you instead grant your *Xbox* permission to connect with your computer.

To let Windows 8 and Xbox communicate, grab your Xbox 360 controller, sit in front of your TV, and follow these steps:

1. **Turn on your Xbox 360, signing in with the same account you've used to sign in to Windows 8.**

   If you've signed in to both your Xbox and computer with *different* Microsoft accounts, you're not left in the lurch. Sign out of that account and create *another* user account in Windows 8 using your Xbox 360 account name and password. (That's a Microsoft account, too.)

   Sign in to that account on Windows 8 whenever you want to use one of the Windows 8 Xbox apps.

2. **On your Xbox 360, go to System Settings, Console Settings, Xbox Companion.**

   There, you see two switches: Available and Unavailable.

3. **Switch from Unavailable to Available.**

4. **Open one of the Windows 8 Xbox apps and choose Connect.**

   After a few moments, the word *Connecting* appears on your television screen, and you're through. Your Xbox apps will find your Xbox in Windows 8.

Adding a printer

Quarrelling printer manufacturers couldn't agree on how printers should be installed. As a result, you install your printer in one of two ways:

✔ Some printer manufacturers say simply to plug in your printer by pushing its rectangular-shaped connector into a little rectangular-shaped USB port on your PC. Windows 8 automatically notices, recognizes, and embraces your new printer. Stock your printer with any needed ink cartridges, toner, or paper, and you're done.

✔ Other manufacturers take an uglier approach, saying you must install their bundled software *before* plugging in your printer. And if you don't install the software first, the printer may not work correctly.

Unfortunately, the only way to know how your printer should be installed is to check the printer's manual. (Sometimes this information appears on a colorful, one-page Quick Installation sheet packed in the printer's box.)

If your printer lacks installation software, install the cartridges, add paper to the tray, and follow these instructions to put it to work:

1. **With Windows 8 up and running, plug your printer into your PC and turn on the printer.**

   Windows 8 may send a message saying that your printer is installed successfully, but follow the next step to test it.

2. **Load the desktop's Control Panel.**

3. **From the Hardware and Sound category, click the View Devices and Printers link.**

The Control Panel displays its categories of devices, including your printer, if you're lucky. If you spot your USB printer listed by its model or brand name, right-click its icon, choose Printer Properties, and click the Print Test Page button. If it prints correctly, you're finished. Congratulations.

Test page *didn't* work? Check that all the packaging is removed from inside your printer and that it has ink cartridges. If it still doesn't print, your printer is probably defective. Contact the store where you bought it and ask who to contact for assistance.

Windows 8 lists a printer named Microsoft XPS Document Writer. It's not really a printer, so it can be safely ignored.

If you have two or more printers attached to your computer, right-click the icon of your most oft-used printer and choose Set As Default Printer from the pop-up menu. Windows 8 then prints to *that* printer automatically, unless you tell it otherwise.

Clock, Language, and Region

Microsoft designed this area mostly for travelers to different time zones and locations. Desktop computer owners will see this information only once — when first setting up your computer. Windows 8 subsequently remembers the time and date, even when your PC is turned off.

Portable computers owners will want to drop by here when visiting different time zones; bilingual computer owners will also appreciate settings allowing characters from different languages.

To visit here, right-click the screen's bottom-left corner; choose Control Panel from the pop-up menu; and click the Clock, Language, and Region category. Three sections appear:

- ✔ **Date and Time:** This area is fairly self-explanatory. (Clicking your taskbar's clock and choosing Change Date and Time Settings lets you visit here, as well.)

- ✔ **Language:** If you're bilingual or multilingual, visit this area when you're working on documents that require characters from different languages.

- ✔ **Region:** Traveling in Italy? Click this category's icon and, on the Formats tab, select Italian from the Formats drop-down list. Windows switches to that country's currency symbols and date format. While you're at the Region window, click the Location tab; and from the Home location drop-down list, select Italy — or whatever country you're currently visiting.

Adding or Removing Programs

Whether you've picked up a new program or you want to purge an old one, the Control Panel's Programs category handles the job fairly well. One of its categories, Programs and Features, lists your currently installed programs. Click the one you want to discard or tweak.

This section describes how to remove or change existing programs and how to install new ones.

Removing apps and programs

Removing an app from your computer doesn't take much effort. Right-click the app's tile from the Start screen; when the App bar rises from the Start screen's bottom edge, click the Uninstall icon.

To remove an unwanted desktop program or change its settings, head for the desktop's Control Panel by following these steps:

1. **Right-click in the screen's bottom-left corner and choose the Control Panel from the pop-up menu.**

2. **When the Control Panel appears, choose Uninstall a Program from the Programs category.**

   The Uninstall or Change a Program window appears, listing your currently installed programs, their publisher, size, installation date, and version number.

   To free up disk space, click the Installed On or Size column header to find old or large programs. Then uninstall those forgotten programs you never or rarely use.

3. **Click the unloved program and then click its Uninstall, Change, or Repair button.**

   The menu bar above the programs' names always displays an Uninstall button, but when you click certain programs, you may also see buttons for Change and Repair. Here's the rundown:

     • **Uninstall:** This completely removes the program from your PC. (Some programs list this button as Uninstall/Change.)

     • **Change:** This lets you change some of the program's features or remove parts of it.

- **Repair:** A handy choice for damaged programs, this tells the program to inspect itself and replace damaged files with new ones. You may need to have the program's original CD or DVD handy, though, because you'll need to insert it into your computer.

4. **When Windows asks whether you're *sure,* click Yes.**

   Depending on which button you've clicked, Windows 8 either boots the program off your PC or summons the program's own installation program to make the changes or repair itself.

   After you delete a program, it's gone for good unless you kept its installation CD. Unlike other deleted items, deleted programs don't linger inside your Recycle Bin.

Always use the Control Panel's Uninstall or Change a Program window to uninstall unwanted programs. Simply deleting their files or folders won't do the trick. In fact, doing so often confuses your computer into sending bothersome error messages.

Installing new programs

Today, most programs install themselves automatically as soon as you slide their discs into your PC's drive or double-click their downloaded installation file.

If you're not sure whether a program has installed, go to the Start screen and look for its tile, usually toward the far right edge. If it's listed there, the program has installed.

But if a program doesn't automatically leap into your computer, here are some tips that can help:

- ✔ You need an Administrator account to install programs. (Most computer owners automatically have an Administrator account.) That keeps the kids, with their Limited or Guest accounts, from installing programs and messing up the computer.

- ✔ Downloaded a program? Windows 8 usually saves them in your Downloads folder, accessible by clicking your username on the Start screen. Double-click the downloaded program's name to install it.

- ✔ Many eager, newly installed programs want to add a desktop shortcut, a Start screen tile, *and* a Quick Launch toolbar shortcut. Say "yes" to all. That way you can start the program from the desktop, avoiding a trip to the Start screen. (Changed your mind? Right-click any unwanted shortcuts and choose either Delete or Unpin to remove them.)

- ✔ It's always a good idea to create a restore point before installing a new program. If your newly installed program goes haywire, use System Restore to return your computer to the peaceful state of mind it enjoyed before you installed the troublemaker.

Modifying Windows 8 for the Physically Challenged

Nearly everybody finds Windows 8 to be particularly challenging, but some people face special physical challenges as well. To assist them, the Control Panel's Ease of Access area offers a variety of welcome changes.

If your eyesight isn't what it used to be, you may appreciate the ways to increase the text size on your computer screen.

Follow these steps to modify the settings in Windows 8:

1. **Load the desktop's Control Panel.**

   You can fetch the Control Panel any of several ways:

   - **Mouse:** Right-click the screen's bottom-left corner and choose Control Panel from the pop-up menu.

   - **Keyboard:** From the desktop, press ⊞+I, scroll up to the words *Control Panel*, and then press Enter.

   - **Touchscreen:** From the desktop, slide your finger from the screen's right edge inward, tap the Settings icon, and tap the words *Control Panel*.

2. **When the Control Panel appears, select the Ease of Access category, and choose the Ease of Access Center icon.**

   The Ease of Access Center appears, as shown in Figure 9-4. The ethereal voice of Windows 8 kicks in, explaining how to change its programs.

Figure 9-4: The Ease of Access Center contains a variety of ways to help users with physical limitations.

3. **Choose the Get Recommendations to Make Your Computer Easier to Use link.**

   Look for the link called Get Recommendations to Make Your Computer Easier to Use (shown with the mouse pointing to it in Figure 9-4). That makes Windows 8 give you a quick interview so that it can gauge what adjustments you may need. When it's through, Windows 8 automatically makes its changes, and you're done.

   If you're not happy with the changes, move to Step 4.

4. **Make your changes manually.**

   The Ease of Access Center offers these toggle switches to make the keyboard, sound, display, and mouse easier to control:

   - **Start Magnifier:** Designed for the visually impaired, this option magnifies the mouse pointer's exact location.

   - **Start Narrator:** The awful built-in narrator in Windows 8 reads onscreen text for people who can't view it clearly.

   - **Start On-Screen Keyboard:** This setting places a clickable keyboard along the screen's bottom, letting you type by pointing and clicking.

   - **Set up High Contrast:** This setting eliminates most screen colors but helps vision-impaired people view the screen and cursor more clearly.

   Choose any of these options to turn on the feature immediately. Close the feature's window if the feature makes matters worse.

   If you're still not happy, proceed to Step 5.

5. **Choose a specific setting in the Explore All Settings area.**

   Here's where Windows 8 gets down to the nitty-gritty, letting you optimize Windows 8 specifically for the following things:

   - Blindness or impaired vision

   - Using an alternative input device rather than a mouse or keyboard

   - Adjusting the keyboard and mouse sensitivity to compensate for limited movements

   - Turning on visual alerts instead of sound notifications

   - Making it easier to focus on reading and typing tasks

   Some centers that assist physically challenged people may offer software or assistance for helping you make these changes.

Part II
Office 2013

Visit www.dummies.com/extras/office2013 for great Dummies content related to Office 2013.

In this part . . .

✔ Become familiar with the basics of using all Office programs.

✔ Find out how to create, edit, and format Word documents.

✔ Discover how to navigate Excel as well as how to set up formulas and use functions.

✔ Create a presentation that has pizazz with PowerPoint.

✔ Organize your e-mail, calendar, and task lists with Outlook.

✔ Set up a database with Access.

Chapter 10

Getting Started with Office 2013

. . . .

In This Chapter

▶ Starting an Office 2013 program

▶ Learning the Ribbon and the Quick Access Toolbar

▶ Selecting data

▶ Editing text

▶ Cutting and pasting

▶ Undoing and redoing work

▶ Adding (and deleting) pictures

▶ Searching the Help window

▶ Exiting from Office 2013

. . . .

*M*icrosoft Office 2013 consists of five core programs:
Word, Excel, PowerPoint, Access, and Outlook,
where each program specializes in manipulating different
data. Word manipulates text; Excel manipulates numbers;
PowerPoint manipulates text and pictures to create a
slide show; Access manipulates organized, repetitive data
such as inventories; and Outlook manipulates personal
information such as e-mail addresses and phone numbers.

Although each Office 2013 program stores and manipulates different types of data, they all work in similar ways. First, you have to enter data into an Office 2013 program by typing on the keyboard or loading data from an existing file. Second, you have to tell Office 2013 how to manipulate your data, such as underlining, sorting, arranging it on the screen, or deleting it. Third, you have to save your data as a file.

This chapter describes how to enter, manipulate, and save data using the standard commands that enable you to quickly jump from Word to PowerPoint to Excel without having to learn entirely new commands for each program. You also find out how to add pictures to your Office 2013 files and how to use the help system.

Starting an Office 2013 Program

Microsoft Office 2013 runs on both Windows 7 and Windows 8. Information in this book focuses on Windows 8.

To load Office 2013 in Windows 8, follow these steps:

1. **Open the Windows 8 tiles by either pressing the Windows key on your keyboard or moving the mouse pointer to the bottom-left corner of the screen and clicking when the Start preview window appears.**

   The Windows 8 tile interface appears.

2. **Scroll sideways until you see the Office 2013 tiles that represent the program you want to start as shown in Figure 10-1.**

Figure 10-1: The tile interface of Windows 8 displays the Office 2013 programs as individual tiles.

3. **Click the tile that represents the Office 2013 program you want to run, such as Microsoft Word 2013 or Microsoft PowerPoint 2013.**

   Your chosen program appears on the screen. At this point, you can open an existing file.

Introducing the Microsoft Office Ribbon

In older Windows programs, such as Microsoft Office 2003, the program displayed pull-down menus at the top of the screen. To find a command, you had to click a pull-down menu and then search for a command buried in the menu. Since this can get tedious and confusing, later versions of Microsoft Office introduced a Ribbon interface.

The basic idea behind this Ribbon interface is to store commonly used commands under separate tabs. Clicking each tab displays icons that represent related commands.

Although every Office 2013 program displays different tabs, the three most common tabs are the File tab, the Home tab, and the Insert tab.

The File tab lets you open, save, and print your files. In addition, the File tab also lets you exit out of the program and customize an Office 2013 program.

The Home tab displays icons that represent the most common commands for that particular Office 2013 program, such as formatting commands.

The Insert tab displays icons that represent common commands for adding items to a file such as pictures and tables.

In addition to the File, Home, and Insert tabs, every Office 2013 program also includes tabs that contain commands specific to that particular program.

The File tab

The various commands available on the File tab include

- ✔ **Info:** Protects your file from changes, inspects a file for compatibility issues with older programs, and manages different versions of your file. The Info command also lets you view the details of your file such as the file's size and the date you created it.
- ✔ **New:** Creates a new file.

✔ **Open:** Loads an existing file.

✔ **Save:** Saves your file.

✔ **Save As:** Save the current file under a new name and/or in a different location such as a different folder or computer.

✔ **Print:** Prints the current file.

✔ **Share:** Sends a file as an e-mail attachment or posts it online.

✔ **Export:** Saves the current file in a different file format.

✔ **Close:** Closes an open file but keeps the Office 2013 program running.

✔ **Account:** Displays information about your SkyDrive account.

SkyDrive is Microsoft's cloud computing service that lets you store files online so you can access them from other types of devices such as a smart phone, a tablet, or another computer.

✔ **Options:** Displays various options for customizing each Office 2013 program.

✔ **Exit:** Closes any open files and exits the Office 2013 program.

Creating a new file

Each time you create a new file, you have the option of choosing different types of templates that are already formatted and designed for specific purposes, such as a calendar, newsletter, sales report, or corporate slide-show presentation, as shown in Figure 10-2.

Figure 10-2: The New command displays a variety of files you can create.

To create a new file, follow these steps:

1. **Click the File tab.**

2. **Click New.**

   A list of templates appears (refer to Figure 10-2).

3. **Double-click the template you want to use.**

   Office 2013 creates a new file based on your chosen template. For some templates, you may need access to the Internet to download the templates from Microsoft's website.

Opening an existing file

To open an existing file, you need to tell Office 2013 the location and name of the file you want to open.

The four options for finding an existing file include

✔ **Recent Documents/Workbooks/Presentations:** Displays a list of files you recently opened.

✔ **Someone's SkyDrive:** Displays a list of files stored on another person's SkyDrive account.

✔ **Computer:** Lets you browse through the folders stored on your computer to find a file.

✔ **Add a place:** Lets you define a new location for storing files in the cloud such as your SkyDrive account.

To open a file, follow these steps:

1. **Click the File tab.**

2. **Click Open.**

   An Open pane appears.

3. **Choose an option such as Recent Documents or Computer.**

   You may need to click the Browse button to access different folders.

4. **Click the file you want to open.**

   Your chosen file appears.

Saving files

Saving a file stores all your data on a hard drive, other storage device, or a SkyDrive account. The first time you save a file, you need to specify three items:

✔ The location in which to store your file

✔ The name of your file

✔ The format in which to save your file

The location can be any folder on your hard drive or in your SkyDrive account. If you save your files to your computer, Office 2013 stores all your files in the Documents folder unless you specify otherwise.

You can give a file any name you want, but it's a good idea to give your file a descriptive name.

The format of your file defines how Office 2013 stores your data. The default file format is simply called Word Document, Excel Workbook, PowerPoint Presentation, or Access Database. Anyone using Office 2013, 2010, or Office 2007 can open these files.

For a quick way to save a file, click the Save icon that appears above the File tab or press Ctrl+S.

Saving a file in other file formats

If you need to share files with people using older versions of Microsoft Office or other word processors, spreadsheets, or database programs, you need to save your files in a different file format. To share files with people using older versions of Microsoft Office, you need to save your files in a format known as *97-2003,* such as *Word 97-2003 Document* or *PowerPoint 97-2003 Presentation.*

To save your Office 2013 files in the 97-2003 format, follow these steps:

1. **Click the File tab.**

2. **Click Export.**

    The middle pane displays different options.

3. **Click Change File Type.**

    A list of different formats appears.

4. **Click the 97-2003 format option, such as Word 97-2003 Document or Excel 97-2003 Workbook.**

5. **Click the Save As button near the bottom of the screen.**

The Save As dialog box appears.

If you want to share your file with different types of programs, you may need to choose a different file format, such as Rich Text Format or Text.

6. **(Optional) Click in the File Name text box and type a descriptive name for your file.**

7. **Click Save.**

Closing a file

When you're done editing a file, you need to close it. Closing a file simply removes the file from your screen but keeps your Office 2013 program running so you can edit or open another file

To close a file, follow these steps:

1. **Click the File tab.**

2. **Click Close.**

    If you haven't saved your file, a dialog box appears asking whether you want to save your changes.

    For a faster way to choose the Close command, press Ctrl+F4.

3. **Click Save to save your changes, Don't Save to discard any changes, or Cancel to keep your file open.**

Using the Ribbon

The Ribbon interface displays tabs that contain groups of related commands. Using the Ribbon is a two-step process. First, you must click the tab that contains the command you want. Second, you click the actual command.

Identifying Ribbon icons

Although some icons include descriptive text (such as Format Painter or Paste), most icons simply look like cryptic symbols from an alien language. To get additional help deciphering icons on the Ribbon, just point the mouse pointer over an icon, and a short explanation appears, called a ScreenTip.

ScreenTips provide the following information:

- ✓ The official name of the command
- ✓ The equivalent keystroke shortcut you can use to run the command
- ✓ A short explanation of what the command does

Shortcut keystrokes let you choose a command from the keyboard without the hassle of clicking a tab and then clicking the icon buried inside that tab. Most shortcut keystrokes consist of two or three keys, such as Ctrl+P or Ctrl+Shift+C.

Displaying dialog boxes

On each tab, the Ribbon displays related commands in a group. Although you can choose the most commonly used commands directly from the Ribbon, Word often contains dozens of additional commands that don't appear on the Ribbon. To access these more obscure commands, you need to open a dialog box.

In the bottom-right corner of a group of icons on the Ribbon, you see the Show Dialog Box icon, which looks like an arrow pointing diagonally downward.

To open a dialog box that contains additional options, follow these steps:

1. **Click a tab on the Ribbon, such as the Home or Page Layout tab.**

2. **Click the Show Dialog Box icon in the bottom-right corner of a group.**

   Office 2013 displays a dialog box.

3. **Choose any options in the dialog box, and then click OK or Cancel when you're done.**

Minimizing the Ribbon

Some people like the Ribbon displaying various icons at all times, but others find that it makes the screen appear too cluttered. In case you want to tuck the Ribbon out of sight so icons only appear when you click a tab, use one of the following methods:

- Double-click the current tab.

- Press Ctrl+F1.

- Click the Full Screen Mode icon that appears on the far right next to the Help (Question Mark) icon.

These three methods also work to make a hidden Ribbon display.

When you choose either of the first two methods, the Ribbon displays its tabs but hides any icons that normally appear underneath. When you click the Full Screen Mode icon, a menu appears and gives you three options:

- **Auto-hide Ribbon:** Completely hides the Ribbon including tabs and icons.

- **Show Tabs:** Displays the Ribbon tabs but hides the icons on each tab.

- **Show Tabs and Commands:** Displays the Ribbon tabs and icons on each tab.

Using the Quick Access Toolbar

The Quick Access toolbar appears in the upper-left corner of the screen. The Quick Access toolbar displays icons that represent commonly used commands such as Save and Undo, as shown in Figure 10-3.

Quick Access toolbar

Figure 10-3: The toolbar provides one-click access to common commands.

Adding icons

The Quick Access toolbar is designed to put your most commonly used commands where you can find them quickly. To add other icons to the Quick Access toolbar, follow these steps:

1. **Click the Customize Quick Access Toolbar arrow.**

   A pull-down menu appears.

2. **Click a command that you want to add to the Quick Access toolbar such as Open or Quick Print.**

   A check mark appears next to each command that currently appears on the Quick Access toolbar. If you want to add more commands that aren't displayed on the Quick Access toolbar menu, continue with the rest of Steps 3 through 7.

3. **Click More Commands.**

   An Options window appears. The panel on the right shows all the current icons on the Quick Access toolbar. The panel on the left shows all the other icons you can add.

4. **Click in the Choose commands from list box and choose a title, such as Home Tab or Insert Tab.**

   The left panel displays a list of icons and commands.

5. **Click an icon and then click the Add button.**

6. **(Optional) Repeat Steps 4 and 5 for each icon you want to add to the Quick Access toolbar.**

7. **Click OK.**

   Your chosen icon (or icons) now appears on the Quick Access toolbar.

Removing icons

You can remove icons from the Quick Access toolbar at any time. To remove an icon, follow these steps:

1. **Right-click an icon on the Quick Access toolbar.**

   A pull-down menu appears.

2. **Click Remove from Quick Access Toolbar.**

   Office 2013 removes your selected icon from the Quick Access toolbar.

Moving the Quick Access toolbar

The Quick Access toolbar can appear above the Ribbon (its default location) or below the Ribbon. To move the Quick Access toolbar, follow these steps:

1. **Click the Customize Quick Access Toolbar arrow.**

   A pull-down menu appears.

2. **Choose Show Below the Ribbon or Show Above the Ribbon.**

Selecting Data

To modify data, you must tell Office 2013 what you want to change by selecting it. Then choose a command that changes your data, such as underlining text or deleting a picture. To select anything in Office 2013, you can use either the mouse or the keyboard.

Selecting data with the mouse

The mouse provides two ways to select data. The first way involves pointing and dragging the mouse:

1. **Point the mouse pointer at the beginning or end of the data you want to select.**

2. **Hold down the left mouse button and drag (move) the mouse pointer over the data to select it.**

You can also select data by clicking the mouse. To select a picture, such as a chart in Microsoft Excel or a photograph added to a Microsoft Word document, just click the picture to select it. Office 2013 displays rectangles, called *handles,* around the border of any selected picture, as shown in Figure 10-4.

Handle

Figure 10-4: Handles appear around a selected picture.

To select text with the mouse, you can click the mouse in one of three ways:

- ✓ **Single-click:** Moves the cursor
- ✓ **Double-click:** Selects the word that you click
- ✓ **Triple-click:** Selects the entire paragraph that contains the word you click

Office 2013 defines a *paragraph* as any chunk of text that begins on a separate line and ends with a Return character (¶), created by pressing the Enter key.

Selecting data with the keyboard

To select data with the keyboard, you need to use the following keys:

- ✔ **The cursor movement keys (up/down/left/right arrow keys, Home/End keys, or Page Up/Page Down keys)**
- ✔ **The Shift key**

To select all the data in a file, press Ctrl+A.

To select data, follow these steps:

1. **Move the cursor to the beginning or end of the data you want to select.**

2. **Hold down the Shift key. (Keep it pressed down.)**

3. **Move the cursor by using any of the cursor movement keys.**

4. **Release the Shift key.**

Selecting multiple chunks of data with the mouse and keyboard

You can use both the mouse and the keyboard to select multiple chunks of data that are not located next to each other. To select two or more chunks of data, follow these steps:

1. **Select a picture or chunk of text, using either the keyboard or the mouse.**

2. **Hold down the Ctrl key.**

3. **Select another picture or chunk of text, using either the keyboard or the mouse.**

4. **Repeat Step 3 for each additional item you want to select.**

5. **Release the Ctrl key when you're done selecting data.**

Editing Text with the Pop-up Toolbar

As soon as you select text with the mouse, Office 2013 displays a pop-up toolbar that displays icons of the most commonly used commands. The closer you move the mouse toward this pop-up toolbar, the darker and sharper the toolbar appears, as shown in Figure 10-5.

Pop-up toolbar

Figure 10-5: Office 2013 displays a toolbar at the upper right of selected text.

To use this pop-up toolbar, follow these steps:

1. **Select data by using the mouse.**

   Selecting data with the keyboard will *not* display the pop-up toolbar.

2. **Move the mouse pointer to the area to the upper right of the selected data.**

   The pop-up toolbar appears.

3. **Click an icon on the pop-up toolbar.**

Whenever you edit a file, save your file periodically by clicking the Save icon in the Quick Access toolbar, pressing Ctrl+S, or clicking the File tab and choosing Save.

Cutting and Pasting (Moving) Data

Moving data in Office 2013 requires a two-step process: cut and paste. When you *cut* data, you delete it but save a copy in a special area of the computer's memory known as the *Clipboard*. When you *paste* data to a new location, you copy the data from the Clipboard and paste it into your file.

To move data, follow these steps:

1. **Select the data you want to move, using the keyboard or mouse.**

2. **Choose one of the following:**

   - Click the Cut icon (on the Home tab).

   - Right-click the mouse and choose Cut.

• Press Ctrl+X.

3. Move the cursor to a new location.

4. Choose one of the following:

> • Click the Paste icon (on the Home tab).
>
> • Right-click the mouse and choose Paste.
>
> • Press Ctrl+V.

If you select data in Step 3, you can replace that selected data with the pasted data you selected in Step 1.

Copying and Pasting Data

Unlike the Cut command, the Copy command leaves your selected data in its original location but places a second copy of that data somewhere else. To copy and paste data, follow these steps:

1. Select the data you want to copy, using the keyboard or mouse.

2. Choose one of the following:

> • Click the Copy icon (on the Home tab).
>
> • Right-click the mouse and choose Copy.
>
> • Press Ctrl+C.

3. Move the cursor to a new location.

4. Choose one of the following:

> • Click the Paste icon.
>
> • Right-click the mouse and choose Paste.
>
> • Press Ctrl+V.

Undo and Redo

To protect you from mistakes, Office 2013 offers a special Undo command, which essentially tells the computer, "Remember that last command I just gave? Pretend I never chose it." The two ways to choose the Undo command are

- ✔ **Click the Undo icon on the Quick Access toolbar.**
- ✔ **Press Ctrl+Z.**

To undo multiple commands, follow these steps:

1. **Click the downward-pointing arrow that appears to the right of the Undo icon.**

   A list of your previously chosen commands appears.

2. **Move the mouse pointer to highlight all the commands that you want to undo.**

3. **Click the left mouse button.**

   Office 2013 undoes your chosen commands.

The Redo command lets you reapply the last command you chose to undo. To choose the Redo command, press Ctrl+Y.

Each time you choose the Redo command, you reverse the effect of the last Undo command. For example, if you use the Undo command four times, you can choose the Redo command only up to four times.

Adding (and Deleting) Pictures

To add a picture to a file, follow these steps:

1. **Click the Insert tab.**
2. **Click the Picture icon.**

   The Insert Picture dialog box appears.

3. **Select the picture file you want to insert.**

   You may need to select a different folder or drive that contains the picture you want to insert.

4. **Click the Insert button.**

   • In Word, your picture appears wherever the cursor appears.

   • In Excel, the upper-left corner of your picture appears in the cell where the cursor appears.

   • In PowerPoint, your picture appears in the center of the currently displayed slide.

To delete a picture in a file, follow these steps:

1. **Select the picture that you want to delete.**

   Handles appear around your selected picture.

2. **Press the Delete or Backspace key.**

Searching in the Help Window

Rather than browse through one or more subcategories to find help, you may want to search for help by typing in one or more keywords. Such keywords can identify a specific topic, such as *Printing* or *Editing charts*.

If you misspell a topic, the Help system may not understand what you want to find, so check your spelling.

To search the Help window by typing in a keyword or two, follow these steps:

1. **Choose one of the following methods to display the Help window:**

   • Click the Help icon.

   • Press F1.

2. **Click in the Search Help list box and type one or more keywords, such as** Formatting **or** Aligning text.

   Type as few words as possible. So rather than type "I want to find help on printing," just type "Printing." Not only will this make it easier for you to search for help, but it will also keep Office 2013 from looking up extra words that have nothing to do with your topic such as "I want to find help on . . . ."

3. **Click Search or press Enter.**

   The Help window displays a list of topics.

4. **Click a Help topic.**

   The Help window displays information for your chosen topic. You may need to click additional topics to get the answer you want.

5. **Click the Close box when you're done, to make the Help window go away.**

Exiting Office 2013

To exit from any Office 2013 program, choose one of the following:

- ✔ Click the Close box in the upper-right corner of the Office 2013 window.

- ✔ Click the program icon in the upper-left corner, and when a menu appears, click Close.

- ✔ Press Alt+F4.

If you try to close an Office 2013 program before saving your file, a dialog box pops up to give you a chance to save your file. If you don't save your file before exiting, you lose any changes you made to that file.

Chapter 11

Working with Word

. . . .

In This Chapter

▶ Moving the cursor with the mouse and keyboard

▶ Finding (and replacing) text

▶ Checking spelling

▶ Viewing a document

▶ Changing font and font size

▶ Changing text style and color

▶ Using styles and templates

▶ Inserting pages and page breaks

. . . .

*T*he whole purpose of Microsoft Word is to let you type in text and make it look pretty so you can print or send it for other people to read. So the first step in using Microsoft Word is finding how to enter text in a Word file, called a *document*.

After you type text into a document, edit it, and check it for spelling errors, you're ready to make it look pretty — a process known as *formatting text* — by changing the font style, size, and color and adjusting the layout and page breaks.

Moving the Cursor with the Mouse

When you move the mouse, Word turns the mouse pointer into an I-beam pointer. If you move the mouse over an area where you cannot type any text, the mouse pointer turns back into the traditional arrow, pointing up to the left.

To move the cursor with the mouse, just point and click the left mouse button once. The blinking cursor appears where you clicked the mouse.

If you have a blank page or a blank area at the end of your document, you can move the cursor anywhere within this blank area by following these steps:

1. **Move the mouse pointer over any blank area past the end of a document.**

   Word defines the *end* of a document as the spot where no more text appears. (Word considers blank spaces as text.) To find the end of a document, press Ctrl+End.

   - *In a new document:* The end of the document is in the upper-left corner where the cursor appears.

   - *In a document with existing text:* The end of the document is the last area where text appears (including spaces or tabs).

2. **Make sure that the correct justification icon appears next to the mouse pointer.**

For example, if you want to center-justify your text, make sure that the Center Justification icon appears at the bottom of the I-beam pointer.

Getting the Left, Center, or Right Justification icon to appear in Step 2 can be tricky. The Left Justification icon appears most of the time. If you move the mouse pointer slightly indented from the left margin of the page, the Left Indent icon appears. To make the Center Justification icon appear, move the mouse pointer to the center of the page. To make the Right Justification icon appear, move the mouse pointer to the right edge of the page.

3. Double-click the mouse pointer.

Word displays your cursor in the area you clicked. Any text you type now appears justified according to the justification icon displayed in Step 3.

Moving the Cursor with the Keyboard

Moving the cursor with the mouse can be fast and easy. However, touch-typists often find that moving the cursor with the keyboard is more convenient (and sometimes faster too). Here's a list of different keystroke combinations you can use to move the cursor.

- ↑: Moves the cursor up one line

- ↓: Moves the cursor down one line

- →: Moves the cursor right one character

- ←: Moves the cursor left one character

- Ctrl+↑: Moves the cursor up to the beginning of the preceding paragraph

- Ctrl+↓: Moves the cursor down to the beginning of the next paragraph

- Ctrl+→: Moves the cursor right one word

- Ctrl+←: Moves the cursor left one word

- Home: Moves the cursor to the beginning of the line

- End: Moves the cursor to the end of the line

- Ctrl+Home: Moves the cursor to the beginning of a document

- Ctrl+End: Moves the cursor to the end of a document

- Page Up: Moves the cursor up one screen

- Page Down: Moves the cursor down one screen

- Ctrl+Page Up: Moves the cursor to the top of the preceding page

- Ctrl+Page Down: Moves the cursor to the top of the next page

You can move the cursor with both the keyboard and the mouse.

Finding and Replacing Text

To help you find text, Word offers a handy Find feature. Not only can this Find feature search for a word or phrase, but it also offers a Replace option so you can make Word find certain words and automatically replace them with other words.

Using the Find command

The Find command can search for a single character, word, or a group of words. To make searching faster, you can either search an entire document or just a specific part of a document. To make searching a document more flexible, Word lets you search for specific words or phrases, headings, or pages.

To search for words or phrases by using the Find command, follow these steps:

1. **Click the Home tab.**

2. **Click the Find icon in the Editing group.**

   The Navigation Pane appears in the left side of the screen.

   If you click the downward-pointing arrow to the right of the Find icon, a menu appears that lets you choose the Find or Go To command.

3. **Click in the Navigation text box, type a word or phrase to find, and press Enter.**

   The Navigation Pane lists all matching text.

   As you type, Word displays all matching text. So if you start typing **he**, Word finds all text that matches "he," such as "hello," "helicopter," or "help."

4. **Click any of the text displayed in the Navigation Pane.**

   Word highlights your chosen text in your document.

5. **Click the X icon that appears in the Navigation text box in the Navigation Pane.**

   Word clears the text you typed in Step 3.

Customizing text searching

If you just want to find a word or phrase, the ordinary Find command works, but if Word finds too much irrelevant text, you may want to take time to customize how Word searches for text. Follow these steps:

1. **Click the Home tab.**

2. **Click the Find icon in the Editing group.**

   The Navigation Pane appears in the left side of the screen.

3. **Click the Magnifying Glass icon in the Search Document text box in the Navigation Pane.**

   A pull-down menu appears.

4. **Click Options.**

   A Find Options dialog box appears, as shown in Figure 11-1.

Figure 11-1: The Find Options dialog box provides options for searching text.

5. **Select one or more options in the Find Options dialog box.**

   • *Match case:* Finds text that exactly matches the upper- and lowercase letters you type.

- *Find whole words only:* Finds text that is not part of another word. Searching for *on* will not find words like *onion*.

- *Use wildcards:* Lets you use the single character (?) or multiple character (*) wildcards, such as searching for *d?g*, which will find *dog* or *dig*; or *b*t*, which will find *but, butt,* or *boost*.

- *Sounds like:* Searches for words based on their phonetic pronunciation, such as finding *elephant* when searching for *elefant*.

- *Find all word forms:* Finds all variations of a word, such as finding *run, ran,* and *running*.

- *Match prefix:* Searches for the prefix of words, such as finding words like *interact* just by searching for *inter*.

- *Match suffix:* Searches for the suffix of words, such as finding words like *runner* or *keeper* just by searching for *er*.

- *Ignore punctuation characters:* Ignores punctuation characters in text, such as finding the phrase *Hello, there* when you searched for *Hello there* in the Navigation Pane.

- *Ignore white-space characters:* Ignores spaces when searching, such as finding the phrase *BotheCat* when you searched for *Bo the Cat* in the Navigation Pane.

6. **Click OK to make the Find Options dialog box**
   disappear.

The next time you search for text, Word uses the options you chose.

Searching by headings

Rather than search for a word or phrase, you may want to browse a long document by headings. After you find the heading you want, then you can edit or read the text underneath that heading.

To search by headings, follow these steps:

1. **Click the Home tab.**
2. **Click the Find icon in the Editing group.**

   The Navigation Pane appears in the left side of the screen.

3. **Click the Headings tab (underneath the Search Document text box) in the Navigation Pane.**

   A list of headings appears in the Navigation Pane

4. **Click a heading in the Navigation Pane.**

   Word displays the heading in your document.

Browsing through pages

In a long document, you often have to scroll or flip through multiple pages to find specific text. To simplify this task, Word can display all pages as thumbnail images. You can browse through these thumbnail images and click the page that you want to view in more detail.

To browse through multiple pages, follow these steps:

1. **Click the Home tab.**
2. **Click the Find icon in the Editing group.**

The Navigation Pane appears in the left side of the screen.

3. **Click the Pages tab (the middle tab) in the Navigation Pane.**

   Word displays thumbnail images of all your pages.

4. **Click the thumbnail image of the page that you want to view.**

   Word displays your chosen page.

Using the Find and Replace command

Rather than just find a word or phrase, you may want to find that text and replace it with something else. To use the Find and Replace command, follow these steps:

1. **Click the Home tab.**

2. **Click the Replace icon in the Editing group. (You can also press Ctrl+H.)**

   The Find and Replace dialog box appears, as shown in Figure 11-2.

Figure 11-2: The Find and Replace dialog box provides options for replacing text.

3. Click in the Find What text box and type a word or phrase to find.

4. Click in the Replace With text box and type a word or phrase to replace the text you typed in Step 3.

5. (Optional) Click the More button and choose any additional options.

   Refer to the "Customizing text searching" section for a list of the additional options.

6. Click one of the following buttons:

   • *Replace:* Replaces the currently highlighted text.

   • *Replace All:* Searches and replaces text throughout the entire document.

   • *Find Next:* Searches from the current cursor location to the end of the document.

7. Click Find Next to search for additional occurrences of the text you typed in Step 3.

8. Click Cancel to make the Find and Replace dialog box disappear.

Checking Your Spelling

As you type, Word tries to correct your spelling automatically. If you type something that Word doesn't recognize, it underlines it with a red squiggly line.

Just because Word underlines a word doesn't necessarily mean that the word is spelled incorrectly. It could be a proper name, a foreign word, or just a word that Word isn't smart enough to recognize.

To correct any words that Word underlines with a red squiggly line, follow these steps:

1. **Right-click any word underlined with a red squiggly line.**

   A pop-up menu appears.

2. **Choose one of the following:**

   - *The word you want:* Click the correct spelling of the word that appears in bold in the pop-up menu.

   - *Ignore All:* This tells Word to ignore this word throughout your document.

   - *Add to Dictionary:* This tells Word to remember this word and never flag it again as a misspelled word.

Viewing a Document

Word can display your document in one of five views, which can help you better understand the layout, margins, and page breaks in your document:

- ✔ **Read Mode:** Displays pages that require you to slide them horizontally to view adjacent pages.

- ✔ **Print Layout:** Displays page breaks as thick, dark horizontal bars so you can clearly see where a page ends and begins (this is the default view).

- ✔ **Web Layout:** Displays your document exactly as it would appear if you saved it as a web page.

- ✔ **Outline:** Displays your document as outline headings and subheadings.

✔ **Draft:** Displays the document without top or bottom page margins where page breaks appear as dotted lines.

Switching between views

Microsoft Word gives you two ways to switch between different document views:

✔ Click the view icons in the bottom-right corner of your document window.

   If you do so, you can only choose Read Mode, Print Layout, and Web Layout. (See Figure 11-3.)

✔ Click the View tab and then click the view you want to use, such as Print Layout or Draft view.

Print Layout view can help you edit and create the design of your pages. If you just want to focus on writing and not see your page margins or headers and footers, you may be happier switching to Draft view instead. The two most unusual views are Read Mode and Outline views.

Using Read Mode view

Read Mode can be handy for making text easier to read just the way you'd see it a book, as shown in Figure 11-3. To "turn the pages" of a document displayed in Read Mode view, click the Previous Screen or Next Screen button on the left and right edges of the screen.

To exit Full Screen Reading view, either press Esc or click the Print Layout or Web Layout buttons

Read Mode | Web Layout

Print Layout

Figure 11-3: Read Mode view lets you read a document in the form of an open book.

Using Outline view

Outline view divides a document into sections defined by headings and text. A *heading* represents a main idea. Text contains one or more paragraphs that are "attached" to a particular heading. A *subheading* lets you divide a main idea (heading) into multiple parts. See Figure 11-4.

Within Outline view you can

- ✔ **Collapse headings** to hide parts (subheadings and text) temporarily from view.

- ✔ **Rearrange headings** to move subheadings and text easily within a large document.

Figure 11-4: A typical outline consists of headings, subheadings, and text that you can expand or collapse to hide subheadings or text from view.

Moving a heading automatically moves all subheadings and text so you don't have to cut and paste multiple paragraphs.

To switch to Outline view, click the View tab and then click the Outline icon.

Defining a heading

Outline view considers each line as either a heading or text. To define a line as either a heading style (Level 1 to Level 9) or text, make sure you have switched to Outline view and then follow these steps:

1. **Move the cursor on the line that you want to define as a heading or text.**

2. **Click in the Outline Level list box and choose a heading level, such as Level 2.**

Word displays Level 1 headings in large type justified to the far-left margin. Level 2 headings appear in smaller type that's slightly indented to the right, Level 3 headings appear in even smaller type that's indented farther to the right, and so on.

To create a heading quickly, move the cursor to the end of an existing heading and press Enter to create an identical heading. For example, if you put the cursor at the end of a Level 3 heading and press Enter, Word creates a new blank Level 3 heading.

Promoting and demoting a heading

After you define a heading (such as a Level 1 or Level 3 heading), you can always change its level, such as changing a Level 1 heading to a Level 2 heading or vice versa:

- ✔ When you raise a heading from one level to another (such as from Level 3 to Level 2), that's *promoting.*

- ✔ When you lower a heading (such as from Level 4 to Level 5), that's *demoting.*

A Level 1 heading cannot be promoted because Level 1 is the highest heading. Likewise, a Level 9 heading cannot be demoted because Level 9 is the lowest heading.

To promote or demote a heading to a different level, follow these steps:

1. **Using either the mouse or the keyboard, move the cursor to the heading you want to promote or demote.**

2. **Choose one of the following methods:**

   - Click the Outline Level list box and click a level (such as Level 2).

- Press Tab (to promote) or Shift+Tab (to demote) the heading.

- Click the Promote or Demote arrow.

- Move the mouse pointer over the circle that appears to the left of the heading, hold down the left mouse button, drag the mouse right or left, and then release the left mouse button.

Promoting or demoting a heading automatically promotes or demotes any subheadings or text attached to the promoted or demoted heading. That way the subheadings or text maintain the same relationship to the heading.

Moving headings up and down

You can move headings up or down within a document.

To move a heading, follow these steps:

1. **Using either the mouse or the keyboard, move the cursor to the heading you want to promote or demote.**

2. **Choose one of the following methods:**

   - Click the Move Up or Move Down arrow.

   - Press Alt+Shift+↑ or Alt+Shift+↓.

   - Move the mouse pointer over the circle that appears to the left of the heading, hold down the left mouse button, drag the mouse up or down, and then release the left mouse button.

If you collapse a heading before moving it, you can move any subheadings or text underneath that heading.

Creating text

Text can consist of a single sentence, multiple sentences, or several paragraphs. Text always appears indented underneath a heading (or subheading). To create text, follow these steps:

1. **Move the cursor to the end of a heading or subheading.**

   This is the heading (or subheading) that your text will be attached to if you move the heading (or subheading).

2. **Press Enter.**

   Word creates a blank heading.

3. **Click the Demote to Body Text button (or click in the Outline Level list box and choose Body Text).**

   Word displays a bullet point, indented underneath the heading you chose in Step 1.

4. **Type your text.**

Collapsing and expanding headings and subheadings

If a heading or subheading contains any subheadings or text underneath, you can collapse that heading. *Collapsing* a heading simply hides any indented subheadings or text from view temporarily. *Expanding* a heading displays any previously hidden subheadings or text.

To collapse a heading along with all subheadings or body text underneath it, double-click the plus (+) icon that appears to the left of the heading.

If you just want to collapse the subheading or body text immediately underneath a heading, choose one of the following:

✔ Move the cursor anywhere in the heading that you want to collapse, and then click the Collapse button.

✔ Press Alt+Shift++ (plus-sign key).

To expand a collapsed heading to reveal all subheadings and body text, double-click the plus icon that appears to the left of the heading.

If you just want to expand the subheading or body text immediately underneath a collapsed heading, choose one of the following:

✔ Move the cursor anywhere in the heading that you want to expand, and then click the Expand button.

✔ Press Alt+Shift+– (minus-sign key).

Changing the Font

The most common way to format text is to change the font. The font defines the uniform style and appearance of letters; examples include Baskerville, Courier, 𝕷𝖎𝖓𝖔𝖙𝖊𝖝𝖙, and **STENCIL**.

To change the font, follow these steps:

1. **Click the Home tab.**

2. **Select the text you want to change.**

3. **Click the Font list box.**

   A list of the fonts available on your computer appears, as shown in Figure 11-5.

4. **Move the mouse pointer over each font.**

Word temporarily changes your selected text (from Step 2) so you can see how the currently highlighted font will look.

5. Click the font you want to use.

Word changes your text to appear in your chosen font.

Figure 11-5: The Font list box displays the appearance of each font.

As a general rule, try not to use more than three fonts in a document. If you use too many fonts, the overall appearance can be ANNOYING and distracting.

Not all computers have the same lists of fonts, so if you plan on sharing documents with others, stick with common fonts that everybody's computers can display.

Changing the Font Size

The *font* changes the appearance of text, but the *font size* defines how big (or small) the text may look.

To change the font size, follow these steps:

1. Click the Home tab.

2. Select the text you want to change.

3. Choose one of the following:

- Click the Font Size list box and then click a number, such as 12 or 24.

- Click the Grow Font or Shrink Font icon.

Changing the Text Style

The text style defines the appearance of text in one or more of the following ways:

- **Bold:** Press Ctrl+B.

- *Italic:* Press Ctrl+I.

- <u>Underline</u>: Press Ctrl+U.

- ~~Strikethrough~~: This formatting draws a line through text.

- Subscript: Use this to create text that falls below the text line, as in the 2 in H_2O.

- Superscript: Use this to create text that sits higher than the top of the text line, as in the 2 in $E = mc^2$.

To change the style of text, follow these steps:

1. Click the Home tab.

2. Select the text you want to change.

3. Click a Style icon, such as Bold or Underline.

4. **Repeat Step 3 for each additional style you want to apply to your text (such as *italic* and <u>underlining</u>).**

If you select any style change without selecting any text, Word applies your style changes to any new text you type from the cursor's current position.

Changing Colors

Color can emphasize text. There are two ways to use color:

✔ Change the color of the text (Font color).

✔ Highlight the text with a different color (Text Highlight color).

Changing the color of text

When you change the color of text, you're physically displaying a different color for each letter. Normally Word displays text in black, but you can change the color to anything you want, such as bright red or dark green.

If you choose a light color for your text, it may be hard to read against a white background.

To change the color of text, follow these steps:

1. **Click the Home tab.**

2. **Select the text you want to color.**

3. **Click the downward-pointing arrow to the right of the Font Color icon.**

   A color palette appears, as shown in Figure 11-6.

4. Click a color.

Word displays your selected text (from Step 2) in your chosen color.

Color palette

Figure 11-6: Use the color palette to make your text stand out.

After you choose a color, that color appears directly on the Font Color icon. Now you can select text and click directly on the Font Color icon (not the downward-pointing arrow) to color your text.

Highlighting text with color

Highlighting text mimics coloring chunks of text with a highlighting marker that students often use to emphasize passages in a book. To highlight text, follow these steps:

1. Click the Home tab.

2. Select the text you want to highlight.

3. Click the downward-pointing arrow to the right of the Text Highlight Color icon.

A color palette appears.

4. Click a color.

Word highlights your selected text (from Step 2) in your chosen color.

5. **Press Esc (or click the Text Highlight Color icon again) to turn off the Text Highlight Color command.**

To remove a highlight, select the text and choose the same color again or choose No Color.

Using Text Effects

If you want a fast way to format text to make it appear colorful like a neon sign, then you can use Text Effects by following these steps:

1. **Click the Home tab.**

2. **Select the text you want to modify.**

3. **Click the Text Effects icon.**

   A menu of different effects appears.

4. **Click an effect.**

   Word changes your selected text (from Step 2) in your chosen visual effect.

Using Styles

As an alternative to choosing fonts, font sizes, and text styles (such as bold) individually, Word offers several predefined formatting styles. To apply a style to your text, follow these steps:

1. **Click the Home tab.**

2. **Select the text that you want to format.**

3. **Click the up/down arrows of the Styles scroll bar to scroll through the different styles available. Or click the More button to display a pull-down menu of all the Quick Formatting styles.**

4. **Move the mouse pointer over a style.**

   Word displays what your text will look like if you choose this style.

5. **Click the style you want to use, such as Heading 1, Title, or Quote.**

   Word formats your text.

Using Templates

In case you need to format an entire document a certain way, you may want to use templates instead. *Templates* act like preformatted documents. Word comes with several templates, but Microsoft offers several through its website as well.

To create a new document from a template, follow these steps:

1. **Click the File tab and then choose New.**

   All available templates appear, as shown in Figure 11-7.

2. **Double-click a template.**

   Word creates a blank document with "dummy" text to show you how the formatting looks.

Figure 11-7: Templates let you create a new document based on the formatting of an existing file.

3. Type new text into your newly created document.

You may need to be connected to the Internet to download some of the available templates.

Removing Formatting from Text

After you format text, you can always remove that formatting. The simplest way to do this is to apply the same formatting you want to remove. For example, you can remove underlining by highlighting all the underlined text and choosing the underline command.

If you want to remove multiple formatting from text, it's much easier to use the Clear Formatting command, which removes all formatting from text, no matter how much formatting there may be.

To use the Clear Formatting command, follow these steps:

1. **Click the Home tab.**
2. **Select the text that contains the formatting you want to remove.**
3. **Click the Clear Formatting icon.**

   Word removes all formatting from your selected text.

   The Clear Formatting command does not remove any highlighting you may have applied over your text.

Inserting New Pages

Word automatically adds new pages to your document as you write. However, Word also gives you the option of adding a new page anywhere in your document, such as in the middle or the beginning.

To insert a new, blank page into your document, follow these steps:

1. **Click the Insert tab.**
2. **Move the cursor to where you want to insert the new page.**
3. **Click the Blank Page icon in the Pages group.**

   Word adds a blank page to your document where the cursor appears. So if you put the cursor between two sentences and insert a blank page, the first sentence appears on one page, a blank page appears next, and the second sentence appears after the blank page.

You don't need to add a page to the end of a document if you're still creating new text. Just move the cursor to the end of your document (Ctrl+End), start typing, and Word automatically adds new pages at the end of your document.

Inserting Page Breaks

Rather than insert a new page, you may want to break text on an existing page into two pages. To insert a page break into your document, follow these steps:

1. **Move the cursor where you want to break your document into two pages.**

2. **Click the Insert tab.**

3. **Click the Page Break icon in the Pages group.**

   Word breaks your document into two pages.

To delete a page break, move the cursor to the top of the page directly following the page break you want to delete. Then press Backspace until Word deletes the page break.

As an alternative to following Steps 2 and 3 in the preceding step list, you can just press Ctrl+Enter to create a page break at the cursor's current location.

Chapter 12

Playing the Numbers with Excel

. . . .

In This Chapter

▶ Typing and formatting data

▶ Moving around a spreadsheet

▶ Searching a spreadsheet

▶ Editing a spreadsheet

▶ Printing

▶ Creating formulas

▶ Using functions

▶ Understanding the parts of a chart

▶ Creating a chart

. . . .

*E*veryone needs to perform simple math. Businesses need to keep track of sales and profits, and individuals need to keep track of budgets. In the old days, people not only had to write down numbers on paper, but they also had to do all their calculations by hand (or with the aid of a calculator).

why people use Excel. By using Excel, you can
n typing in the correct numbers and let Excel
worry about calculating accurate results quickly with its
functions and formulas. Even better is that Excel has the
capability to help you visualize your data with a variety
of charts.

Besides calculating numbers, spreadsheets can also store
lists of data organized in rows and columns.

Understanding Spreadsheets

Excel organizes numbers in rows and columns. An entire
page of rows and columns is called a *spreadsheet* or a
worksheet. (A collection of one or more worksheets is
stored in a file called a *workbook.*) Each row is identified
by a number such as 1 or 249; and each column is identified by letters, such as A or BF. The intersection of each
row and column defines rectangular spaces called *cells,*
each of which contains one of three items:

- ✔ Numbers
- ✔ Text (labels)
- ✔ Formulas

Numbers provide the data, and *formulas* calculate that
data to produce a useful result, such as adding sales
results for the week. Labels identify what numbers represent. Figure 12-1 shows the parts of a typical spreadsheet.

Formulas usually appear as numbers, so at first glance,
it may be difficult to tell the difference between ordinary
numbers and numbers that represent a calculation by a
formula.

The strength of spreadsheets comes by playing "What-if?" games with your data, such as "What if I gave myself a $20-per-hour raise and cut everyone else's salary by 25%? How much money would that save the company every month?" Because spreadsheets can rapidly calculate new results, you can experiment with different numbers to see how they create different answers.

Labels

Numbers

Formula

Figure 12-1: The parts of a typical spreadsheet.

Storing Stuff in a Spreadsheet

Every cell can contain a number, a label, or a formula. To type anything into a spreadsheet, you must first select or click in the cell (or cells) and then type a number or text.

Typing data into a single cell

To type data in a single cell, follow these steps:

1. **Choose one of the following to select a single cell:**

   - Click a cell.

   - Press the up/down/right/left arrow keys to highlight a cell.

2. **Type a number (such as** 34.29 **or** 198**), a label (such as** Tax Returns**), or a formula.**

   You can find out how to create formulas later in this chapter in the "Creating a Formula" section.

Typing data in multiple cells

After you type data in a cell, you can press one of the following four keystrokes to select a different cell:

- ✔ **Enter:** Selects the cell below in the same column

- ✔ **Tab:** Selects the cell to the right in the same row

- ✔ **Shift+Enter:** Selects the cell above in the same column

- ✔ **Shift+Tab:** Selects the cell to the left in the same row

Excel lets you select a *range* of cells, which essentially tells Excel, "See all the cells I just highlighted? I only want to type data in those cells." After you select multiple cells, you can type data and press Enter. Excel selects the next cell down in that same column. When Excel reaches the last cell in the column, it selects the top cell of the column to the right.

To select multiple cells for typing data in, follow these steps:

1. **Highlight multiple cells using the mouse or keyboard.**

Excel selects the cell that appears in the upper-left corner of your selected cells.

2. **Type a number, label, or formula.**

3. **Press Enter.**

Excel selects the cell directly below the preceding cell. If the preceding cell appeared at the bottom of the selected column, Excel highlights the top cell in the column that appears to the right.

You can also move backward by pressing Shift+Enter instead.

4. **Repeat Steps 2 and 3 until you fill your selected cells with data.**

5. **Click outside the selected cells or press an arrow key to tell Excel not to select the cells anymore.**

Typing in sequences with AutoFill

If you need to type a sequence of things (such as months, days, or numbers), Excel offers a shortcut to save you from typing all the data yourself. With this shortcut, you just type one month or day (or the first few numbers in the sequence) and then drag the mouse to highlight all the adjacent cells. Then Excel enters the rest of the information in those cells.

To use this shortcut, follow these steps:

1. **Click a cell and type a month (such as** January **or just** Jan) **or a day (such as** Monday **or just** Mon).

The Fill Handle, a block box, appears in the bottom-right corner of the cell.

You can also type in a sequence of numbers in Step 1. So if you typed the numbers 2, 4, and 6 in adjacent cells, highlighted all these adjacent cells, and grabbed the Fill Handle, Excel is smart enough to detect the pattern and display the numbers 8, 10, and 12 in the next three adjacent cells.

2. **Move the mouse pointer over the Fill Handle until the mouse pointer turns into a black crosshair icon.**

3. **Hold down the left mouse button and drag (move) the mouse down a column or across the row.**

   Excel automatically fills in the rest of the sequence.

Formatting Numbers and Labels

When you first create a spreadsheet, numbers and labels appear as plain text. Plain labels may look boring, but plain numbers (such as 8495 or 0.39) can be difficult to read and understand if the numbers are supposed to represent currency amounts ($8,495) or percentages (39%).

To make labels visually interesting and numbers appear more descriptive of what they actually represent (such as currency or percentages), you need to format your data after you type it into a spreadsheet.

You can format a cell or range of cells after you've already typed in data or before you type in any data. If you format cells before typing any data, any data you type in that cell will appear in your chosen format.

Formatting numbers

To format the appearance of numbers, follow these steps:

1. **Select one or more cells by using the mouse or keyboard.**

   To select multiple cells, drag the mouse or hold the Shift key while pressing the arrow keys.

2. **Click the Home tab.**

3. **Click the Number Format list box in the Number group.**

   A pull-down menu appears so you can choose the format you want to use for the numbers.

   The Number group also displays three icons that let you format numbers as Currency, Percentage, or with Commas in one click. Click the downward-pointing arrow to the right of the Accounting Number Format icon to choose different currency symbols to use, such as $, £, or €.

4. **Click a number format style, such as Percentage or Scientific.**

   Excel displays your numbers in your chosen format.

Formatting decimal numbers

If you format cells to display numbers with decimal places, such as 23.09 or 23.09185, you can modify how many decimal places appear. To define the number of decimal places, follow these steps:

1. **Select the cell or cells that contain the numbers you want to format.**

2. **Click the Home tab.**

3. **Click in the Number Format list box and choose a format that displays decimal places, such as Number or Percentage.**

   Excel formats the numbers in your chosen cells.

You can click the Increase Decimal (increases the number of decimal places displayed) or Decrease Decimal icon (decreases the number of decimal places displayed) in the Number group on the Home tab.

Formatting cells

To make your data look prettier, Excel can format the appearance of cells to change the font, background color, text color, or font size used to display data in a cell. You can use Excel's built-in formatting styles, or you can apply different types of formatting individually.

Formatting cells with built-in styles

Excel provides a variety of predesigned formatting styles that you can apply to one or more cells. To format cells with a built-in style, follow these steps:

1. **Select the cell or cells that you want to format with a built-in style.**

2. **Click the Home tab.**

3. **Click the Cell Styles icon in the Styles group.**

   A pull-down menu appears listing all the different styles you can choose, as shown in Figure 12-2.

4. **Move the mouse pointer over a style.**

   Excel displays a Live Preview of how your selected cells will look with that particular style.

5. **Click the style you want.**

   Excel applies your chosen style to the selected cells.

Figure 12-2: The Cell Styles menu offers different ways to format your cells quickly.

Formatting fonts and text styles

Different fonts can emphasize parts of your spreadsheet, such as using one font to label columns and rows and another font or font size to display the actual data. Text styles (bold, underline, and italic) can also emphasize data that appears in the same font or font size.

To change the font, font size, and text style of one or more cells, follow these steps:

1. **Select the cell or cells that you want to change the font and font size.**

2. **Click the Home tab.**

3. **Click the Font list box.**

   A pull-down menu of different fonts appears.

4. **Click the font you want to use.**

5. **Choose one of the following methods to change the font size:**

   • Click the Font Size list box and then choose a font size, such as 12 or 16.

- Click the Font Size list box and type a value such as 7 or 15.

- Click the Increase Font Size or Decrease Font Size icon until your data appears in the size you want.

6. **Click one or more text style icons (Bold, Italic, Underline).**

Formatting with color

Each cell displays data in a Font color and a Fill color. The *Font color* defines the color of the numbers and letters that appear inside a cell. The *Fill color* defines the color that fills the background of the cell.

To change the Font and Fill colors of cells, follow these steps:

1. **Select the cell or cells that you want to color.**

2. **Click the Home tab.**

3. **Click the downward-pointing arrow that appears to the right of the Font Color icon.**

   A color palette appears.

4. **Click the color you want to use for your text.**

The color you select appears directly on the Font Color icon. The next time you want to apply this same color to a cell, you can click the Font Color icon directly instead of the downward-pointing arrow to the right of the Font Color icon.

5. **Click the downward-pointing arrow that appears to the right of the Fill Color icon.**

   A color palette appears.

6. **Click a color to use to fill the background of your cell.**

Adding borders

For another way to highlight one or more cells, you can add borders. Borders can surround the entire cell or just the top, bottom, left, or right side of a cell. To add borders to a cell, follow these steps:

1. **Select one or more cells.**

2. **Click the Home tab.**

3. **Click the downward-pointing arrow to the right of the Border icon.**

   A pull-down menu appears.

4. **Click a border style.**

   Excel displays your chosen borders around the cells you selected in Step 1.

Navigating a Spreadsheet

If you have a large spreadsheet, chances are good that some information may be hidden by the limitations of your computer screen. To help you view and select cells in different parts of your spreadsheet, Excel offers various ways to navigate a spreadsheet by using the mouse and keyboard.

Using the mouse to move around a spreadsheet

To navigate a spreadsheet with the mouse, you can click the onscreen scroll bars or use the scroll wheel on your mouse (if it has one). To use the scroll bars, you have three choices:

- ✔ **Click the up/down or right/left arrows on the horizontal or vertical scroll bars.**

  This moves the spreadsheet one row (up or down) or column (right or left) at a time.

- ✔ **Drag the scroll box of a scroll bar.**

- ✔ **Click the scroll area (any area to the left/right or above/below the scroll box on the scroll bar).**

  This moves the spreadsheet one screen left/right or up/down.

If your mouse has a scroll wheel, you can use this wheel to move through a spreadsheet by two methods:

- ✔ Roll the mouse's scroll wheel forward or back to scroll your spreadsheet up or down.

- ✔ Press the scroll wheel to display a four-way pointing arrow, and then move the mouse up, down, right, or left. (When you're done, click the scroll wheel again.)

Using the keyboard to move around a spreadsheet

Sometimes trying to line up the mouse just right can be frustrating. For that reason, you can also use the keyboard to move around a spreadsheet. For example, the arrow keys and Page Up/Page Down keys move you around as you'd expect. The following are some of the other ways to move around a spreadsheet:

✔ Ctrl+↑: Jumps to the top of a column that contains data

✔ Ctrl+↓: Jumps to the bottom of a column that contains data

✔ Ctrl+←: Jumps to the left of a row that contains data

✔ Ctrl+→: Jumps to the right of a row that contains data

✔ Ctrl+Page Up: Displays the previous worksheet

✔ Ctrl+Page Down: Displays the next worksheet

✔ Home: Moves to the A column of the current row

✔ Ctrl+Home: Moves to the A1 cell

✔ Ctrl+End: Moves to the bottom-right cell of your spreadsheet

If you know the specific cell you want to move to, you can jump to that cell by using the Go To command. To use the Go To command, follow these steps:

1. **Click the Home tab.**

2. **Click the Find & Select icon in the Editing group.**

   A pull-down menu appears.

3. **Click Go To.**

   The Go To dialog box appears.

   You can also choose the Go To command by pressing Ctrl+G.

4. **Click in the Reference text box and type the cell you want to move to, such as C13 or F4.**

   If you've used the Go To command before, Excel lists the last cell references you typed. Now you can just click one of those cell references to jump to that cell.

5. Click OK.

Excel highlights the cell you typed in Step 4.

Naming cells

One problem with the Go To command is that most people won't know which cell contains the data they want to find. For example, if you want to view the cell that contains the total amount of money you owe for your income taxes, you probably don't want to memorize that this cell is G68 or P92.

To help you identify certain cells, Excel lets you give them descriptive names. To name a cell or range of cells, follow these steps:

1. **Select the cell or cells that you want to name.**

2. **Click in the Name box, which appears directly above the A column heading.**

3. **Type a descriptive name without any spaces and then press Enter.**

After you name a cell, you can jump to it quickly by following these steps:

1. **Click the downward-pointing arrow to the right of the Name box.**

   A list of named cells appears.

2. **Click the named cell you want to view.**

   Excel displays your chosen cell.

Eventually, you may want to edit or delete a name for your cells. To delete or edit a name, follow these steps:

1. **Click the Formulas tab.**

2. **Click the Name Manager icon.**

   The Name Manager dialog box appears.

3. **Edit or delete the named cell as follows:**

   • To edit the name, click the cell name you want
     to edit and then click the Edit button. An Edit
     Name dialog box appears, where you can
     change the name or the cell reference.

   • To delete the name, click the cell name you
     want to delete and then click the Delete
     button.

4. **Click Close.**

Searching a Spreadsheet

Rather than search for a specific cell, you may want to
search for a particular label or number in a spreadsheet.

Searching for text

You can search for a specific label or number anywhere
in your spreadsheet. To search for text or numbers,
follow these steps:

1. **Click the Home tab.**

2. **Click the Find & Select icon in the Editing group.**

   A pull-down menu appears.

3. **Click Find.**

   The Find and Replace dialog box appears.

If you click the Replace tab, you can define the text or number to find and new text or numbers to replace it.

4. Click in the Find What text box and type the text or number you want to find.

If you click the Options button, the Find and Replace dialog box expands to provide additional options for searching, such as searching in the displayed sheet or the entire workbook.

5. Click one of the following:

- *Find Next:* Finds and selects the first cell, starting from the currently selected cell that contains the text you typed in Step 4.

- *Find All:* Finds and lists all cells that contain the text you typed in Step 4.

6. Click Close to make the Find and Replace dialog box go away.

Searching for formulas

Formulas appear just like numbers; to help you find which cells contain formulas, Excel gives you two choices:

- Display formulas in your cells (instead of numbers)
- Highlight the cells that contain formulas

To display formulas in a spreadsheet, press Ctrl+` (the accent character that's on the same key as the ~ sign). Figure 12-3 shows what a spreadsheet looks like when formulas appear inside of cells.

Formula

Figure 12-3: By displaying formulas in cells, you can identify which cells display calculations.

To highlight all cells that contain formulas, follow these steps:

1. **Click the Home tab.**

2. **Click the Find & Select icon in the Editing group.**

   A pull-down menu appears.

3. **Click Formulas.**

   Excel highlights all the cells that contain formulas.

Editing a Spreadsheet

The two ways to edit a spreadsheet are

- ✔ Edit the data itself, such as the labels, numbers, and formulas that make up a spreadsheet.

- ✔ Edit the physical layout of the spreadsheet, such as adding or deleting rows and columns, or widening or shrinking the width or height of rows and columns.

Editing data in a cell

To edit data in a single cell, follow these steps:

1. **Double-click the cell that contains the data you want to edit.**

   Excel displays a cursor in your selected cell.

2. **Edit your data by using the Backspace or Delete key, or by typing new data.**

If you click a cell, Excel displays the contents of that cell in the Formula bar. You can click and edit data directly in the Formula bar, which can be more convenient for editing large amounts of data such as a formula.

Changing the size of rows and columns

Using the mouse can be a quick way to modify the sizes of rows and columns. To change the height of a row or the width of a column, follow these steps:

1. **Move the mouse pointer over the bottom line of a row heading, such as the 2 or 18 heading. (Or move the mouse pointer over the right line of the column heading, as for column A or D.)**

   The mouse pointer turns into a two-way pointing arrow.

2. **Hold down the left mouse button and drag (move) the mouse.**

   Excel resizes your row or column.

3. **Release the left mouse button when you're happy with the size of your row or column.**

If you need to resize a row or column to a precise value, it's easier to type a specific value into the Row Height or Column Width dialog box instead. To type a value into a Row Height or Column Width dialog box, follow these steps:

1. **Click the Home tab.**

2. **Click the row or column heading that you want to resize.**

   Excel highlights your entire row or column.

3. **Click the Format icon that appears in the Cells group.**

   A pull-down menu appears.

4. **Click Row Height (if you selected a row) or Column Width (if you selected a column).**

   The Row Height or Column Width dialog box appears.

5. **Type a value and then click OK.**

   Excel resizes your row or column.

Adding and deleting rows and columns

After you type in labels, numbers, and formulas, you may realize that you need to add or delete extra rows or columns. To add a row or column, follow these steps:

1. **Click the Home tab.**

2. **Click the row or column heading where you want to add another row or column.**

   Excel highlights the entire row or column.

3. **Click the bottom half of the Insert icon in the Cells group.**

   A menu appears.

4. **Choose Insert Sheet Rows or Insert Sheet Columns.**

   Excel inserts a new row above the selected row or inserts a column to the left of the selected column.

To delete a row or column, follow these steps:

1. **Click the Home tab.**

2. **Click the row or column heading that you want to delete.**

3. **Click the bottom half of the Delete icon in the Cells group.**

   A menu appears.

4. **Choose Delete Sheet Rows or Delete Sheet Columns.**

Deleting a row or column deletes any data stored in that row or column.

Adding sheets

When you load Excel, it automatically provides you with a sheet, but you can add more sheets to your workbook if you need them.

To add a new sheet, choose one of the following:

  ✔ **Click the New sheet icon (it looks like a plus sign inside a circle) that appears to the right of your existing tabs (or press Shift+F11).**

> ✔ **Click the Home tab, click the bottom half of the
> Insert icon in the Cells group, and when a menu
> appears, choose Insert Sheet.**

Renaming sheets

By default, Excel gives each sheet a generic name such
as Sheet1. To give your sheets a more descriptive name,
follow these steps:

1. Choose one of the following:

   • *Double-click the sheet tab that you want to
     rename.*

     Excel highlights the entire sheet name.

   • *Click the sheet tab you want to rename, click
     the Home tab, click the Format icon in the Cells
     group, and choose Rename Sheet.*

   • *Right-click the sheet tab you want to rename;
     when a pop-up menu appears, choose Rename
     Sheet.*

**2. Type a new name for your sheet and press Enter
when you're done.**

   Your new name appears on the sheet tab.

Rearranging sheets

You can rearrange the order that your sheets appear in
your workbook. To rearrange a sheet, follow these steps:

**1. Move the mouse pointer over the sheet tab that
you want to move.**

2. **Hold down the left mouse button and drag the mouse.**

   The downward-pointing black arrow points where Excel will place your sheet.

3. **Release the left mouse button to place your sheet in a new order.**

Deleting a sheet

Using multiple sheets may be handy, but you may want to delete a sheet if you don't need it.

If you delete a sheet, you also delete all the data stored on that sheet.

To delete a sheet, follow these steps:

1. **Click on the sheet that you want to delete.**

2. **Choose one of the following:**

   - *Right-click the tab of the sheet you want to delete. When a pop-up menu appears, click Delete.*

   - *Click the Home tab, click the bottom of the Delete icon in the Cells group; when a menu appears, choose Delete Sheet.*

   If your sheet is empty, Excel deletes the sheet right away. If your sheet contains data, a dialog box appears to warn you that you'll lose any data stored on that sheet.

3. **Click Delete.**

   Excel deletes your sheet along with any data on it.

Printing Workbooks

After you create a spreadsheet, you can print it. When printing spreadsheets, you need to take special care how your spreadsheet appears on a page because a large spreadsheet will likely get printed on two or more sheets of paper; take time to align your data so that it prints correctly on every page.

Using Page Layout view

Excel can display your spreadsheets in two ways: Normal view and Page Layout view. Normal view is the default appearance, which simply fills your screen with rows and columns so you can see as much of your spreadsheet as possible.

Page Layout view displays your spreadsheet exactly as it will appear if you print it. Not only can you see where your page breaks occur, but you can also add any headers to the top of your spreadsheet.

To switch back and forth from Normal view to Page Layout view, follow these steps:

1. **Click the View tab.**

2. **Click the Normal or Page Layout View icon in the Workbook Views group, as shown in Figure 12-4.**

You can also click the Normal or Page Layout View icons in the bottom-right corner of the Excel window.

Figure 12-4: The Page Layout view clearly shows where page breaks occur at the bottom and sides of your spreadsheet.

Adding a header (or footer)

Headers and footers are useful when printing out your spreadsheet. A header may explain the information in the spreadsheet and a footer may display page numbers. To create a header or footer, follow these steps:

1. **Click the Insert tab.**

2. **Click the Header & Footer icon in the Text group.**

   Excel displays the Design tab and creates a text box for your header and footer.

3. **Type your header text in the header text box.**

4. **Click the Go To Footer icon in the Navigation group.**

   Excel displays your footer text box.

5. **Type your footer text in the footer text box.**

If you switch to Page Layout view, you can click directly in the header or footer box at the top or bottom of the page.

Printing gridlines

Gridlines appear on the screen to help you align data in rows and columns. However, when you print your worksheet, you can choose to omit gridlines or print them to make your data easier to understand.

To print gridlines and/or row and column headings, follow these steps:

1. **Click the Page Layout tab.**

2. **(Optional) Select the Print check box under the Gridlines category.**

3. **(Optional) Select the Print check box under the Heading category.**

Defining a print area

Sometimes you may not want to print your entire spreadsheet but just a certain part of it, called the *print area.* To define the print area, follow these steps:

1. **Select the cells that you want to print.**

2. **Click the Page Layout tab.**

3. **Click the Print Area icon in the Page Setup group.**

    A pull-down menu appears.

4. **Choose Set Print Area.**

    Excel displays a line around your print area.

5. Click the File tab and then click Print.

A print preview image of your chosen print area appears.

6. Click Print.

After you define a print area, you can see which cells are part of your print area by clicking the downward-pointing arrow of the Name box and choosing Print_Area.

After you define a print area, you can always add to it by following these steps:

1. Select the cells adjacent to the print area.

2. Click the Page Layout tab.

3. Click the Print Area icon in the Page Setup group.

A pull-down menu appears.

4. Choose Add to Print Area.

Excel displays a line around your newly defined print area.

After you define the print area, you can always remove it by following these steps:

1. Click the Page Layout tab.

2. Click Print Area.

A pull-down menu appears.

3. Choose Clear Print Area.

Inserting (and removing) page breaks

One problem with large spreadsheets is that when you print them, parts may get cut off when printed on separate pages. To correct this problem, you can tell Excel exactly where page breaks should occur.

To insert page breaks, follow these steps:

1. **Move the cursor in the cell to define where the vertical and horizontal page breaks will appear.**

2. **Click the Page Layout tab.**

3. **Click the Breaks icon in the Page Setup group.**

   A pull-down menu appears.

4. **Choose Insert Page Break.**

   Excel inserts a horizontal page directly above the cell you selected in Step 1, as well as a vertical page break to the left of that cell.

To remove a page break, follow these steps:

1. **Choose one of the following:**

   • *To remove a horizontal page break:* Click in any cell that appears directly below that horizontal page break.

   • *To remove a vertical page break:* Click in any cell that appears directly to the right of that horizontal page break.

- *To remove both a vertical and horizontal page
break:* Click in the cell that appears to the
right of the vertical page break and directly
underneath the horizontal page break.

2. **Click the Page Layout tab.**

3. **Click the Breaks icon in the Page Setup group.**

   A pull-down menu appears.

4. **Choose Remove Page Break.**

   Excel removes your chosen page break.

Printing row and column headings

If you have a large spreadsheet that fills two or more
pages, Excel may print your spreadsheet data on separate
pages. Although the first page may print your labels to
identify what each row and column may represent, any
additional pages that Excel prints won't bear those same
identifying labels. As a result, you may wind up printing
rows and columns of numbers without any labels that
identify what those numbers mean.

To fix this problem, you can define labels to print on
every page by following these steps:

1. **Click the Page Layout tab.**

2. **Click the Print Titles icon in the Page Setup group.**

   The Page Setup dialog box appears.

3. **Click the Collapse/Expand button that appears to
   the far right of the Rows to Repeat at Top text box.**

   The Page Setup dialog box shrinks.

4. **Click in the row that contains the labels you want to print at the top of every page.**

5. **Click the Collapse/Expand button again.**

   The Page Setup dialog box reappears.

6. **Click the Collapse/Expand button that appears to the far right of the Columns to Repeat at Left text box.**

   The Page Setup dialog box shrinks.

7. **Click in the column that contains the labels you want to print on the left of every page.**

8. **Click the Collapse/Expand button again.**

   The Page Setup dialog box reappears.

9. **Click OK.**

Defining printing margins

To help you squeeze or expand your spreadsheet to fill a printed page, you can define different margins for each printed page. To define margins, follow these steps:

1. **Click the Page Layout tab.**

2. **Click the Margins icon in the Page Setup group.**

   A pull-down menu appears.

3. **Choose a page margin style you want to use.**

If you choose Custom Margins in Step 3, you can define your own margins for a printed page.

Defining paper orientation and size

Paper *orientation* can be either *landscape* (the paper width is greater than its height) or *portrait* mode (the paper width is less than its height). Paper *size* defines the physical dimensions of the page.

To change the paper orientation and size, follow these steps:

1. **Click the Page Layout tab.**

2. **Click the Orientation icon in the Page Setup group.**

   A pull-down menu appears.

3. **Choose Portrait or Landscape.**

4. **Click the Size icon in the Page Setup group.**

   A pull-down menu appears

5. **Click a paper size.**

Printing in Excel

When you finish defining how to print your spreadsheet, you'll probably want to print it. To print a worksheet, follow these steps:

1. **Click the File tab.**

   The Backstage View appears.

2. **Click Print.**

   The Print Preview appears in the right pane.

3. **Click the Print icon near the top of the middle pane.**

Creating a Formula

Formulas consist of three crucial bits of information:

- ✔ An equal sign (=)
- ✔ One or more cell references
- ✔ The type of calculation to do on the data (addition, subtraction, and so on)

The equal sign (=) simply tells Excel not to treat the formula as text but as instructions for calculating something.

A *cell reference* is simply the unique row and column heading that identifies a single cell, such as A4 or D9.

The four common calculations that a formula can use are addition (+), subtraction (–), multiplication (*), and division (/). Table 12-1 lists other mathematical operators you can use in a formula.

Table 12-1   Common Mathematical Operators

Operator	What It Does
+	Addition
–	Subtraction
*	Multiplication
/	Division
%	Percentage
^	Exponentiation

(continued)

Table 12-1 *(continued)*

Operator	*What It Does*
=	Equal
>	Greater than
<	Less than
>=	Greater than or equal to
<=	Less than or equal to
<>	Not equal to
&	Text concatenation

A simple formula uses a single mathematical operator and two cell references such as:

=A4+C7

To type a formula in a cell, follow these steps:

1. **Click in the cell where you want to store the formula.**

   Excel highlights your selected cell.

2. **Type the equal sign (=).**

   This tells Excel that you are creating a formula.

3. **Type your formula that includes cell references that identify cells that contain data.**

   For example, if you want to add the numbers stored in cells A4 and E8, you would type =**A4+E8**.

4. **Press Enter.**

As a faster alternative to typing cell references, you can use the mouse to click any cell that contains data; Excel enters that cell reference into your formula.

To use the mouse to click cell references when creating a formula, follow these steps:

1. **Click in the cell where you want to store the formula. (You can also select the cell by pressing the arrow keys.)**

   Excel highlights your selected cell.

2. **Type the equal sign (=).**

   This tells Excel that anything you type after the equal sign is part of your formula.

3. **Type any mathematical operators and click any cells that contain data, such as A4 or E8.**

   If you want to create the formula =A4+E8, you would do the following:

   a. Type =.

      This tells Excel that you're creating a formula.

   b. Click cell A4.

      Excel types the A4 cell reference in your formula automatically.

   c. Type +.

   d. Click cell E8.

      Excel types in the E8 cell reference in your formula automatically.

4. **Press Enter.**

After you finish creating a formula, you can type data into the cell references used in your formula to calculate a new result.

Organizing formulas with parentheses

Formulas can be as simple as a single mathematical operator such as =D3*E4. However, you can also use multiple mathematical operators, such as

=A3+A4*B4+B5

There are two problems with using multiple mathematical operators. First, they make a formula harder to read and understand. Second, Excel calculates mathematical operators from left to right, based on precedence, which means a formula may calculate results differently from what you intended. For example, in the example formula, Excel first multiplies A$*B4 and then adds the result to A3 and B5.

Precedence tells Excel which mathematical operators to calculate first, as listed in Table 12-2.

Table 12-2	Operator Precedence in Excel
Mathematical Operator	*Description*
: (colon) (single space) , (comma)	Reference operators
−	Negation
%	Percent

Mathematical Operator	Description
^	Exponentiation
* /	Multiplication and division
+ −	Addition and subtraction
&	Text concatenation
= < > <= >= <>	Comparison

Typing parentheses around cell references and mathematical operators not only organizes your formulas, but also tells Excel specifically how you want to calculate a formula. In the example =A3+A4*B4+B5, if you want Excel to first add A3 and A4, then add B4 and B5, and finally multiply the two results together, you have to use parentheses, like this:

=(A3+A4)*(B4+B5)

Copying formulas

In many spreadsheets, you may need to create similar formulas that use different data. You can type nearly identical formulas in multiple cells, but that's tedious and error-prone. When you copy a formula and paste it in another cell, Excel automatically changes the cell references.

To copy and paste a formula so that each formula changes cell references automatically, follow these steps:

1. Select the cell that contains the formula you want to copy.

2. **Press Ctrl+C (or click the Copy icon under the Home tab).**

   Excel displays a dotted line around your selected cell.

3. **Select the cell (or cells) where you want to paste your formula.**

   If you select multiple cells, Excel pastes a copy of your formula in each of those cells.

4. **Press Ctrl+V (or click the Paste icon under the Home tab).**

   Excel pastes your formula and automatically changes the cell references.

5. **Press Esc or double-click away from the cell with the dotted line to make the dotted line go away.**

Using Functions

Creating simple formulas is easy, but creating complex formulas is hard. To make complex formulas easier to create, Excel comes with prebuilt formulas called *functions*. Table 12-3 lists some of the many functions available.

Table 12-3	Common Excel Functions
Function Name	*What It Does*
AVERAGE	Calculates the average value of numbers stored in two or more cells
COUNT	Counts how many cells contain a number instead of a label (text)

Function Name	What It Does
MAX	Finds the largest number stored in two or more cells
MIN	Finds the smallest number stored in two or more cells
ROUND	Rounds a decimal number to a specific number of digits
SQRT	Calculates the square root of a number
SUM	Adds the values stored in two or more cells

Excel provides hundreds of functions that you can use by themselves or as part of your own formulas. A *function* typically uses one or more cell references:

✔ **Single cell references** such as =ROUND(C4,2), which rounds the number found in cell C4 to two decimal places.

✔ *Contiguous* (adjacent) **cell ranges** such as =SUM(A4:A9), which adds all the numbers found in cells A4, A5, A6, A7, A8, and A9.

✔ **Noncontiguous cell ranges** such as =SUM(A4,B7,C11), which adds all the numbers found in cells A4, B7, and C11.

To use a function, follow these steps:

1. **Click in the cell where you want to create a formula using a function.**

2. **Click the Formulas tab.**

3. **Click one of the following function icons in the Function Library group:**

- *Financial:* Calculates business-related equations, such as the amount of interest earned over a specified time period.

- *Logical:* Provides logical operators to manipulate True and False (also known as *Boolean)* values.

- *Text:* Searches and manipulates text.

- *Date & Time:* Provides date and time information.

- *Lookup & Reference:* Provides information about cells, such as their row headings.

- *Math & Trig:* Offers mathematical equations.

- *More Functions:* Provides access to statistical and engineering functions.

4. **Click a function category, such as Financial or Math & Trig.**

A pull-down menu appears.

5. **Click a function.**

The Function Arguments dialog box appears, as shown in Figure 12-5.

Figure 12-5: Specify which cell references contain the data your function needs to calculate a result.

6. **Click the cell references you want to use.**

7. **Repeat Step 6 as many times as necessary.**

8. **Click OK.**

   Excel displays the calculation of your function in the cell you selected in Step 1.

Using the AutoSum command

One of the most useful and commonly used commands is the AutoSum command. The *AutoSum command* uses the SUM function to add two or more cell references without making you type those cell references yourself. The most common use for the AutoSum function is to add a column or row of numbers.

To add a column or row of numbers with the AutoSum function, follow these steps:

1. **Create a column or row of numbers that you want to add.**

2. **Click at the bottom of the column or the right of the row.**

3. **Click the Formulas tab.**

4. **Click the AutoSum icon in the Function Library group.**

   Excel automatically creates a SUM function in the cell you chose in Step 2 and highlights all the cells where it will retrieve data to add, as shown in Figure 12-6. (If you accidentally click the downward-pointing arrow under the AutoSum icon, a pull-down menu appears. Just choose Sum.)

Figure 12-6: The AutoSum command automatically creates cell references.

5. Press Enter.

Excel automatically sums all the cell references.

The AutoSum icon also appears on the Home tab in the Editing group.

Using recently used functions

Excel tries to simplify your life by creating a special Recently Used list that contains a list of the functions you've used most often. To use the list of recently used functions, follow these steps:

1. Click the cell where you want to store a function.

2. Click the Formulas tab.

3. Click the Recently Used icon in the Function Library group.

A pull-down menu appears.

4. Choose a function.

Understanding the Parts of a Chart

To create charts that clarify your data (rather than confuse you even more), you need to understand the parts of a chart and their purposes, as shown in Figure 12-7:

- ✔ **Data Series:** The numeric data that Excel uses to create the chart

- ✔ **X-axis:** Defines the width of a chart

- ✔ **Y-axis:** Defines the height of a chart

- ✔ **Legend:** Provides text to explain what each visual part of a chart means

- ✔ **Chart Title:** Explains the purpose of the entire chart

Data series   Y-axis   X-axis

Figure 12-7: Each part of a typical Excel chart displays information about your data.

Charts typically use two data series to create a chart. For example, one data series (on the Y-axis) may be sales made that month, while a second data series (on the X-axis) may be the products actually sold.

The chart itself could display different colors that represent products sold in different months, and the legend would explain what each color represents.

By glancing at the column chart in Figure 12-7, you can quickly identify which products sell best, how each product sells in each month, and whether sales of a particular product are improving.

Although Figure 12-7 shows a column chart, Excel can create a variety of other types of charts so you can look at your data in different ways, as shown in Figure 12-8. Some other types of charts Excel can create include

- **Column chart:** Displays quantities as vertical columns that "grow" upward. Useful for creating charts that compare two items, such as sales per month or sales per salesperson.

- **Line chart:** Displays quantities as lines. Essentially shows the tops of a column chart.

- **Area chart:** Identical to a line chart except that it shades the area underneath each line.

- **Bar chart:** Essentially a column chart turned on its side where bars "grow" from left to right.

- **Pie chart:** Compares multiple items in relation to a whole, such as which product sales make up a percentage of a company's overall profits.

Figure 12-8: Common types of charts that Excel can create to help you visualize your data in different ways.

Excel can create both two- and three-dimensional charts. A 3-D chart can look neat, but sometimes the 3-D visual can obscure the true purpose of the chart, which is to simplify data and make it easy for you to understand in the first place.

Creating a Chart

Before you create a chart, you need to type in some numbers and identifying labels because Excel uses those labels to identify the parts of your chart.

To create a chart, follow these steps:

1. **Select the numbers and labels that you want to use to create a chart.**

2. **Click the Insert tab.**

   A list of chart type icons appears in the Charts group.

3. **Click a Chart icon, such as the Pie or Line icon.**

   A menu appears, displaying the different types of charts you can choose as shown in Figure 12-9.

Figure 12-9: Clicking a chart icon displays different chart options.

4. Click a chart type.

Excel creates your chart and displays a Chart Tools Design/Format tab, as shown in Figure 12-10.

Figure 12-10: The Chart Tools Design/Format tab appears so you can modify a chart after you create it.

In case you aren't sure what type of chart would best display your data, click the Recommended Charts icon on the Insert tab. This displays an Insert Chart dialog box that lists the recommended chart types as shown in Figure 12-11.

Figure 12-11: The Insert Chart dialog box displays a list of recommended charts for your data.

Chapter 13

Making Presentations with PowerPoint

. . . .

In This Chapter

▶ Creating a PowerPoint presentation

▶ Adding text

▶ Using themes

▶ Adding graphics

▶ Showing movies on a slide

▶ Adding sound to a presentation

▶ Organizing slides

▶ Adding visual transitions

▶ Viewing presentations

. . . .

*P*owerPoint works as a visual aid for giving presentations. (If you never give presentations, you probably don't need PowerPoint.) Instead of fumbling around creating, organizing, and displaying transparencies with an overhead projector, you can use PowerPoint on your computer to create, organize, and display slides that present information as text and graphics.

1ake your presentations look more visually appealing
:ngaging to your audience, PowerPoint enables you
d color, graphics, video, and audio to your slides.
The bells and whistles can't turn a worthless presentation
into an informative one, but they can enhance an
informative presentation and make it easier for people to
watch.

Creating a PowerPoint Presentation

A PowerPoint *presentation* consists of one or more slides
where each slide can display text and graphics. Creating
a presentation means adding slides and typing text or
pasting graphics on each slide.

If you've been working on another presentation in
PowerPoint and you need to start a new, blank
presentation from scratch, follow these steps:

1. **Click the File tab.**

2. **Click New.**

   PowerPoint displays different templates you can
   choose.

3. **Click Blank Presentation.**

   PowerPoint displays a blank slide with a title and
   subtitle box.

After you create a new presentation, you need to fill it
with *content* (text and graphics). view, edit, and design
your presentation in Slide view or Outline view.

Both views let you add, delete, rearrange, and edit slides. The main difference is that *Slide view* lets you add graphics and modify the visual appearance of a slide. *Outline view* displays your entire presentation as an outline in which each slide appears as an outline heading, and additional text on each slide appears as a subheading. Outline view makes it easy to focus on the text of your presentation without the distraction of the visual appearance of your slides.

You can create an entire presentation in Slide view without ever using Outline view at all (or use Outline view without ever using Slide view at all). Outline view is most useful for creating and organizing a presentation. Slide view is most useful for viewing the appearance of multiple slides at once.

Designing a presentation with Slide view

Slide view shows your entire slide show as thumbnails in the left pane and the currently selected slide in full-size view in the right pane.

To create a new slide within Slide view, follow these steps:

1. **Click an existing slide in the thumbnail pane.**

2. **Click the Home tab.**

3. **Click the New Slide icon in the Slides group.**

   PowerPoint inserts your new slide after the slide you selected in Step 1.

Rearranging slides

You can rearrange the order of your slides by following these steps:

1. **In the thumbnail pane, click the slide that you want to move to a new position in your presentation.**

2. **Hold down the left mouse button and drag (move) the mouse up or down within the thumbnail pane.**

   PowerPoint displays a horizontal line between slides to show you where your slide will appear.

3. **Release the left mouse button when you're happy with the slide's new position.**

Hiding or deleting a slide

If you have a slide that you no longer want in your presentation, you can either hide or delete it. Hiding a slide keeps the slide but doesn't display that slide when you give your presentation. You may want to hide a slide in case you need it later or so you can reference the information on this slide with the rest of your presentation.

To hide a slide, follow these steps:

1. **In the thumbnail pane, click the slide that you want to hide.**

2. **Click the Slide Show tab.**

3. **Click Hide Slide in the Set Up group.**

   PowerPoint dims your chosen slide and highlights the Hide Slide icon.

To unhide a slide, repeat the preceding steps.

If you're sure that you want to get rid of a slide, you can just delete it. To delete a slide, follow these steps:

1. **In the thumbnail pane, click the slide that you want to delete.**

2. **Press the Delete key.**

    PowerPoint deletes your chosen slide.

If you press Ctrl+Z or click the Undo icon right away, you can recover a deleted slide.

Designing a presentation with Outline view

The Outline pane only displays the text on each slide. Clicking a slide in the Outline pane displays the entire slide, including graphics, as shown in Figure 13-1.

Expanded outline heading

Collapsed outline heading

Figure 13-1: Outline view lets you view just the titles and subtitles of your entire presentation.

The biggest advantage of Outline view is that it lets you rearrange and organize your slides by focusing on their content (title, subtitles, and text). To switch from Slide view to Outline view, click the View tab and then click the Outline View icon. To switch from Outline view to Slide view, click the View tab and then click the Normal icon.

Creating a new slide

In Outline view, each outline heading represents a slide. To create a new slide in Outline view, follow these steps:

1. **Click a slide title in the Outline pane.**

2. **Choose one of the following:**

   - *Press Home to move the cursor to the front of the outline heading.* This creates a new slide before the currently displayed slide.

   - *Press End to move the cursor to the end of the outline heading.* This creates a new slide after the currently displayed slide.

3. **Press Enter.**

   PowerPoint adds a new, blank slide to your presentation.

Creating subtitles on a slide

Outline view lets you create slides and add subtitles to each slide as well. To add a subtitle to a slide, follow these steps:

1. **Click a slide title and then press End to move the cursor to the end of the slide title.**

2. **Press Enter.**

   PowerPoint creates a blank slide title underneath.

3. **Press Tab.**

PowerPoint indents your slide title and turns it into subtitle text under the preceding outline heading.

Collapsing and expanding subtitles

A large presentation consisting of multiple slides with subtitles can be hard to read. To simplify the appearance of your outline, PowerPoint lets you collapse or expand outline headings. To collapse or expand an outline heading, double-click the slide icon of a slide title in the Outline pane.

PowerPoint collapses any subtitles that appear under your chosen outline heading and displays a gray wavy line under your outline heading to let you know that its subtitle text is *collapsed* (hidden).

To expand a collapsed slide title, just double-click its slide icon.

Rearranging slides

Outline view makes it easy to rearrange slides just by moving slide titles up or down. To move a slide title, follow these steps:

1. **Move the mouse pointer over the slide icon that appears to the left of the slide title (or slide subtitle) that you want to move.**

The mouse turns into a four-way-pointing arrow.

2. **Hold down the left mouse button and drag (move) the mouse up or down.**

PowerPoint displays a horizontal gray line to show where the new position of the slide will appear in your presentation.

3. **Release the left mouse button.**

   PowerPoint moves your outline heading to its new position in your presentation.

Deleting a slide

To delete a slide in Outline view, follow these steps:

1. **Click the slide icon that appears to the left of the slide title (or subtitle) you want to delete.**

2. **Press Delete.**

Working with Text

Most slides contain exactly one title and one subtitle text box. The title text box typically defines the information that the slide presents, and the subtitle text box displays supporting information.

When you create a new slide, both the title and subtitle text boxes display the message `Click to add title` or `Click to add subtitle`. (This text won't appear on your slides if you don't type anything there.)

To add text inside a title or subtitle text box, follow these steps:

1. **Click in the title or subtitle text box, directly on the slide.**

   PowerPoint displays a cursor in your chosen text box.

2. **Type your text.**

Typing text in a text box

Aside from typing text in the default text boxes on a slide, you can create your own text box and place it anywhere on the slide.

To create and place a text box on a slide, follow these steps:

1. **Click the Insert tab.**
2. **Click the Text Box icon in the Text group.**

   The mouse pointer turns into a downward-pointing arrow.

3. **Move the mouse pointer over the area on the slide where you want to create a text box.**
4. **Hold down the left mouse button and drag (move) the mouse to draw a text box on a slide.**
5. **Release the left mouse button.**

   PowerPoint displays a text box.

6. **Type your text inside the text box.**

Any text you type into a text box that you create will not appear in Outline view.

PowerPoint lets you move text boxes anywhere on the slide. To move a text box, move the mouse pointer over the edge of the text box you want to move and then drag while you hold down the left mouse button. Release the button when you're happy with the location.

You can also rotate a text box on your slide. To rotate a text box, follow these steps:

1. **Click the text box you want to rotate.**

   PowerPoint displays a rotate handle at the top of your text box.

2. **Move the mouse pointer over the rotate handle.**

   The mouse pointer turns into a circular arrow.

3. **Hold down the left mouse button and drag (move) the mouse to rotate your text box.**

   If you hold down the Shift key while dragging the mouse, you can rotate the text box in 15-degree increments.

4. **Release the left mouse button when you're happy with the rotated position of your text box (or press Esc to cancel the rotation).**

Formatting text

You can format text that you type on a slide by choosing different fonts, font sizes, and colors. To change the appearance of text, follow these steps:

1. **Click the Home tab.**

2. **Click in a text box and select the text you want to format.**

3. **Click one of the font tools, such as Bold, Shadow, or Font Color.**

Aligning text

PowerPoint can align text both horizontally and vertically inside a text box. To align text, follow these steps:

1. **Click the Home tab.**

2. **Click in a text box and select the text you want to align.**

3. **Click one of the text-alignment tools in the Paragraph group.**

4. **Click the Align Text icon in the Paragraph group.**

    A pop-up menu appears.

5. **Click a vertical alignment option, such as Top or Middle.**

Adjusting line spacing

Line spacing defines the space that appears between each line in a text box. To define the line space in a text box, follow these steps:

1. **Click the text box that contains text.**

2. **Click the Home tab.**

3. **Click the Line Spacing icon in the Paragraph group.**

    A pull-down menu appears.

4. **Select a line spacing value, such as 1.5 or 2.**

    PowerPoint adjusts line spacing in your chosen text box.

Making numbered and bulleted lists

PowerPoint can display text as bulleted or numbered lists. The two ways to create such a list are before you type any text or after you've already typed some text.

To create a bulleted or numbered list as you type new text, follow these steps:

1. **Click in a text box.**

2. **Click the Home tab.**

3. **Click the Bullets or Numbering icon in the Paragraph group.**

   A pull-down menu appears.

4. **Click a bullet or numbering option.**

   PowerPoint displays a bullet or number.

5. **Type any text and press Enter.**

   As soon as you press Enter, PowerPoint displays a new bullet or number.

If you have existing text, you can convert it to a bulleted or numbered list. To convert existing text into a list, follow these steps:

1. **Click in the text box that contains the text you want to convert into a bulleted or numbered list.**

2. **Select the text you want to convert into a list.**

3. **Click the Home tab.**

4. **Click the Bullets or Numbering icon in the Paragraph group.**

   PowerPoint converts your text into a list.

PowerPoint displays each paragraph as a separate item in a bulleted or numbered list. A *paragraph* is any amount of text that ends with a paragraph mark (¶), which is an invisible character that you create when you press the Enter key.

Making columns

You can divide a text box into multiple columns, which can be especially useful if you need to display large lists on a slide. To divide a text box into columns, follow these steps:

1. **Click the text box that you want to divide into columns.**

2. **Click the Home tab.**

3. **Click the Columns icon in the Paragraph group.**

   A menu appears.

4. **Click a column option, such as Two Columns or Three Columns.**

   PowerPoint divides your text box into columns.

Applying a Theme

By default, PowerPoint displays each slide with a white background. Although you can change the colors and appearance of each slide individually, it's much easier to change every slide in your presentation by using a theme. A *theme* provides predesigned colors and designs that are applied to each slide to give your presentation a uniform and professional look.

To define a theme for a presentation, follow these steps:

1. **Click the Design tab.**

   If you click a slide in the thumbnail view and hold down the Ctrl key, you can select which slides you'll change. If you don't select any slide, PowerPoint changes all your slides.

2. Click the More button under the Themes group.

A menu appears, as shown in Figure 13-2.

Figure 13-2: Themes provide predesigned backgrounds for your presentation.

If you move the mouse pointer over a theme, PowerPoint shows how your presentation will look.

3. Click a theme.

PowerPoint displays your chosen theme on your slides.

4. Move the mouse pointer over a theme displayed in the Variants group.

PowerPoint shows how the theme will change the appearance of your slides.

5. Click a theme.

PowerPoint displays your new theme colors.

Adding Graphics to a Slide

Another way to spice up the appearance of your presentation is to include graphics on one or more slides. Such graphics can be informative, such as a chart that displays sales results; or they can be decorative, such as a cartoon smiley face that emphasizes the presentation's good news.

Three common types of graphics you can add to a PowerPoint slide include

- ✔ **Picture files:** Includes clip art images as well as images you may have stored on your hard drive, such as photographs from your digital camera

- ✔ **Charts:** Displays bar, column, line, pie, and other types of charts

- ✔ **WordArt:** Displays text as colorful text

Placing picture files on a slide

To liven up a presentation, you can add pictures you may have already stored on your computer. To add a picture to a slide, follow these steps:

1. **Click a slide (in either Slide or Outline view) to which you want to add a picture.**

2. **Click the Insert tab.**

3. **Click the Picture icon in the Images group.**

   The Insert Picture dialog box appears. You may need to change folders or drives to find the picture file you want.

4. **Choose the picture file you want and then click Open.**

   PowerPoint displays your chosen picture on the currently displayed slide. You may need to resize or move your picture.

Placing clip art on a slide

Clip art consists of drawings that come with PowerPoint. To add a clip-art image to a slide, follow these steps:

1. **Click a slide (in either Slide or Outline view) to which you want to add a picture.**

2. **Click the Insert tab.**

3. **Click the Online Pictures icon in the Images group.**

   An Insert Pictures window appears, giving you a choice of typing a picture description to look for clip art, either on Office.com or through the Bing image-search engine.

   You need an Internet connection to search for clip art.

4. **Click in the Office.com Clip Art or Bing Image Search text box and type a word that describes the type of image you want to find.**

5. **Press Enter.**

   The window displays all the clip-art images it can find that match the descriptive word you typed in Step 4.

6. **Choose the clip-art image you want to use and click the Insert button.**

   PowerPoint displays your chosen image on the current slide. (You may need to move or resize the image.)

Creating WordArt

Unlike ordinary text that you can format, WordArt lets you create graphically oriented text to use as headlines for added emphasis. To create WordArt, follow these steps:

1. **Click the slide (in either Slide or Outline view) to which you want to add WordArt.**

2. **Click the Insert tab.**

3. **Click the WordArt icon in the Text group.**

   A WordArt menu appears.

4. **Click a WordArt style to use.**

   PowerPoint displays a WordArt text box on the current slide.

5. **Click in the WordArt text box and type text.**

Capturing screenshots

Sometimes you may want to show an image of an actual computer screen to show how a program works, or to show what a competitor's website looks like. To capture a screenshot, follow these steps:

1. **Click the slide (in either Slide or Outline view) to which you want to add a screenshot.**

2. **Click the Insert tab.**

3. **Click the Screenshot icon in the Images group.**

   A menu appears, showing all currently open windows.

4. **Click a screenshot that you want to capture.**

   PowerPoint displays the screenshot on the current slide.

If you choose Screen Clipping from the bottom of the menu, you can drag the mouse to select just a portion of a screen to capture and store on your slide.

The instructions for moving and rotating graphics are the same as what was described earlier in the "Working with Text" section. Please refer to that section for more information.

Resizing, moving, and deleting graphic images

When you add graphics to a slide, you may need to resize or move them to another location. To resize a graphic image, follow these steps:

1. **Click the graphic that you want to resize.**

   PowerPoint displays handles around your chosen object.

2. **Move the mouse pointer over a handle.**

   The mouse pointer turns into a two-way-pointing arrow.

3. **Hold down the left mouse button and drag the mouse.**

   PowerPoint resizes your chosen graphic image.

4. **Release the left mouse button when you're happy with the new size of your graphic image.**

To move a graphic image, follow these steps:

1. **Move the mouse pointer over the edge of the graphic image you want to move.**

   The mouse turns into a four-way-pointing arrow.

2. **Hold down the left mouse button and drag (move) the mouse.**

PowerPoint moves your graphic image.

3. **Release the left mouse button when you're happy with the new position of your graphic image.**

After you add a graphic image to a slide, you may later decide to delete it. To delete a graphic image, follow these steps:

1. **Click the graphic image you want to delete.**

   PowerPoint displays handles around your chosen graphic image.

2. **Press Delete.**

   PowerPoint deletes your chosen graphic image.

Rotating graphics

You may want to rotate graphic images for added visual effects. To rotate images or to flip them vertically or horizontally, follow these steps:

1. **Click the graphic image you want to rotate.**

   PowerPoint displays handles around your image along with a green rotate handle.

2. **Move the mouse pointer over the rotate handle.**

   The mouse pointer turns into a circular arrow.

3. **Hold down the left mouse button and move (drag) the mouse.**

   PowerPoint rotates your graphic image.

   If you hold down the Shift key while dragging the mouse, you can rotate an image at 15-degree increments.

  4. **Release the left mouse button when you're happy with the rotation of the image.**

Layering objects

PowerPoint treats graphics and text boxes (see Chapter 11) as objects that you can move around on a slide. If you move one object over another, it may block part of another object.

When one object covers another one, PowerPoint considers the first object to be on top and the other object (the one being obscured) to be on the bottom. By moving objects from top to bottom (or vice versa), you can create unique visual effects (or just cover up parts of other objects by mistake).

To move a graphic image to the top or bottom when layered over another object, follow these steps:

  1. **Click the graphic image you want to move.**

     The Picture Tools Format tab appears.

  2. **Click the Format tab.**

  3. **Click the Bring Forward or Send Backward icon in the Arrange group.**

     PowerPoint rearranges the layering of your graphic images.

     You can also right-click an object and choose the Bring Forward or Send Backward command.

Adding Movies to a Slide

Besides adding static graphic images, you can also add movies to a slide so that they play as part of your presentation. To get a video, you can either search for one over the Internet or look for one stored on your computer.

Searching for a video on the Internet

PowerPoint can access a library of videos over the Internet. Make sure you have an Internet connection and then follow these steps:

1. **Click the slide (in either Slide or Outline view) to which you want to add a video.**

2. **Click the Insert tab.**

3. **Click the Video icon in the Media group.**

4. **Choose Online Videos from the menu.**

   An Insert Video window appears.

5. **Click in a text box (such as the Bing Video Search) and type a description of the video you want such as "dogs," and then press Enter.**

   A list of videos appears.

6. **Click the video you want to place on your slide and click the Insert button.**

   PowerPoint displays the video on your slide. You may need to move or resize it.

You won't see the video in action until you view your presentation by pressing F5 or (if you click the video) you click the Playback tab and then click the Play icon.

Searching for video on your computer

You may want to search for a video stored on your computer instead of searching for one over the Internet.

PowerPoint can use movies stored in common video formats such as AVI, MPEG, ASF (streaming video), QuickTime, Flash, and WMV files. If your movie is stored in a different file format, such as Real Video, you must convert the file before you add it to a PowerPoint presentation.

To add a movie stored on your computer, follow these steps:

1. **Click the slide (in either Slide or Outline view) to which you want to add a movie.**

2. **Click the Insert tab.**

3. **Click the Video icon in the Media group.**

4. **Choose Videos on My PC from the menu.**

   An Insert Video dialog box appears.

5. **Click the movie file you want to add and then click the Insert button.**

   PowerPoint displays your video on the slide.

   If you click the Play button on the Format or Playback tab, you can view your video.

Trimming a video

In case you add a video to your presentation and suddenly realize that the video is too long, PowerPoint lets you trim a video from the beginning or end.

You can trim only those videos retrieved from your computer, not videos retrieved off the Internet.

To trim a video, follow these steps:

1. **Click the slide (in either Slide or Outline view) that contains the video you want to trim.**

2. **Click the video.**

   The Video Tools Format and Playback tabs appear.

3. **Click the Playback tab and then click the Trim Video icon.**

   The Trim Video dialog box appears, as shown in Figure 13-3.

Figure 13-3: The Trim Video dialog box.

4. **To trim the beginning of the video, drag the Beginning Marker to the right or click the Up/Down arrows in the Start Time box.**

5. **To trim the end of the video, drag the Ending Marker to the right or click the Up/Down arrows in the End Time box.**

6. **Click the OK button.**

   PowerPoint displays your trimmed video on the slide.

Coloring a video

To spice up the appearance of a video, you can modify its brightness, contrast, or color. Modifying one or more of these options can correct flaws in a video or just create unique visual effects that may make your video more memorable.

To change the color of a video, follow these steps:

1. **Click the slide (in either Slide or Outline view) that contains the video you want to trim.**

2. **Click the video that you want to format.**

   The Video Tools Format and Playback tabs appear.

3. **Click the Format tab.**

4. **Click the Corrections icon in the Adjust group.**

   A menu appears, letting you choose different brightness and contrast settings.

5. **Click a brightness and contrast option.**

6. **Click the Color icon in the Adjust group.**

A menu appears, letting you choose different color settings.

Formatting the shape of a video

To make your video appear even more visually interesting, PowerPoint lets you modify the shape of the video. Instead of appearing as a boring rectangle, your video can now appear with shadows, in shapes like a triangle or arrow, or with a frame around it.

To format the shape of a video, follow these steps:

1. **Click the slide (in either Slide or Outline view) that contains the video you want to trim.**

2. **Click the video that you want to format.**

   The Video Tools Format and Playback tabs appear.

3. **Click the Format tab.**

4. **Click the Video Shape icon in the Video Styles group.**

   A menu appears, letting you choose a shape to format your video.

5. **Click the Video Border icon in the Video Styles group.**

   A color palette appears, letting you choose a color for your border. If you click the Weight or Dashes option from this color palette, you can choose a border thickness and style, such as a dotted line.

6. **Click the Video Effects icon in the Video Styles group.**

   A menu appears, letting you choose from different effects such as Shadow or Rotation.

If you click a style in the Video Styles group, you can choose a predefined appearance for your video.

Adding Sound to a Slide

Sound can be as simple as a sound effect or a recorded speech from the CEO.

PowerPoint can use audio files stored in common formats such as AIFF, MIDI, MP3, and WAV files. If your audio file is stored in a different file format, such as Real Audio, you have to convert the file before you add it to a PowerPoint presentation.

Adding an audio file off the Internet

Microsoft provides plenty of audio clips stored on the Internet that you can download and use in your PowerPoint presentation.

To add an audio file off the Internet, make sure you have an Internet connection and then follow these steps:

1. **Click the slide (in either Slide or Outline view) to which you want to add an audio file.**

2. **Click the Insert tab.**

3. **Click the Audio icon in the Media group.**

   A menu appears.

4. **Choose Online Audio.**

   An Insert Audio window appears.

5. **Click in the Office.com Clip Art text box and type a description of the audio you want, such as "barking," and then press Enter.**

   A list of audio clips appears.

6. **Click the audio clip you want to place on your slide and click the Insert button.**

   PowerPoint displays your audio clip as an audio icon that won't appear during your presentation.

   You may want to move the audio icon on your slide so you can edit and view the rest of your slide.

Adding audio from a file

If you already have music, sound effects, or a speech stored as a file, such as an MP3 file, you can add it to your presentation. To add an audio file stored on your computer, follow these steps:

1. **Click the slide (in either Slide or Outline view) to which you want to add an audio file.**

2. **Click the Insert tab.**

   A menu appears.

3. **Choose Audio on My PC.**

   An Insert Audio dialog box appears.

4. **Click the audio clip you want to place on your slide and click the Insert button.**

   PowerPoint displays your audio clip as an audio icon that won't appear during your presentation. However, you may want to move the audio icon on your slide so you can edit and view the rest of your slide.

To hear your audio file, click the audio file to display a Play button underneath. Then click the Play button.

Recording audio

For greater flexibility, PowerPoint lets you record audio directly from your computer's microphone (if you have one, of course).

To record audio for your presentation, follow these steps:

1. **Click the slide (in either Slide or Outline view) to which you want to add an audio file.**

2. **Click the Insert tab.**

3. **Click the Audio icon in the Media group.**

   A menu appears.

4. **Choose Record Audio.**

   The Record Sound dialog box appears, as shown in Figure 13-4.

Record

Stop

Play

Figure 13-4: The Record Sound dialog box.

5. **Click in the Name text box and type a description for your recording.**

6. **Click the Record button and start talking.**

7. **Click the Stop button and click OK.**

   PowerPoint displays your recording as a horn icon on the slide. You may want to move this audio icon to keep it from obscuring part of your slide.

The audio icon that represents an audio file won't appear when you show off your presentation.

Organizing Slides in Sections

PowerPoint displays all the slides of your presentation in the Slides or Outline view. Although this makes it easy to see all the slides that make up your presentation, such a long list of slides can make it hard for you to find any particular slide.

To help you avoid searching for a single slide among a huge list, PowerPoint gives you the option of organizing in groups called *sections.* After grouping slides into sections, you can selectively hide or display all slides in a section. Sections simply help you organize a large presentation of slides so you can find and edit particular slides at any given time.

Adding a section

By default, presentations don't contain any sections. When you add a section, PowerPoint groups all slides in that section, starting with the first slide you picked all the way to the end of your presentation or the next section heading, whichever comes first.

To add a section to a presentation, follow these steps:

1. **Click the slide that you want to define the beginning of a section.**

2. **Click the Home tab and click the Section icon under the Slides group.**

   A pull-down menu appears.

3. **Choose Add Section.**

   PowerPoint displays a section heading (named Untitled Section) above the slide you selected in Step 1.

4. **Click the selection heading, click the Section icon in the Slides group, and choose Rename Section.**

   The Rename Section dialog box appears.

5. **Click in the Section Name: text box and type a descriptive name for your section. Then click Rename.**

   PowerPoint renames your chosen section.

When you add a section to a presentation, PowerPoint automatically creates a Default Section that contains the first slide and all additional slides up to the section heading you just created.

Expanding and collapsing a section

After you've created at least one section, you can collapse and expand it. Collapsing a section temporarily hides those slides in that section from view so you can focus on the rest of your slides. Expanding a section makes the slides in that section appear again.

To expand and collapse a section, follow these steps:

1. **Click the Collapse Section arrow that appears to the left of the section name.**

   PowerPoint collapses your chosen section and displays the number of slides (in parentheses) hidden in that collapsed section.

2. **Click the Expand Section arrow that appears to the left of the collapsed section name.**

   The section expands, displaying all slides within that section.

Deleting a section

Sections can help divide a large presentation into more manageable chunks, but you may eventually decide you don't need a section anymore. When you delete a section, you have the option of just deleting the section (and leaving the slides intact) or deleting both the section and all slides inside that section.

To delete a section, follow these steps:

1. **Right-click the section name that you want to delete.**

   PowerPoint displays a pop-up menu.

2. **Choose Remove Section (to remove your chosen section), Remove All Sections (to remove all sections), or Remove Section & Slides (to remove your chosen section and all the slides in that section).**

   PowerPoint deletes your section (or sections).

Adding Transitions

Transitions define how slides or part of a slide (text or graphics) appear during your presentation. By default, slides appear one at a time with all the text and graphics displayed at once, which can get monotonous.

When creating a transition, you need to define the following:

- ✔ The actual visual appearance of the transition
- ✔ The speed of the transition (Slow, Medium, or Fast)
- ✔ Any sound effects you want to play during the transition (these can get really annoying, so use them sparingly)
- ✔ When to display the transition (after a certain time period or when you click the mouse)

To spice up your presentation, PowerPoint offers two types of transitions:

- ✔ Slide transitions (these occur between two different slides)
- ✔ Text and picture animations (these occur on a single slide)

Use transitions sparingly. Transitions may be visually interesting, but too many transitions can be distracting.

Adding slide transitions

Slide transitions can make a slide appear to melt or break into multiple pieces that slip away, revealing the next slide underneath.

To create a slide transition, follow these steps:

1. **Click a slide (in the Slide or Outline view pane).**

   Any transition you choose will end by displaying the slide you choose in this step.

2. **Click the Transitions tab.**

   PowerPoint displays the different animation (transition) tools.

3. **Click the More button of the Transition To This Slide group.**

   A pull-down menu appears, listing all the different transitions available.

4. **Click the transition you want.**

   PowerPoint shows you how your transition will look.

5. **(Optional) Click in the Sound list box in the Timing group.**

   A pull-down menu appears, listing all the sound effects you can choose.

6. **(Optional) Select the On Mouse Click or After check box in the Timing group of the Transitions tab.**

   If you select the After check box, you have to specify a time to wait before running the transition.

   You can select both the On Mouse Click and Automatically After check boxes, so the slide transition waits until you click the mouse or until a specified amount of time passes.

7. **(Optional) Click Apply to All to apply your transitions to every slide in your presentation.**

Applying the same transition throughout your presentation can give your slide show a consistent look, but it's best for only simple, visual transitions and not for transitions that involve noisy sound effects that can get tedious.

Text and graphic transitions

Besides animating how your slides appear and disappear, you can also add transitions to your text boxes or graphics so they fly or drop into place across a slide.

To create a simple text or graphic transition, follow these steps:

1. **Click a text box or picture on a slide.**

   PowerPoint displays handles around your chosen item.

2. **Click the Animations tab.**

3. **Click the More button in the Animations group to display a menu of options.**

4. **Click an animation, such as Fly In or Wipe.**

   PowerPoint displays a number near your chosen item. These numbers define the order that your transitions will appear.

5. **Click the Preview icon to see how your animation will look.**

To remove an animation, just select that text box or graphic, click the Animations tab, and choose None from the Animation group.

Using the Animation Painter

If you create an animation that you want to apply to other text boxes or graphic objects, you can tediously re-create that transition all over again. However, it's much simpler to use the Animation Painter, which lets you copy animations from one object to another.

To use the Animation Painter, follow these steps:

1. **Click a text box or picture that contains the animation you want to copy.**

   PowerPoint displays handles around your chosen item.

2. **Click the Animations tab.**

3. **Click the Animation Painter icon under the Advanced Animation group.**

4. **Click a text box or picture.**

   PowerPoint applies the transition, from the object you selected in Step 1, to the object you selected in Step 4.

Viewing a Presentation

After you finish arranging your slides, adding transitions, and adding hyperlinks, you're ready to test how your entire presentation looks. To view your entire presentation, follow these steps:

1. **Click the Slide Show tab.**

2. **Click the From Beginning icon in the Start Slide Show group.**

PowerPoint displays the first slide of your presentation.

You can also choose the From Beginning command by pressing F5.

3. Choose one of the following:

- Click the mouse or press the spacebar to view the next slide.

- Press Esc to exit your presentation.

If you have a large presentation consisting of 300 slides, you may not want to view the first 290 slides just to test how your last 10 slides look. To avoid this problem, click the slide you want to view and then click the From Current Slide icon in Step 2.

Creating a custom slide show

You may have a presentation organized for one audience but need to give the same presentation to a different audience. As a simple solution, PowerPoint lets you create custom slide shows based on an existing presentation. Such a custom slide show can selectively show slides in a different order. To create a custom slide show, you need to define the order you want to display the slides.

To arrange the order of a custom slide show, follow these steps:

1. Click the Slide Show tab.

2. Click the Custom Slide Show icon in the Start Slide Show group.

A pull-down menu appears.

3. **Choose Custom Shows.**

   The Custom Shows dialog box appears.

4. **Click New.**

   The Define Custom Show dialog box appears.

5. **Click in the Slide Show Name: text box and type a name for your custom slide show.**

6. **Click in the check box for a slide in the Slides in Presentation list box and then click the Add button.**

   This tells PowerPoint which existing slides you want to use in your custom slide show.

7. **Repeat Step 6 for each slide you want to include in your custom slide show.**

8. **(Optional) Click a slide in the Slides in Custom Show list box and click the Up or Down arrow button to rearrange their order.**

9. **Repeat Step 8 for each slide you want to rearrange in your custom slide show.**

10. **Click OK.**

    The Custom Shows dialog box appears again.

11. **Click the name of your custom slide show and then click Close.**

To present a custom slide show, follow these steps:

1. **Click the Slide Show tab.**

2. **Click the Custom Slide Show icon in the Start Slide Show group.**

   A pull-down menu appears that lists the names of all the custom slide shows you've created.

3. **Click the name of the custom slide show you want to view.**

4. **Choose one of the following:**

   - Click the mouse or press the spacebar to view the next slide.

   - Press Esc to exit your presentation.

Eventually you may need to delete a custom slide show. When you delete a custom slide show, you don't delete any slides used in your original presentation.

To delete a custom slide show, follow these steps:

1. **Click the Slide Show tab.**

2. **Click the Custom Slide Show icon in the Start Slide Show group.**

   A pull-down menu appears, listing the names of all the custom slide shows you've created.

3. **Click Custom Shows.**

   The Custom Shows dialog box appears.

4. **Click the name of the custom slide show you want to delete and click the Remove button.**

5. **Click the Close button.**

Hiding a slide

PowerPoint can hide a slide, which lets you keep your slide but not display it during a presentation. Hiding a slide can be especially handy when you need to create a custom slide show and need a slide to appear only in the custom slide show but not the original presentation (or vice versa).

To hide a slide, follow these steps:

1. **Click the slide that you want to hide (in Slide or Outline view).**

2. **Click the Slide Show tab.**

3. **Click the Hide Slide icon in the Set Up group.**

   PowerPoint dims your selected slide.

To unhide a slide, just repeat the preceding three steps.

Organizing with Slide Sorter view

After you view your presentation, you may want to rearrange slides. To help you organize your presentation, switch to Slide Sorter view, which numbers each slide to show you the order that they appear, as shown in Figure 13-5.

Figure 13-5: Slide Sorter view lets you rearrange the order of your slides.

To use Slide Sorter view, follow these steps:

1. **Click the View tab.**

2. **Click the Slide Sorter view icon in the Presentation Views group.**

   You can also click the Slide Sorter icon in the bottom-right corner of the PowerPoint window.

3. **(Optional) To delete a slide, click a slide and press Delete.**

4. **(Optional) To hide a slide, click a slide, click the Slide Show tab, and click Hide Slide.**

5. **(Optional) To move a slide**

   a. *Move the mouse pointer over a slide.*

   b. *Hold down the left mouse button and move (drag) the mouse.*

      PowerPoint displays a vertical line where it will place your slide.

   c. *Release the left mouse button.*

6. **Click the Normal icon on the View tab to switch out of Slide Sorter view.**

Chapter 14

Getting Organized with Outlook

● ●

In This Chapter

▶ Configuring e-mail account settings

▶ Creating e-mail

▶ Adding file attachments

▶ Reading e-mail

▶ Deleting e-mail

▶ Setting an appointment

▶ Storing names and addresses

▶ Managing tasks

● ●

*M*icrosoft Outlook is the personal organizer portion of Office 2013 for tracking appointments, storing names and addresses of important people, and keeping a list of to-do tasks. However, the most popular uses for Outlook are reading, writing, and organizing your e-mail.

ɟuring E-Mail Settings

The first time you run Outlook, you need to configure your e-mail account information. To retrieve e-mail from your account within Outlook, you may need to know the following:

- ✔ Your name
- ✔ The username of your e-mail account, which may be JSmith (for Joe Smith)
- ✔ Your e-mail address (such as `JSmith@micro soft.com`)
- ✔ Your e-mail account password
- ✔ Your e-mail account type (such as POP3 or IMAP)
- ✔ Your incoming mail server name (such as `pop. microsoft.com`)
- ✔ Your outgoing mail server name (such as `smtp. microsoft.com`)

Outlook can often recognize many popular e-mail accounts such as Yahoo! Mail, but if Outlook can't set up your e-mail account automatically, you will need to ask your Internet service provider (ISP) for all these details.

Adding an e-mail account

Before you can use Outlook to manage your e-mail, you must add your e-mail account. The first time you run Outlook, the program will try to set up an e-mail account to use.

If you want to add a new e-mail account later, follow these steps:

1. **Load Outlook and click the File tab.**

2. **Click Info and then click the Add Account button.**

   An Add Account dialog box appears

3. **Type in the appropriate information and click Next.**

   You may need to wade through several sets of questions before Outlook can properly configure your e-mail account.

To delete an e-mail account, click the File tab, click Info, click Account Settings, and when a pop-up menu appears, choose Account Settings. When an Account Settings dialog box appears, click the e-mail account you want to delete, and then click the Remove icon.

Creating E-Mail

After you set up an e-mail account, you can start sending e-mail. The three ways to create and send e-mail are

- ✔ **Create a message and type the recipient's e-mail address manually.**

- ✔ **Reply to a previously received message.** Outlook then adds the recipient's e-mail address automatically.

- ✔ **Create a message and use a previously stored e-mail address.** Outlook adds the e-mail address automatically.

Creating a new e-mail message

The most straightforward way to send a message is to type the recipient's e-mail address and then type your message by following these steps:

1. **Click the Mail icon in the bottom-left corner of the Outlook window.**

2. **Click the Home tab and then click the New Email icon.**

   Outlook displays a message window, as shown in Figure 14-1. Notice that the message window displays a Ribbon with File, Message, Insert, Options, Format Text, and Review tabs.

Figure 14-1: The message window lets you type and format a message.

3. **Click in the To text box and type the e-mail address of the person you want to receive your message.**

   Make sure that you type the e-mail address correctly. One incorrect character, and your message won't go to your intended recipient.

4. **(Optional) Click in the Cc text box and type another e-mail address to send the message to more than one person.**

5. **Click in the Subject text box and type a brief description of your message.**

Many people use spam filters that examine the Subject line of a message, so it's a good idea not to type your subject text in ALL CAPITAL LETTERS or use multiple exclamation points!!! Otherwise your recipient's spam filter may inadvertently flag your message as spam and delete it before anyone can even read it.

6. **Click in the message text box and type your message.**

If you click the Save icon on the Quick Access toolbar (or press Ctrl+S), you can store the message in your Drafts folder so you can edit and send it at a later time.

7. **Click the Send icon to send your message.**

Replying to an e-mail message

Oftentimes, you may receive a message from someone else and want to send a reply to that person. When you send a reply, Outlook automatically copies the original message as part of your e-mail; that way, the recipient can read the original message that you're responding to.

Even better, when you reply to a message, you won't have to retype the recipient's e-mail address and risk misspelling it. To reply to an e-mail message, follow these steps:

1. **Click the Mail icon in the bottom-left corner of the Outlook window.**

2. **Click the Home tab.**

   Outlook displays the Mail pane.

3. **Click a message that you want to reply to.**

   Outlook displays the contents of that message in a pane on the right side of the Outlook window.

4. **Click the Reply icon in the Respond category.**

   Outlook displays a message window with the recipient's e-mail address and subject line already typed in, along with a copy of the original message.

   If you click the Forward icon instead of the Reply icon, you can send a message to another person instead of the person who originally sent you the message.

5. **Click in the message text box and type your message.**

   If you click the Save icon on the Quick Access toolbar in the upper-left corner of the screen, you can store the message in your Drafts folder so you can edit and send it at a later time.

6. **Click the Send icon.**

Using a stored e-mail address to create a new e-mail message

If you send e-mail to certain people regularly, you can type a particular person's e-mail address once, store it, and then have Outlook type that e-mail address whenever you need it again.

To store an e-mail address, follow these steps:

1. **Click the Mail icon in the bottom-left corner of the Outlook window.**

2. **Click the Home tab and click the Address Book icon in the Find category.**

   The Address Book: Contacts window appears.

3. **Choose File⇨New Entry.**

   A New Entry dialog box appears.

4. **Choose New Contact and click OK.**

   A Contact window appears.

5. **Click in the Full Name text box and type a person's name.**

6. **Click in the E-mail text box and type a person's e-mail address.**

7. **Click the Save & Close icon.**

   Your newly added name appears in the Address Book: Contacts window.

8. **Choose File⇨Close.**

After you have stored at least one name and e-mail address, you can retrieve that e-mail address to send a message by following these steps:

1. **Click the Mail icon in the bottom-left corner of the Outlook window.**

2. **Click the Home tab and click the New Email icon in the New category.**

   The Message window appears.

3. **Click the To button.**

The Select Names: Contacts dialog box appears, listing all your stored names and e-mail addresses.

4. Click a name to select it.

5. Click the To button at the bottom of the Select Names: Contacts dialog box.

6. Click OK.

Outlook automatically enters your chosen e-mail address in the To text box.

7. Click in the Subject text box and type a brief description of your message.

8. Click in the message text box and type your message.

If you click the Save icon on the Quick Access toolbar, you can store the message in your Drafts folder so you can edit and send it at a later time.

9. Click the Send icon to send your message.

Attaching Files to Messages

Rather than just send plain text, you can also *attach* a file to your message. This file can be anything from a picture, a song (stored as an audio file), a program, a video file, or even another e-mail message.

Be careful when attaching files to messages because many Internet service providers (ISPs) put a limit on the maximum size of an e-mail message, such as 10MB. Also try to keep any file attachments small because if the recipient has a slow Internet connection, downloading a large file attachment can take a really long time.

If you want to send someone a picture, video, audio file, compressed file, or even an entire program, you need to attach that file to a message by following these steps:

1. **Follow the steps in the earlier section, "Creating E-Mail," to create a new e-mail message.**

2. **Click the Insert tab.**

3. **Click the Attach File icon in the Include group.**

   The Insert File dialog box appears.

4. **Click the file you want to attach to your message and then click Insert.**

   Outlook displays an Attached text box in the message window, as shown in Figure 14-2.

   If you hold down the Ctrl or Shift key while clicking a file, you can select multiple files at once.

Figure 14-2: The Attached text box displays the filename attached to the message.

5. **(Optional) Right-click any file in the Attached text box; when a pop-up menu appears, choose Remove if you change your mind about attaching a file to a message.**

6. **Click the Send icon.**

Rather than select multiple files to attach to a message, you can compress or *zip* multiple files into a single compressed file by using a separate program such as the free Jzip program (www.jzip.com) or by using the built-in Zip compression feature in Windows.

Reading and Organizing E-Mail

One of the biggest problems with receiving e-mail is trying to sort through all the important messages. To help you organize your e-mail, Outlook offers several ways to group related messages together and search for specific text in messages so you can find exactly what you need.

Grouping messages into categories

Outlook can display messages with the newest message on top and the oldest message at the bottom (or vice versa). In addition, Outlook can also group messages according to Date, Subject, Size, or even by e-mail accounts.

To view and sort your e-mail messages, follow these steps:

1. **Click the Mail icon in the bottom-left corner of the Outlook window.**

2. **Click the View tab.**

   The different ways to arrange e-mail messages appear in the Arrangement category.

3. **Click a category such as Date, Size, From, or Account.**

   Outlook sorts your messages.

4. **(Optional) Click Reverse Sort.**

   Outlook sorts your messages in reverse order, such as oldest to newest or newest to oldest.

Changing the appearance of the Reading Pane

To make reading e-mail messages easier, Outlook can display your messages in three different ways:

- ✓ **Right:** Lists of messages appear in the left side of the Outlook window and the currently selected message appears in the right side of the Outlook window.

- ✓ **Bottom:** Lists of messages appear in the top of the Outlook window and the currently selected message appears in the bottom of the Outlook window.

- ✓ **Off:** Only lists of messages appear in the Outlook window. To see the contents of a single message, you have to double-click that message.

To change the way Outlook displays your e-mail messages, follow these steps:

1. **Click the Mail icon in the bottom-left corner of the Outlook window.**

2. **Click the View tab.**

3. **Click the Reading Pane icon in the Layout category.**

   A menu appears.

4. **Choose an option such as Right, Bottom, or Off.**

   Outlook displays your messages in your chosen configuration.

Retrieving a file attachment from a message

Rather than just send text, people may send you file attachments. When you receive a message with a file attachment, Outlook displays a paper clip icon next to the message.

Never open a file attachment unless you absolutely trust its contents. Many malicious hackers send viruses, worms, spyware, and Trojan horses as file attachments, so if you aren't careful, you can accidentally infect your computer and lose your data.

To open a file attachment, follow these steps:

1. **Click a message that displays a paper clip icon.**

   Outlook displays the message's contents with the file attachments listed.

2. **Double-click the file (paper clip) icon displayed in the message.**

   An Opening Mail Attachment dialog box appears, giving you the option to open the file directly or save it. Unless you trust the file contents, it's usually best to save the file in a directory and scan it with your antivirus program.

If you right-click a file attachment icon, a pop-up menu appears. Then you can click Preview and see a preview of the file contents without opening it. This only works with popular file formats such as text files or Word documents.

Deleting E-Mail Messages

To keep your Inbox folder from getting too cluttered, you can always delete messages. To delete a message, follow these steps:

1. **Click the Mail icon in the bottom-left corner of the Outlook window.**

2. **Click the Home tab.**

3. **Click the message you want to delete.**

4. **Press Delete or click the Delete icon in the Delete group.**

If you accidentally delete the wrong e-mail message, you can undelete it by pressing Ctrl+Z or clicking the Undo icon in the Quick Access toolbar.

Setting Appointments

Everyone can get busy and miss deadlines and appointments. To avoid this problem, let Outlook keep track of your schedule.

Making an appointment

Before you can add an appointment to Outlook, you need to decide which day that appointment will occur and what time it will start. To do this, you need to look at the Outlook calendar.

Outlook offers several ways to display its calendar:

- ✔ **Day:** Displays a single day divided into 24 hours
- ✔ **Week:** Displays a single week divided into five or seven days
- ✔ **Month:** Displays a single month divided into days

To set an appointment, follow these steps:

1. **Click the Calendar icon in the bottom-left corner of the Outlook window.**

   Outlook displays the Calendar view.

2. **Click the Home tab and then click the Day, Work Week (5 days), Week (7 days), or Month icon in the Arrange category.**

   Outlook displays the Calendar based on the time frame you chose, such as Month, as shown in Figure 14-3.

Figure 14-3: The month Calendar view in Outlook.

You can also click the New Appointment icon on the Home tab to define an appointment.

3. **Double-click the day (or time if you're in the Day calendar) where you want to schedule an appointment.**

   Outlook displays the Appointment window.

4. **Click in the Subject text box and type a brief description of your event.**

5. **(Optional) Click in the Location text box and type the location of your appointment.**

If you often set appointments for specific locations, Outlook remembers these locations. In the future, just click the downward-pointing arrow in the Location text box and then click a previously used location in the list that appears.

6. **Click in the Start Time list box and choose a time.**

   You can also type a time directly in the Start Time list box or even choose a different date.

If the Start Time and End Time list boxes appear dimmed, make sure you clear the All Day Event check box.

7. **Click in the End Time list box and choose a time.**

   You can also type a time directly in the End Time list box or even choose a different date.

8. **Click in the big text box and type any additional information you want to store about your event, such as items you need to bring or information you want to recall about the person you're meeting.**

9. **Click the Save & Close icon in the Actions group.**

Outlook displays your appointment in Day, Week, or Month view of the calendar.

If you need to edit an appointment, just double-click it to display the Appointment window again. You can also drag an appointment from one location on the calendar to another to switch it to a different time or date.

Viewing appointments

If you store several appointments on the same day, you may find it hard to keep track of them all. When you use the Schedule View icon in the Arrange group, Outlook displays your appointments so you can quickly spot your free and busy times.

You can also view your appointments by moving the mouse pointer over the Calendar icon in the bottom-left corner of the Outlook window, and when a calendar pops up, click a date to view your appointments for that day.

Deleting an appointment

After an appointment has passed or been canceled, you can delete it. To delete an appointment, follow these steps:

1. **Double-click an appointment to open the Appointment window.**

2. **Click the Delete icon (or press Ctrl+D).**

Outlook deletes your appointment.

For another way to delete an appointment, follow these steps:

1. Click an appointment on the calendar.

Outlook displays a black border around your chosen appointment and displays the Appointment tab.

2. Click the Delete icon.

Outlook deletes your appointment.

If you delete an appointment by mistake, press Ctrl+Z to recover it.

Storing Names and Addresses

Everyone has important names, addresses, e-mail addresses, and phone numbers that need to be saved. You can store this information in Outlook.

Adding a name

To store a name in Outlook, follow these steps:

1. Click the People icon in the bottom-left corner of the Outlook window.

Outlook displays the Contacts view.

2. Click the Home tab and click the New Contact icon in the New group.

Outlook displays a Contact window.

3. Type the information you want to store about each person, such as the name in the Full Name text box.

You can store as much or as little data about a person as you want.

4. Click the Save & Close icon.

Outlook saves your information.

If you click the Save & New icon instead of the Save & Close icon in Step 4, another blank Contact window appears so you can keep adding new names to your Outlook contact list.

Viewing names

After you've stored one or more names in Outlook, you'll probably need to find it again. If you just want to browse through your list of names, follow these steps:

1. Click the People icon in the bottom-left corner of the Outlook window.

Outlook displays the Contacts view.

2. Click the Home tab and click the People, Business Card, Card, Phone, or List icon in the Current View group.

The People view displays lists of people alphabetically. The Business Card displays names and additional information as large windows, as shown in Figure 14-4. The Card view displays names as smaller windows, allowing you to see more names on the screen. The Phone view helps you find a specific phone number. The List view organizes people by company.

Figure 14-4: The Business Card view.

If you click a name, you can delete it by clicking the Delete icon on the Home tab.

3. Double-click a name to open the Contacts window.

The Contacts window opens, allowing you to edit or add new information to your chosen contact.

Searching names

If you know all or part of a name or other information about a person, you can exhaustively browse through your entire list of stored contacts. However, it's much easier to just search for that information instead.

To search for a name, follow these steps:

1. Click the People icon in the bottom-left corner of the Outlook window.

Outlook displays the Contacts view.

2. Click the Home tab and click in the Search Contacts text box in the Find group (or press Ctrl+ E).

The cursor appears in the Search Contacts text box.

3. **Type as much data as you can about the person you want to find, typing (for example) all or part of a name or phone number.**

4. **Press Enter.**

   Outlook displays all contacts that match your search criteria that you typed in Step 3.

5. **Click the Close icon at the far right of the Search Contacts text box.**

   Outlook displays all your contacts once more.

You can also search for a name by clicking on the People icon in the bottom-left corner of the Outlook window. A window pops up with a search text box on top; there you can type all or part of a name.

Managing Tasks

Everyone's busy. However, the big difference between busy, efficient people and overwhelmed people is that busy people simply know how to manage their tasks so they get things done.

To help you manage your tasks, Outlook lets you store your most important tasks and assign due dates and priorities. Now at a glance, you can see what's most important for you to focus on.

Storing a task

When storing tasks in Outlook, you need to define what it is that you want to do and set a date for when you want to complete it.

Microsoft OneNote 2013

If you need to take notes in meetings, you're probably dragging your laptop around and typing notes in a Microsoft Word document. There's nothing wrong with that, except that by the end of the meeting, your notes will appear in one long document and you'll need to edit those notes so you can keep track of everything you wrote.

You may prefer using a more specialized note-taking program called Microsoft OneNote 2013. OneNote lets you divide your notes into sections to help you find what you need. Instead of typing everything on a single page (as Microsoft Word forces you to do), OneNote lets you create one section for action items and another section for upcoming meetings to keep the project on track.

Now when you want to read your notes, you don't have to scroll through endless pages (the way you do in Microsoft Word). Instead, you can just flip to the section that contains the information you want to find. Think of the difference between trying to find information printed on a scroll of paper (Microsoft Word) or information organized in separate sections like tabs in a notebook (OneNote).

If you have a microphone and a webcam, you can even capture audio and video to store in your notes. That way you can capture an entire classroom lecture or meeting in audio or video, and then jot down notes at the same time. And because notes don't always rely on words, OneNote also lets you draw pictures, which can be handy for capturing ideas visually.

More important, OneNote can link to Outlook to share data. If you're in a meeting, you may need to write down a task for yourself and a future appointment. When you work with Outlook, OneNote lets you capture information and store it in Outlook so you can keep track of your busy schedule. OneNote can be a great note-taking program by itself, but when combined with Outlook, the two programs make an efficient information-gathering system.

To store a task in Outlook, follow these steps:

1. **Click Tasks in the bottom-left corner of the Outlook window.**

   Outlook displays the Tasks view.

   If you just need to store a quick task, click in the Type a New Task text box in the middle pane, type a brief description of your task, and press Enter.

2. **Click the Home tab and click the New Tasks icon in the New group.**

   Outlook displays a Task window.

3. **Click in the Subject text box and type a brief description of your task.**

4. **(Optional) Click in the Start Date list box and click a date to start your task. Then click in the Due Date list box and click a date when you want to complete that task.**

   You don't have to add a start and end date, but it's a good idea to do so to help you measure your progress (or lack of progress) on your task.

5. **(Optional) Click in the Status list box and choose an option.**

6. **(Optional) Click in the Priority list box and choose an option.**

7. **(Optional) Click in the % Complete box and click the up/down arrows to define what percentage you've completed of the task.**

8. **Click in the big text box to describe more details about your task.**

9. **Click the Save & Close icon.**

   Outlook displays your task, as shown in Figure 14-5.

Figure 14-5: Outlook displays a list of tasks.

If you double-click a task, you can open the Tasks window so you can edit or add information to your chosen task.

Searching tasks

If you have a lot of tasks, you may want to find a particular one, which you can do by searching.

To search for a task, follow these steps:

1. **Click Tasks in the bottom-left corner of the Outlook window.**

   Outlook displays the Tasks view. You can browse through this list of tasks to find the one you want. However, if you have many tasks, you may want to let Outlook search for them instead.

2. **Click the Home tab and click in the Search To-Do List text box (or press Ctrl+ E).**

   The cursor appears in the Search To-Do text box.

3. **Type as much data as you can about the task you want to find.**

   Outlook displays all tasks that match the search criteria that you typed in Step 3.

4. Click the Close icon in the Search text field.

Outlook displays all your tasks once more.

Viewing tasks

There may be times when you want to see only certain types of tasks, such as tasks due in the next seven days; Outlook can show different views of your task list.

To change views of your list of tasks, follow these steps:

1. Click Tasks in the bottom-left corner of the Outlook window.

Outlook displays the Tasks view.

2. Click the Home tab.

3. Click the More button in the Current View list.

Outlook displays a list of different ways to view your tasks.

4. Click on a view icon such as Next 7 Days or Overdue.

Outlook displays all your tasks that meet your chosen criteria.

Chapter 15

Storing Stuff in Access

. . . .

In This Chapter

▶ Understanding how databases work

▶ Designing a database

▶ Editing a database

▶ Typing information into a database

▶ Closing a database

▶ Searching and filtering a database

▶ Creating a report with the Report Wizard

. . . .

A *database* is a program that stores information
such as names, addresses, and phone numbers, or
inventory part numbers, shipping dates, customer codes,
and any other type of information that you think is worth
saving.

To help you store information in a database, Office 2013
comes with the *Access* database program. Access
provides three advantages over storing information on
paper. First, Access can store literally billions of chunks
of information (try doing that with a filing cabinet).
Second, Access makes it easy to search and sort through
your information in the blink of an eye. Third, you can
easily generate reports to help you make sense of your
data.

The three main advantages of a computer database over a paper database are

✔ **Massive storage:** The largest computer database can fit on a hard drive, but a paper database may take a roomful of file cabinets.

✔ **Fast retrieval:** Searching for a single name in a computer database is fast and easy. Doing the same thing in a paper database is difficult, error prone, and nearly impossible with a large database.

✔ **Reporting:** A *report* can help you make sense out of your data, such as showing a list of customers who earn a certain amount of money and live in a specific area. Trying to find this information in a paper database is time-consuming and error-prone.

Understanding the Basics of a Database

A database is nothing more than a file that contains useful information that you need to save and retrieve in the future. A database can consist of a single name and address or several million names and addresses.

A typical Access database file consists of several parts:

✔ **Fields:** A *field* contains a single chunk of information, such as name, street address, or phone number.

✔ **Records:** A *record* consists of one or more fields. A business card is a paper version of a database record that stores fields (name, address, phone number, and so on) about a single person (record).

- ✔ **Tables:** A *table* displays records in rows and columns, much like a spreadsheet. Tables group related records, such as records of all your customers or records of all your invoices.

- ✔ **Forms:** A *form* displays all the fields of a single record onscreen, mimicking a paper form, so that you can add, edit, or view a single record at a time.

- ✔ **Queries:** A *query* lets you retrieve certain information based on your criteria, such as only retrieving names and addresses of people who earn more than $50,000 a year and have children.

- ✔ **Reports:** A *report* arranges your data in a certain way, such as showing all customers who placed more than 1,000 orders last year or all customers who live within a certain zip code.

Access is known as a *relational* database. Basically, this means that you can store data in separate tables and link or "relate" them together to avoid duplicating data in multiple tables. One table may contain customer names and addresses while a separate, related table may contain those same customers' purchase orders.

Here are the two basic steps to using a database. First, you need to design your database, which means deciding what type of information your database will hold, such as names, addresses, e-mail addresses, telephone numbers, and so on.

After you design a database, the second step is filling it with actual data, such as typing the name **Bob Jones** in the Name field or the e-mail address **BJones@somecompany.com** in the E-mail field.

When you first create a database, you'll probably start out with a single table that contains customer information. Inside the Customer Information table will be multiple records where each record represents a single customer. Each record will consist of multiple fields, such as Last Name, Company Name, Phone Number, and E-mail Address.

To help you edit and view your database information, you may eventually want to create a form that displays your fields onscreen, mimicking a paper form that's easy to read.

If you find yourself searching for the same type of information on a regular basis, you can store this search criteria as a query. Then you can just click the query name and make Access show you exactly what you want to find.

Finally, you may want to print your data in a way that makes sense to you, such as printing a quarterly sales report. By saving your printing criteria in a report, you can make Access print selected data on a page that's easy for you to read and understand.

Features such as forms, queries, and reports are optional but handy. Features like tables, records, and fields are necessary to store your information in your database.

Designing a Database

To design a database, you need to first create a database table and then define the names of all the fields you want to store in that particular table. Database tables let you divide a file into separate parts. For example, one database table may hold the names and addresses of all your customers, a second database table may hold the names and addresses of all your employees, and a third database table may hold the names and addresses of your suppliers. Access stores all this related information in a single Access file that's saved on your hard drive.

To design your database, you can create a database from scratch or use an existing template, which you can modify. *Designing* a database means defining both the number of fields to use for storing information and the maximum amount of data each field can hold.

In general, store information in separate fields. So rather than create a single field to hold someone's full name, create two separate fields: One field holds a first name, and the second field holds the last name.

Access can create a blank database or a special database by using one of many templates available from the Microsoft website. No matter how you create a database, you will likely need to modify it to customize it for the type of data you want to store.

When you start Access, it gives you a choice of opening an existing database or creating a new one.

To create a database with Access already running, follow these steps:

1. **Click the File tab.**

2. **Choose New.**

   Access displays a variety of options.

3. **Click an icon such as Blank desktop database or any database template.**

   If you click a template, the right pane shows a preview of your template.

4. **Click in the File Name text box and type a descriptive name for your database.**

   If you click the folder icon that appears to the right of the File Name text box, you can open a dialog box that enables you to define a specific drive and folder in which to store your database file.

5. **Click the Create button to create your database file.**

   Access displays a blank database with a generic field name of Field1.

6. **Double-click the Field1 column heading and type a name for your field (such as** First Name **or** Salary**).**

7. **Click the Click to Add column heading to define another field for your database.**

   A menu appears, letting you choose the type of data to store in that field.

8. **Click a data type to store in your field such as Number, Currency, or Long Text.**

9. **Double-click the Field column heading and type a name for your field such as** Last Name.

10. **Repeat Steps 7 through 9 for each additional field you want to create.**

Editing and Modifying a Database

After you create a database from scratch or from a template, you may need to modify it by giving each field a descriptive name, defining the size of each field, or adding and deleting a field.

Naming a field

If you create a database from scratch, Access displays generic field names such as *Field1*. If you create a database from a template, you see the descriptive field names, but you may still want to rename the fields to something else.

To rename a field, follow these steps:

1. **In the All Access Objects pane on the left of the screen, double-click the table that contains the fields you want to rename.**

   Access displays the Datasheet view of your database.

2. **Double-click the field (column head) that you want to rename.**

   Access highlights the column heading.

3. **Type a new name for your field and then press Enter when you're done.**

Adding and deleting a field

Sometimes you may need to add a field to make room to store new information. At other times, you may want to delete a field that you don't really want after all. To add a field to a database table, follow these steps:

1. **Click the downward-pointing arrow that appears to the right of the Click to Add heading.**

   A menu appears.

2. **Choose the type of field you want to add, such as Currency or Text.**

Access inserts your field and gives it a generic name like `Field3`.

To delete a field from a database table, follow these steps:

1. **Click the field (column head) you want to delete.**

   Access highlights the entire column in your database table.

2. **Click the Delete button in the Add & Delete group.**

   If you have stored data in that field, a dialog box appears, asking whether you want to permanently delete all the data in the field.

   If you delete a field, you also delete any data that may be stored in that field. Depending on how much data you have stored, you can wipe out a lot of information by deleting a single field, so be careful.

3. **Click Yes (or No).**

   If you click Yes, Access deletes your chosen field.

Defining the type and size of a field

The *data type* of a field defines what kind of data the field can hold (numbers, text, dates, and so on), and the *size* of a field defines the amount of data the field can hold (no numbers larger than 250 digits, any text string with fewer than 120 characters, and so on).

The purpose of defining the type and size of a field is to make sure that you store only valid data in a particular field. To define the type and amount of data a field can store, follow these steps:

1. **Click the Home tab.**

2. **In the All Access Objects pane on the left of the screen, double-click the table that contains the fields you want to define.**

   Access displays the Datasheet view of your table.

3. **Click the column heading of the field you want to define.**

   Access highlights the entire column.

4. **Click the Fields tab that appears under the Table Tools heading on the Ribbon interface.**

   The Fields tab displays options for modifying your field.

5. **Click the arrow that appears to the right of the Data Type combo box.**

   A pull-down menu appears, listing all the different types of data you can define to store in a field.

6. **Choose a data type, such as Number, Text, or Date/ Time.**

   Depending on the data type you choose, you can choose additional options by clicking in the Format combo box.

Typing Data into a Database

After you create a database table and define fields within that table to hold chunks of information, you're ready to type in actual names, phone numbers, and e-mail addresses. You can use Datasheet view or Form view.

Datasheet view displays information in rows and columns, where each row represents a single record and each column defines a specific field name. Datasheet view can be especially handy for examining multiple records at once.

Form view displays all the fields of a single record onscreen. Form view is most useful when you just need to view or edit a single record, as when you're typing in the phone number of your cousin or boss.

Using Datasheet view

Datasheet view displays all your database information in rows and columns, much like a spreadsheet. To view and enter data in Datasheet view, follow these steps:

1. **In the All Access Objects pane on the left of the screen, double-click a table name.**

   Access displays the Datasheet view of your table.

2. **Click the bottom half of the View icon (that displays a downward-pointing arrow), which appears in the Views group.**

   A pull-down menu appears.

3. **Click Datasheet View.**

   Access displays the Datasheet view of your database table.

4. **Click in a field defined by the column and row.**

   Each column defines a field, such as a name or address. Each row represents a single record.

   If you click in a field that already contains data, you can edit or delete that data.

5. **Press Tab to select the next field (or Shift+Tab to select the preceding field).**

6. **Type or edit the data in the field.**

Using Form view

The biggest problem with Datasheet view is that it can be confusing to find a field for a specific record. Because most people are familiar with paper forms or index cards that arrange related data (fields) on a page, Access offers you Form view.

Form view simply displays the fields of a single record onscreen, arranged like the information typically stored on a business card. To use Form view, you must first create a form and arrange your fields on that form. After you create a form, you can add, edit, and view data through that form.

Creating a form

The simplest way to create a form is to let Access design one for you, which you can modify. To create a form quickly, follow these steps:

1. **In the All Access Objects pane on the left of the screen, double-click a table.**

   Access displays the Datasheet view of your database.

2. **Click the Create tab.**

3. **Click the Form icon in the Forms group.**

   Access creates a form, as shown in Figure 15-1. Notice that the form name automatically uses the name of the database table you chose in Step 3.

Figure 15-1: Form view displays multiple fields of a single record.

4. **Click the Save icon on the Quick Access toolbar (or press Ctrl+S).**

   The Save As dialog box appears, asking you to type a name for your form.

5. **Type a descriptive name for your form in the Form Name text box and then click OK.**

   Access displays your form's name underneath the All Tables pane. The next time you open this database and want to view the form, you can double-click the form's name in the left pane.

Viewing and editing data in a form

After you create a form, you can use it to edit and add data at any time. To view a form, follow these steps:

1. **In the All Access Objects pane on the left of the screen, double-click the name of the form you want to use.**

   Access displays the Form view of your database.

2. **Click one of the following icons (they appear near the bottom of the screen) to display a record:**

- *First Record:* Displays the first record stored in your file

- *Previous Record:* Displays the preceding record in the file

- *Next Record:* Displays the next record in the file

- *Last Record:* Displays the last record that contains data

- *New (Blank) Record:* Displays a blank form so you can type in data that will create a new record in your file

3. Click in a field and type the information you want to store, such as a name or phone number.

You don't need to use the Save command to save your changes because Access automatically saves any data you add or edit in your file as soon as you type or edit the data and move the cursor to a new field or record.

Editing a form

A form can be a convenient way to view all the fields of a single record. However, you can always rearrange the position of certain fields onscreen (to make them easier to find), or you can delete one or more fields altogether.

Deleting a field

If you delete a field from a form, you simply prevent the form from displaying any data stored in that field.

Deleting a field on a form doesn't erase any data; it just keeps you from seeing that data on a particular form.

To delete a field from a form, follow these steps:

1. **In the All Access Objects pane on the left of the screen, double-click the name of the form you want to use.**

   Access displays the Form view of your database.

2. **Click the Home tab.**

3. **Click the downward-pointing arrow underneath the View icon in the Views group.**

   A pull-down menu appears.

4. **Choose Design View.**

   Access shows your chosen form in Design view, which displays a background grid to help you align fields on your form.

5. **Hold down the Ctrl key and click the field label and field that you want to delete.**

   Access highlights your chosen field.

Each field consists of a field label *and* the actual field itself. The *field label* contains descriptive text that defines the data, such as Name, Age, or Sales. The field is the text box that holds the actual data.

6. **Click the Home tab, and then click the Delete icon in the Records group.**

   Access deletes your chosen field.

If you press Ctrl+Z right away, you can undelete any field that you just deleted.

7. **Click the downward-pointing arrow underneath the View icon in the Views group.**

   A pull-down menu appears.

8. Choose Form View.

Access shows your form with the deleted field missing.

Adding a field

Before you can add a field to a form, you must make sure that the field already exists in your database table.

To add a field to a form, follow these steps:

1. In the All Access Objects pane on the left of the screen, double-click the name of the form you want to use.

Access displays the Form view of your database.

2. Click the Home tab.

3. Click the downward-pointing arrow underneath the View icon in the Views group.

A pull-down menu appears.

4. Choose Design View.

Access displays your form in Design view.

5. Click the Design tab.

6. Click the Add Existing Fields icon in the Tools group.

The Field List pane appears on the right side of the screen.

7. Double-click a field.

Access displays the field label and a field on your form.

8. **Move the mouse pointer over the edge of the field and drag the mouse (hold down the left mouse button and move the mouse) to move the field and field label on your form.**

9. **Click the downward-pointing arrow underneath the View icon in the Views group and choose Form View.**

   Access displays the Form view. Notice that the form displays both your newly added field and any data stored in that field.

Searching a Database

Searching a database is crucial to make your data useful, so Access provides two ways to search a database:

- ✔ Search for a specific record.
- ✔ Use a filter to show one or more records that meet a specific criterion.

Searching for a specific record

The simplest type of search looks for a specific record. To search for a record, you need to know the data stored in at least one of its fields.

The more information you already know, the more likely Access will find the one record you want. If you search for all records that contain the first name *Bill,* Access could find dozens of records. If you just search for all records that contain the first name *Bill,* the last name *Johnson,* and a state address of *Alaska,* Access will likely find just the record you want.

To search for a specific record in a database table, follow these steps:

1. **In the All Access Objects pane on the left of the screen, double-click the name of the database table you want to search.**

   Access displays the Datasheet view of your database.

2. **Click the Home tab.**

3. **Click the Find icon in the Find group.**

   The Find and Replace dialog box appears.

4. **Click in the Find What text box and type the data you know is stored in the record you want.**

5. **Click the Look In list box and choose Current field or Current document (searches in all fields).**

6. **(Optional) Click in the Match list box and choose one of the following:**

   - *Any Part of Field:* The Find What text can appear in any part of a field.

   - *Whole Field:* The Find What text is the only text stored in a field.

   - *Start of Field:* The Find What text can be only at the beginning of a field.

7. **(Optional) Click in the Search list box and choose one of the following:**

   - *Up:* Searches from the record where the cursor appears, up to the beginning of the database table

   - *Down:* Searches from the record where the cursor appears, down to the end of the database table

   - *All:* Searches the entire database table

8. **Click Find Next.**

   Access highlights the field where it finds the text you typed in Step 4.

9. **Repeat Step 8 to search for more records that may contain the text you typed in Step 4.**

10. **Click Cancel or the Close button.**

Filtering a database

Searching a database is easy but somewhat limited because you can retrieve only a record that matches any text that you want to find. If you want to find multiple records, you can use a filter. A *filter* lets you tell Access to display only those records that meet certain criteria.

To filter a database table, you must tell Access which field to use as a filter, and then you must define the criteria for that filter.

Filtering simply hides all records in a database table that don't match your criteria. Filtering doesn't delete or erase any records.

Using an exact match for a filter

The simplest filtering criterion searches for an exact match. When you filter a field by an exact match, you're telling Access, "I want to see only those records that contain this specific chunk of data in this particular field."

To filter a database table, follow these steps:

1. **In the All Access Objects pane on the left of the screen, double-click the name of the database table you want to filter.**

   Access displays the Datasheet view of your database.

2. **Click the Home tab.**

3. **Click in the field (column) that you want to use as a filter.**

4. **Click the Filter icon in the Sort & Filter group.**

   A pop-up menu appears.

5. **(Optional) Clear one or more of the check boxes that appear to the left of the list of data that appears in the field you chose in Step 3.**

6. **Click OK.**

   Access displays the filtered view of your database table of only those items that appeared selected in Step 5.

7. **Repeat Steps 3 through 6 for each additional field you want to filter.**

You can click the Toggle Filter on the Home tab in the Sort & Filter group to view all the data in your database table.

Filtering by form

One problem with defining filters in Datasheet view is that you have all your database table records cluttering the screen. To avoid this problem, Access lets you define filters by using a *form,* which basically displays an empty record so you can click the fields that you want to use to filter your database table.

To define a filter by form, follow these steps:

1. **In the All Access Objects pane on the left of the screen, double-click the name of the database table that you want to filter.**

   Access displays the Datasheet view of your database.

2. **Click the Home tab.**

3. **Click the Advanced icon in the Sort & Filter group.**

   A pull-down menu appears.

4. **Choose Filter By Form.**

   Access displays a blank record.

5. **Click in any field.**

   A downward-pointing arrow appears.

6. **Click the downward-pointing arrow.**

   A pull-down menu appears, listing all the data currently stored in that field.

7. **Click the data you want.**

   You can only click one entry in the list.

8. **Click the Toggle Filter icon in the Sort & Filter group.**

   Access displays a filtered view of your database table.

You can click the Toggle Filter icon again to view all the data in your database table.

Using filter criteria

Searching for an exact match in a field can be handy, but sometimes you may want to see records that meet certain criteria. Instead of filtering by an exact match, you have to define the filter criteria.

The type of data stored in each field determines the type of criteria you can create. Three common types of data stored in fields include Text, Numbers, and Dates, which you can filter in different ways, as shown in Tables 15-1, 15-2, and 15-3.

Table 15-1 Common Criteria for Filtering Text Data

Filtering Criterion	*Description*
Equals	Field must match filter text exactly.
Does Not Equal	Field must not match filter text.
Begins With	Field must start with the filter text.
Does Not Begin With	Field must not begin with the filter text.
Contains	Field must contain the filter text.
Does Not Contain	Field must not contain any part of the filter text.
Ends With	Field ends with the filter text.
Does Not End With	Field does not end with the filter text.

Table 15-2	Common Criteria for Filtering Numeric Data
Filtering Criterion	*Description*
Equals	Field must equal filter number.
Does Not Equal	Field must not equal filter number.
Less Than or Equal To	Field must contain a number less than or equal to the filter number.
Greater Than or Equal To	Field must contain a number greater than or equal to the filter number.
Between	Field must contain a number that falls between two filter numbers.

Table 15-3 Common Criteria for Filtering Field Data	
Filtering Criterion	*Description*
Equals	Field must equal the filter date.
Does Not Equal	Field must not equal the filter date.
On or Before	Field date must be equal or earlier than the filter date.
On or After	Field date must be equal or later than the filter date.

To create the filter criteria, follow these steps:

1. **In the All Access Objects pane on the left of the screen, double-click the name of the database table you want to filter.**

Access displays the Datasheet view of your
database.

2. **Click the Home tab.**

3. **Click in the field (column) that you want to use as a filter.**

4. **Click the Filter icon in the Sort & Filter group.**

   A pop-up menu appears.

5. **Select the Filters option, such as Text Filters or Number Filters.**

   A submenu of filter options appears.

6. **Click a filter option, such as Between or Less Than.**

   The Custom Filter dialog box appears. The Custom
   Filter dialog box contains the name of your filter
   option, such as Between Numbers or Less Than.

7. **Type in one or more values in each text box displayed in the Custom Filter dialog box and then click OK.**

   Access filters your database table according to your
   criteria.

8. **Repeat Steps 5 through 7 for each additional filter you want to add.**

You can click the Toggle Filter icon again to view all the
data in your database table.

Clearing a filter

When you apply a filter to a database table, you see only
those records that match that filter. Access displays a
Filtered message at the bottom of the screen to let you
know when you're looking at a filtered database table.

To remove a filter so you can see all the records, choose one of the following:

- ✔ Click the Toggle Filter icon in the Sort & Filter group.
- ✔ Click the Filtered or Unfiltered button on the status bar near the bottom of the screen.

Access temporarily turns off any filters so you can see all the information stored in your database table.

When you choose the Save command (Ctrl+S) to save a database table, Access also saves your last filter. The next time you open that database table, you'll be able to use the last filter you created.

Using the Report Wizard

The easiest way to create a report is to use the Report Wizard, which guides you step by step through arranging and selecting which data to print on a report, along with sorting your data at the same time. To use the Report Wizard, follow these steps:

1. **Click the Create tab.**
2. **Click the Report Wizard icon in the Reports group.**

   The Report Wizard dialog box appears, as shown in Figure 15-2.

3. **Click in the Tables/Queries list box and choose the table or query that contains the data you want to print in a report.**
4. **Click in a field in the Available Fields box and then click the > button. Repeat this step for each additional field you want to display in your report.**

Figure 15-2: The Report Wizard lets you choose where to retrieve your data for your report.

5. **Click Next.**

   Another dialog box appears, asking whether you want to group your data by a specific field, such as by Last Name or Employee Number.

6. **Click a field name displayed in the box and then click the > button. Repeat this step for each additional field you want to use to group your data on the report.**

7. **Click Next.**

   Another dialog box appears, asking you to choose up to four fields to use for sorting your data in your report.

8. **Click in a list box and choose a field to sort your data.**

   Data will be sorted by the order chosen here for each additional field you sort on.

9. **(Optional) Click the Ascending button to change the sorting criteria from Ascending to Descending and vice versa.**

10. **Click Next.**

Another dialog box appears, asking you how to lay out your report.

11. **Select a radio button under the Layout group, such as Stepped or Block.**

12. **(Optional) Select a radio button in the Orientation group, such as Portrait or Landscape.**

13. **Click Next.**

    Another dialog box appears, asking for a descriptive name for your report.

14. **Type a descriptive name for your report and then click Finish.**

    Access displays your report, as shown in Figure 15-3.

Figure 15-3: Access displays your report onscreen.

If you change any data, you can see those updated changes in your report by following these steps:

1. **Right-click the tab that represents your currently displayed report.**

   A pop-up menu appears.

2. **Choose Close.**

3. Double-click the report name in the left pane of the Access window.

Your chosen report appears again, displaying any data you updated or modified since the last time you viewed the report.

Access won't automatically update your reports just because you modified any data that the report displays.

Part III

The Part of Tens

Find more content related to Windows 8 and enjoy an additional Office 2013 Part of Tens chapter online at www.dummies.com.

In this part . . .

✔ Discover ten things you'll hate about Windows 8.

✔ Get ten shortcuts and tips that make it easier to work with Office 2013.

Chapter 16

Ten Things You'll Hate about Windows 8

*Y*ou may find yourself thinking Windows 8 would be perfect if only . . . *(insert your pet peeve here)*. If you find yourself thinking (or saying) those words frequently, read this chapter. Here, you find not only a list of ten or so of the most aggravating things about Windows 8, but also ways you can fix them.

I Want to Avoid the Start Screen!

If you find the mysterious new Start screen to be more startling than helpful, here's how to avoid it. This section explains how to stay on the desktop as long as possible.

Bringing back the Start button

Even before Windows 8 hit the stores, a cottage industry began creating ways to put the Start button and its menu back onto the desktop's taskbar, conveniently bypassing the new Start screen.

A Google search for *"Windows 8 Start Button"* turns up several programs, including Lee-Soft's ViSoft (http://lee-soft.com/visoft). Shown in Figure 16-1, the program restores the Start button and menu to Windows 8. Yet, the program leaves the Start screen in place, just in case you must revisit that strange land.

Figure 16-1: Several Windows 8 programs and apps put the Start button and menu back onto the taskbar.

If you want the best of both worlds — desktop and apps —
try Start8 by StarDock (`www.stardock.com/products/
start8`). Start8 restores the Start button to its usual
place. Clicking the Start button, however, fetches the
Start screen showing icons for *all* your programs and
apps.

Knowing when the Start screen reappears unexpectedly

The Start screen and the desktop aren't self-contained
entities. No, the two worlds intertwine, and one wrong
click on the desktop tosses you back onto the Start
screen's sharp-edged tiles.

So, no matter how many Start screen–avoiding tactics
you may employ, you'll still find yourself tossed back
onto the Start screen when you do any of the following
things:

- ✔ **Add user accounts.** The desktop's Control Panel
  lets you manage a user account. You can toggle a
  user account between Standard and Administrator,
  change its name, and even delete it completely. But
  if you need to *add* a user account — or even change
  your own account's picture — you're dropped off
  at the Start screen's PC Settings screen to finish
  the job.

- ✔ **Play a music file or view a photo.** Windows 8 sets
  itself up to use the Start screen's Music and Pictures
  apps. Open one photo or MP3 file on the desktop,
  and you'll find yourself back in Start screen land.

- ✔ **Troubleshoot.** Although the Start screen specializes
  in rather anemic fare, it also contains two of the

most powerful troubleshooting tools in Windows 8: Refresh and Remove Everything. These two tools offer last-ditch cure-alls for ailing computers. You won't find any way to access these tools from the desktop, however.

In short, even adding a Start button back to the desktop won't keep you from being dropped off into the land of the Start screen. Be prepared for these occasional unavoidable journeys.

I Want to Avoid the Desktop!

On a touchscreen tablet, it's enticing to stay on the Start screen with its finger-sized tiles and easy-to-touch icons. Smartphone owners have enjoyed the app lifestyle for years. Easily downloadable apps offer help for nearly every niche, from bird watching to car repair.

But staying nestled within the Start screen's world of apps can be more difficult than it appears. No matter how hard you try to avoid the desktop and its pin-sized controls, you'll find yourself dragged there when you do any of the following things from the Start screen:

✔ **Click the Desktop tile.** This app brings you straight to the desktop zone. To hide this tile or any other Start screen tile, right-click the unwanted app to reveal the App bar and then click the Unpin from Start icon.

✔ **Browse files.** The Start screen isn't sophisticated enough to browse your files. As soon as you plug in a flash drive or portable hard drive, the desktop's File Explorer leaps onscreen to handle the job.

✔ **Manage a user account.** You can *create* new accounts from the Start screen, but to *delete* or *change* an existing account, you need the desktop's Control Panel.

✔ **Watch Flash videos.** The Start screen's version of Internet Explorer handles most websites well. But on some websites, it can't play videos that employ Adobe Flash technology. When a video won't play, right-click a blank part of the website to reveal the App bar. Then click the Page Tool icon, and choose View on the Desktop. The desktop's Internet Explorer jumps in to finish the task.

✔ **Manage gadgetry.** The Start screen's PC Settings screen lists all the devices connected to your computer, from printers to mice to portable hard drives. But it shows only their names; to change the *settings* of any of those devices requires a trip to the desktop's Control Panel.

✔ **Manage files.** You can access your photos and music files from the Start screen's Photos and Music apps, respectively. But *changing* those files in any way — renaming a file or folder, perhaps — requires a trip to the desktop. You'll find yourself there when looking for the date you snapped a photo, as well.

In short, the Start screen works well for most simple computing tasks. But when it comes to fine-tuning your computer's settings, performing maintenance work, or even browsing files, you'll find yourself returning to the desktop.

If you find yourself constantly returning to the desktop for certain tasks, keep visiting the Windows Store to search for an app that can accomplish the same task. Microsoft stocks the store with more apps every day;

as the apps fill more niches, you'll find yourself relying on the desktop less often.

But until the apps catch up with the desktop, tablet owners might want to pop a portable Bluetooth mouse into their gadget bags for those inevitable trips to the desktop.

I Can't Copy Music to My iPod

You won't find the word *iPod* mentioned in the Windows 8 menus, help screens, or even in the Help areas of Microsoft's website. That's because Microsoft's competitor, Apple, makes the tremendously popular iPod. Microsoft's strategy is to ignore the little gizmo in the hope that it will go away.

What won't go away, though, are the problems you'll face if you ever try to copy songs onto an iPod with Media Player. You face two hurdles:

- ✔ Windows Media Player won't recognize your iPod, much less send it any songs or videos.

- ✔ When you plug in your iPod, Windows might recognize the slick gadget as a portable hard drive. It may even let you copy songs to it. But your iPod won't be able to find or play them.

The easiest solution is to download and install iTunes software from Apple's website (www.apple.com/ itunes). Because iTunes and Media Player will bicker over which program can play your files, you'll probably end up choosing iTunes. Also, keep checking the Windows Store for iPod management apps. Third-party companies will eventually fill the void.

Windows Makes Me Sign In All the Time

The power-conscious Windows 8 normally blanks your screen when you haven't touched a key for a few minutes. And, when you belatedly press a key to bring the screen back to life, you're faced with the lock screen. And to move past the lock screen, you need to type your password to sign back in to your account.

Some people prefer that extra level of security. If the lock screen kicks in while you're spending too much time at the water cooler, you're protected: Nobody can walk over and snoop through your e-mail. Other people don't need that extra security, and they simply want to return to work quickly.

If you don't *ever* want to see the lock screen, use a single user account without a password. That defeats all the security offered by the user account system, but it's more convenient if you live alone.

To keep Windows from asking for a password whenever it wakes back up, follow these steps:

1. **Right-click in any screen's bottom-left corner and then choose Control Panel.**

2. **From the Control Panel, click System and Security and then click Power Options.**

3. **From the screen's left edge, click Require a Password on Wakeup.**

   When the window appears, most of the options are *grayed out* — inaccessible.

4. **Select the option labeled Change Settings That Are Currently Unavailable.**

5. **Select the Don't Require a Password option and then click the Save Changes button.**

That leaves you with a more easy-going Windows. When your computer wakes up from sleep, you're left at the same place where you stopped working, and you don't have to enter your password anymore. Unfortunately, it also leaves you with a less-secure Windows. Anybody who walks by your computer will have access to all your files.

To return to the safer-but-less-friendly Windows, follow these same steps, but in Step 5, select the Require a Password (Recommended) option. Then click the Save Changes button.

The Taskbar Keeps Disappearing

The taskbar is a handy Windows 8 feature that usually squats along the bottom of your desktop. Sometimes, unfortunately, it up and wanders off into the woods. Here are a few ways to track it down and bring it home.

If your taskbar suddenly clings to the *side* of the screen — or even the ceiling — try dragging it back in place: Instead of dragging an edge, drag the entire taskbar from its middle. As your mouse pointer reaches your desktop's bottom edge, the taskbar suddenly snaps back into place. Let go of the mouse, and you've recaptured it.

Follow these tips to prevent your taskbar from wandering:

✔ To keep the taskbar locked into place so that it won't float away, right-click a blank part of the taskbar and select Lock the Taskbar. Remember, though, that before you can make any future changes to the taskbar, you must first unlock it.

✔ If your taskbar drops from sight whenever the mouse pointer doesn't hover nearby, turn off the taskbar's Auto Hide feature: Right-click a blank part of the taskbar and choose Properties from the pop-up menu. When the Taskbar Properties dialog box appears, deselect the Auto-Hide the Taskbar check box. (Or, to turn on the Auto Hide feature, select the check box.)

1 Can't Keep Track of Open Windows

You don't *have* to keep track of all those open windows. Windows 8 does it for you with a secret key combination: Hold the Alt key and press the Tab key, and a little bar appears, displaying the icons for all your open windows. Keep pressing Tab; when Windows highlights the icon of the window you're after, release the keys. The window pops up.

Or visit the taskbar, that long strip along the bottom of your screen. Mentioned in Chapter 3, the taskbar lists the name of every open window. Click the name of the window you want, and that window hops to the top of the pile.

If a program icon on the taskbar contains several open windows — you're simultaneously editing several documents in Microsoft Word, for example — right-click the

Microsoft Word icon. A pop-up menu appears, letting you click the document you want to access.

Can't find a previously opened Start screen app? Hold down the ⊞ key and press the Tab key: Thumbnail images of all your open apps appear on a strip along the screen's left edge. Keep pressing the Tab key until you've highlighted the desired app; let go of the Tab key, and the selected app fills the screen.

I Can't Line Up Two Windows on the Screen

With its arsenal of dragging-and-dropping tools, Windows simplifies grabbing information from one window and copying it to another. You can drag an address from an address book and drop it atop a letter in your word processor, for example.

However, the hardest part of dragging and dropping comes when you're lining up two windows on the screen, side by side, for dragging.

Windows 8 offers an easy way to align windows for easy dragging and dropping:

1. **Drag one window against a left or right edge.**

   When your mouse pointer touches the screen's edge, the window reshapes itself to fill half the screen.

2. **Drag the other window against the opposite edge.**

   When your mouse pointer reaches the opposite edge, the two windows are aligned side by side.

You can also minimize all the windows except for the two you want to align side by side. Then right-click a blank spot on the taskbar, and choose Show Windows Side By Side. The two windows line up on the screen perfectly.

It Won't Let Me Do Something Unless I'm an Administrator!

Windows 8 gets really picky about who gets to do what on your computer. The computer's owner gets the Administrator account. And the administrator usually gives everybody else a Standard account. What does that mean? Well, only the administrator can do the following things on the computer:

✔ Install programs and hardware

✔ Create or change accounts for other people

✔ Start an Internet connection

✔ Install some hardware, such as digital cameras and MP3 players

✔ Perform actions affecting other people on the PC

People with Standard accounts, by nature, are limited to fairly basic activities. They can do these things:

✔ Run previously installed programs

✔ Change their account's picture and password

Guest accounts are meant for the babysitter or visitors who don't permanently use the computer. If you have a broadband or other "always on" Internet account, guests can browse the Internet, run programs, or check their e-mail. (Guest accounts aren't allowed to *start* an Internet session, but they can use an existing one.)

If Windows says only an administrator may do something on your PC, you have two choices: find an administrator to type his or her password and authorize the action; or convince an administrator to upgrade your account to an Administrator account.

1 Don't Know What Version of Windows 1 Have

Windows has been sold in more than a dozen flavors since its debut in November 1985. How can you tell what version is installed on your computer?

Right-click in the bottom-left corner of any screen. When the pop-up menu appears, choose System. When the System window appears, look near the top to see which version of Windows 8 you own: Windows 8 (for consumers), Windows Pro (for small businesses), Enterprise (for large businesses), or Windows RT.

I describe the different Windows versions in Chapter 1.

My Print Screen Key Doesn't Work

Contrary to its name, the Print Screen key doesn't shuttle a picture of your screen to your printer. Instead, the Print Screen key (usually labeled PrintScreen, PrtScr, or PrtSc) sends the screen's picture to the Windows 8 memory.

From there, you can paste it into a graphics program, such as Paint, letting the graphics program send the picture to the printer.

Windows 8 introduces something new, though: If you want to capture an image of the entire screen and save it as a file, press ⊞+PrtScr.

That tells Windows to snap a picture of your current screen and save it in your Pictures library with the name *Screenshot.* (Windows saves those images in the PNG format, if you're interested, and it captures your mouse pointer, as well.) Subsequent screenshots include a number after the name, like Screenshot (2) and Screenshot (3). When saved, your screenshot can head for your printer when you right-click the file and choose Print from the pop-up menu.

Chapter 17

Ten Tips for Using Office 2013

*M*icrosoft Office is famous for burying tons of useful features that most people never know about, so this chapter is about exposing some of Office 2013's features so you can take advantage of them and make Office 2013 more convenient (and safer) for you to use.

Saving Office 2013 Files

Most people dump their documents inside a folder in the Documents folder. To make retrieving files easier, it's a good idea to store different data in its own folders.

Left to its own devices, of course, Office 2013 will cheerfully save all your files in the Documents folder, so you'll need to tell Office 2013 where you want it to save files.

In addition to defining a default folder to store files, you can also define a default file format for your Office 2013 programs. This can be especially useful if you need to share files with others, such as people still stuck using an older version of Microsoft Office (97/2000/XP/2003).

Finally, to protect your data (as much as possible) from inevitable computer crashes and hard drive failures, Office 2013 programs include a special AutoRecover feature, which saves a temporary copy of your file at fixed intervals, such as every ten minutes.

Access doesn't offer an AutoRecover feature because it automatically saves any changes to your data anyway.

To customize the location, format, and AutoRecover feature of an Office 2013 program, follow these steps:

1. **Load the Office 2013 program you want to customize (such as Word or PowerPoint).**

2. **Click the File tab.**

3. **Click Options.**

   An Options dialog box appears.

4. **Click Save in the left pane.**

   The Options dialog box displays various Save options.

5. **(Optional) Click in the Save Files in This Format list box and choose a file format, such as the 97–2003 format.**

6. **(Optional) Click in the Default File Location text box and type the drive and folder that you want to define as your default folder. (Or click the Browse button and then choose a folder.)**

7. **(Optional) Select the Save AutoRecover information every check box, click in the Minutes text box, and type a value or click the up/down arrows to define a value, such as 7 minutes.**

8. **Click OK.**

Password-Protecting Your Files

To prevent prying eyes from peeking at your Word, Excel, or PowerPoint files, you can password-protect them. If someone doesn't know your password, she won't be able to view — let alone edit — your files.

You (or anyone) can buy programs off the Internet that can crack an Office 2013 password-protected file. For real security, don't rely on Office 2013's password-protection feature.

To password-protect a file, follow these steps:

1. **Load Word, Excel, or PowerPoint.**

2. **Click the File tab.**

3. **Choose Save As.**

   The Save As window appears.

4. **Click the Browse button.**

   The Save As dialog box appears.

5. **Click the Tools button.**

   A pull-down menu appears.

6. **Choose General Options.**

   The General Options dialog box appears.

7. **(Optional) Click in the Password to Open text box and type a password.**

   Another dialog box appears and asks you to confirm the password by typing it again.

8. **Type the password again and then click OK.**

9. **(Optional) Click in the Password to Modify text box and type a password.**

   This password can be different from the password you typed in Step 6. Another dialog box appears and asks you to confirm the password by typing it again.

10. **Type the password again and then click OK.**

11. **Click Save.**

Guarding Against Macro Viruses

Macro viruses are malicious programs designed to attach themselves to Word, Excel, and PowerPoint files. When an unsuspecting victim opens an infected file, the virus can spread and do something nasty.

To stop these pests from wrecking your files, turn on Office 2013's built-in macro-protection feature, which can disable macros or restrict what macro viruses and worms can do even if they infect your computer.

To turn on macro protection, follow these steps:

1. **Load Word or PowerPoint.**

2. **Click the File tab.**

3. **Click Options.**

   The Options dialog box appears.

4. **Click Trust Center.**

   The Trust Center options appear in the right pane.

5. **Click the Trust Center Settings button.**

   The Trust Center dialog box appears with the Macro Settings options displayed.

6. **Select one of the following radio buttons:**

   • *Disable All Macros without Notification:* Prevents any macros from running when you open the file; the safest setting.

   • *Disable All Macros with Notification:* The default setting, which displays a dialog box to turn on macros if you trust that the file isn't infected.

   • *Disable All Macros except Digitally Signed Macros:* Blocks all macros except for the ones "authenticated" (previously defined as "trusted") by the user.

   • *Enable All Macros:* Runs all macros, which is the most dangerous setting.

7. **Click OK until you return to the Save As dialog box.**

8. **Click Save.**

Customize the Ribbon

You can customize which icons appear on the Ribbon so it only displays those features you need (and use) most often.

To customize the Ribbon interface, follow these steps:

1. **Load an Office 2013 program, such as Word or Excel.**

2. **Click the File tab.**

3. **Click Options.**

   The Options dialog box appears.

4. **Click Customize Ribbon in the left pane.**

   The Options dialog box displays two columns. The left column displays all additional commands you can place on the Ribbon, and the right column lists all currently displayed tabs and commands, as shown in Figure 17-1.

Figure 17-1: You can customize which tabs and commands appear on the Ribbon.

5. **(Optional) Clear a check box in the right column to hide an entire tab from view.**

6. **(Optional) Click the New Tab button to create a new tab. Then you can click a command in the left column and click the Add button to place commands on a new tab of your own design.**

7. **(Optional) Click the Reset button.**

   The Reset button lets you restore the default settings of a single tab or the entire Ribbon.

8. **Click OK.**

Save to SkyDrive

If you need to access, edit, or create files on more than one computer or device, you may find it easier to save your important files to SkyDrive, which is Microsoft's cloud storage service. By signing up for a SkyDrive account, you can get 7GB of free storage and pay if you need more.

The basic idea behind SkyDrive is that you store a single file on your SkyDrive. No matter where you are in the world or which device you have with you, you can access that file as long as you have an Internet connection. By editing a file stored in a single location, you can avoid the hassles of copying a file to store on multiple devices and then worrying about which file has your latest changes.

You can download the SkyDrive app from www.windows.microsoft.com/en-US/skydrive/download.

To open a file stored on SkyDrive, follow these steps:

1. **Load an Office 2013 program, such as Word or Excel.**

2. **Click the File tab.**

3. **Click Open.**

   The Open window appears.

4. **Click Add a place.**

5. **Click SkyDrive.**

   At this point, you'll have to type in your SkyDrive username and password to access your file.

To save a file to SkyDrive, follow these steps:

1. **Load an Office 2013 program, such as Word or Excel.**

2. **Click the File tab.**

3. **Click Save As.**

   The Save As window appears.

4. **Click Add a Place.**

5. **Click SkyDrive.**

   At this point, you have to type in your SkyDrive username and password to save your file to your SkyDrive account.

When in Doubt, Right-Click the Mouse

As a shortcut to giving commands to Office 2013, remember this simple guideline: First select, and then right-click.

So if you want to change text or a picture, first select it to tell Office 2013 what you want to modify. Then right-click the mouse to display a pop-up menu of the commands. These pop-up menus display a list of only relevant commands for the item you just selected.

Freezing Row and Column Headings in Excel

One problem with creating large spreadsheets in Excel is that your identifying row and column headings may scroll out of sight if you scroll down or to the right of your worksheet. To prevent this from happening, you can "freeze" a row or column that contains identifying labels.

To freeze a row or column in an Excel worksheet, follow these steps:

1. **Click the View tab.**

2. **Click the Freeze Panes icon in the Window group.**

3. **Click one of the following:**

    • *Freeze Panes:* Divides a worksheet into multiple panes

    • *Freeze Top Row:* Always displays the top row, no matter how far down you scroll

    • *Freeze First Column:* Always displays the first column, no matter how far to the right you scroll

To unfreeze a row or column, repeat Steps 1 through 3 but click Unfreeze Panes in Step 2.

Displaying Slides Out of Order in PowerPoint

When you display a PowerPoint presentation, your slides typically appear in the order that you arranged them, starting with the first slide. If you want to display your slides in a different order in the middle of a presentation, follow these steps:

1. **Load your presentation in PowerPoint and press F5.**

   The first slide of your presentation appears.

2. **Type the number of the slide you want to view and press Enter.**

   If you want to jump to the fifth slide in your presentation, type **5** and press Enter. If you jump to the fifth slide, clicking the mouse or pressing the spacebar next displays the sixth slide, and then the seventh, and so on.

Print a list of your slide titles and slide numbers on a sheet of paper so that you know which slide number to type to view a particular slide.

Reduce Spam in Outlook

If you have an e-mail account, you will get *spam,* that unwanted e-mail that clogs millions of Inboxes every day with obnoxious offers for things you don't need. Outlook can filter your e-mail for you.

Setting up Outlook's junk e-mail filter

Outlook can move suspected spam to a special junk e-mail folder automatically. Because Outlook looks for keywords in spam, be aware that it will never be 100 percent effective in identifying spam, but it can identify the more blatant spam and save you the time and effort of deleting the messages yourself.

To define Outlook's spam filter, follow these steps:

1. **Click the Home tab.**

2. **Click the Junk icon.**

   A menu appears.

3. **Click Junk E-mail Options.**

   The Junk E-mail Options dialog box appears.

4. **Select one of the following radio buttons:**

   - *No Automatic Filtering:* Turns off the Outlook spam filter.

   - *Low:* Identifies and moves the most obvious spam to the Junk E-mail folder.

   - *High:* Identifies and moves nearly all spam into the Junk E-mail folder along with some regular e-mail messages, too, so check the Junk E-mail folder periodically to look for valid messages.

   - *Safe Lists Only:* Identifies and moves e-mail messages into the Junk E-mail folder, except for those messages sent from addresses listed in your Safe Senders List or Safe Recipients List.

5. **Click OK.**

The Options dialog box appears again.

6. **Click OK.**

Creating a Safe Senders list

A Safe Senders list lets you define all the e-mail addresses you want to accept messages from. The advantage of a Safe Senders list is that it guarantees you will never receive spam. On the downside, though, it also guarantees that if someone tries to contact you whose e-mail address doesn't appear on your Safe Senders list, you will never get that valid message.

To create a Safe Senders list, follow Steps 1 through 4 in the preceding section, "Setting up Outlook's junk e-mail filter," to display the Junk E-mail Options dialog box. Then follow these steps:

1. **In the Junk E-mail Options dialog box, click the Safe Senders tab.**

The Safe Senders tab of the Junk E-mail Options dialog box appears.

2. **(Optional) Select (or clear) the Also Trust E-mail from My Contacts check box.**

Selecting this check box tells Outlook that if you store someone's e-mail address in your Contacts list, you will also accept e-mail from that person, too.

3. **(Optional) Select (or clear) the Automatically Add People I E-mail to the Safe Senders List check box.**

This tells Outlook that if you send e-mail to someone, you'll accept his or her messages in return.

4. **(Optional) Click the Add button.**

   The Add Address or Domain dialog box appears.

5. **Type a complete e-mail address or type a domain
   name.**

6. **Click OK.**

7. **Repeat Steps 4 through 6 for each additional e-mail
   address or domain you want to add.**

8. **Click OK until all the dialog boxes disappear.**

If you click the Safe Recipients tab, you can repeat these
steps to define another list of e-mail addresses that you'll
accept as valid.

Creating a Blocked Senders list

If a particular e-mail address persists in sending you
spam, you can choose to selectively block that single
e-mail address or domain. To create a Blocked Senders
list, follow Steps 1 through 4 in the earlier section,
"Setting up Outlook's junk e-mail filter," to display the
Junk E-mail Options dialog box. Then follow these steps:

1. **In the Junk E-mail Options dialog box, click the
   Blocked Senders tab.**

   The Blocked Senders tab of the Junk E-mail Options
   dialog box appears.

2. **Click the Add button.**

   The Add Address or Domain dialog box appears.

3. **Type an e-mail address or domain name and then
   click OK.**

The Options dialog box appears again.

4. Click OK until all the dialog boxes disappear.

Using Office Web and Windows RT

Office 2013 gobbles up a huge chunk of hard drive space and bombards you with waves of features that you'll probably never need (or use) in a million years. In case you want to use Microsoft Office but find it too complicated, try the free Office Web (`http://office.microsoft.com/en-us/web-apps/`) version instead.

Office Web provides simplified versions of Word, Excel, and PowerPoint that you use over the Internet. As long as you have an Internet connection, a browser, and a free Windows Live ID, you can use Office Web to create, edit, and share files with others.

Perhaps the greatest advantage of Office Web is that multiple people can collaborate on a single document from anywhere in the world. Instead of swapping files back and forth (and risk losing track of which file may be the latest one), Office Web lets you store a single copy of your document online for everyone to access.

Of course, the biggest drawback of Office Web is that you need an Internet connection to use it. However, as Internet access becomes cheaper and more accessible, this disadvantage shouldn't be a problem for most people.

In case you don't like the idea of accessing Office 2013 through the Internet, grab a tablet running Windows RT, which comes with a bundled version of Office 2013. By using Office 2013 on your Windows RT tablet, you can take your programs and files with you and save them in either of these ways:

- ✔ Save your files to a USB flash drive so you can transfer them to your computer at a later time.
- ✔ Save your files to SkyDrive.

By using the version of Office 2013 that comes bundled with Windows RT, you can still be productive with your favorite Microsoft Office programs without lugging around a heavy and bulky laptop computer running the full version of Windows 8.

Index

Take Dummies with you everywhere you go!

Whether you're excited about e-books, want more from the web, must have your mobile apps, or swept up in social media, Dummies makes everything easier .

Visit Us

Like Us

Follow Us

Watch Us

Join Us

Pin Us

Circle Us

Shop Us